THE FIJI MACROECONOMY

AN INTRODUCTION

THE FIJI MACROECONOMY

AN INTRODUCTION

AZMAT GANI

Nova Science Publishers, Inc.
New York

For permission to use material from this book please contact us:
Telephone 631-231-7269; Fax 631-231-8175
Web Site: http://www.novapublishers.com

Library of Congress Cataloging-in-Publication Data
Gani, Azmat.
The Fiji macroeconomy : an introduction / Azmat Gani.
p. cm.
Includes index.
ISBN 13 978-1-60021-464-6
ISBN 10 1-60021-464-9
1. Fiji--Economic conditions. 2. Finance--Fiji. I. Title.
HC685.5.G36 2006
339.099611--dc22 2006030789

Published by Nova Science Publishers, Inc. ✦ New York

CONTENTS

ACKNOWLEDGEMENTS

I am pleased to acknowledge those who aided me in preparing this book.

I thank Shamshad for inspired and tireless research assistance. I would like to thank my colleague Michael D. Clemes of Lincoln University, New Zealand whose thoughtful and insightful suggestion and encouragement was of incalculable help. I am also grateful to John Gibson (University of Wiakato, New Zealand); Basu Sharma (University of New Brunswick, Canada); Biman Chand Prasad (The University of the South Pacific, Fiji); Christopher Ngassam (Florida A&M University, USA); and Greg Barrett (University of Canberra, Australia) - for their generous advise and help while I was preparing the manuscript. The editorial and production team at Nova Science was enormously helpful as they guided me with patience and tact. It has been a pleasure to work with Maya Columbus, Acquisitions; Susan Boriotti, Senior Editor and Donna Dennis, Editorial Production Manager. This book is dedicated to Shanza.

Chapter 1

FIJI: AN INTRODUCTION

1.1. INTRODUCTION

This chapter gives a general introduction to the Fiji economy. It covers several aspects that give a broad description of the country particularly to the new readers. It outlines the physical position, the economic structure, trends in real per capita GDP, constraints to economic progress, its links with the global economy and development achievements. Important issues highlighted in this chapter are raised further for detailed discussions in the chapters that follow.

1.2. THE PHYSICAL SETTING

Fiji, with a land area of approximately 18,000 square kilometers comprising of some 400 islands, is located in the tropical latitudes, approximately 2,200 kilometers north of New Zealand and 3,500 kilometers to the North East of Australia. It is also thousands of kilometers away from some of its major trading partners (United States of America, the European Union, Japan and China). Under the World Bank's criteria of classification of countries (The World Bank, 2006), Fiji falls in the lower-middle-income category of countries, meaning that, its per capita gross national product (GNP) is some where between US$746 to US$3,035. Latest available statistics reveal that Fiji's per capita income in 2005 was US$3280 (The World Bank, 2006). Where appropriate, the average achievements in the lower-middle-income economies macroeconomic indicators are used in this chapter as comparisons so as to put Fiji in perspective with the lower-middle-income countries.

Given the difficulties in defining size, the literature has settled on a country's population as the primary measure of its size with GNP as the secondary measure (Srinivasan, 1986 and Streetan, 1997). Countries with population of between 1.5 million and 5 million are considered as small while countries with fewer than 1.5 million are considered to be very small. Based on this criterion, Fiji is a very small country with an estimated population in 2004 of 838,317 (Fiji Islands Bureau of Statistics, 2006). It is very small in terms of land area (18,300 square kilometers) as well as gross output (gross national income of US$2.6 billion in

2004, see The World Bank (2006)). At the same time it is highly open economy in the South Pacific region and is grouped with the Asia and the Pacific regional category of countries.

Fiji's population reveals its degree of smallness. With less than a million people, its population has grown at an average annual rate of 1 percent in the 1990-2004 periods. The population density is 45 people per square kilometer, below the average of 48 people per square kilometer for countries in the lower-middle-income category (Asian Development Bank, 2005). Fiji is multicultural, with the ethnic Fijians (Melanesians), the dominant ethnic group, comprising of 53.2 percent of total population in 2004 (Fiji Islands Bureau of Statistics, 2006). The people of Indian descent, hereafter known as Fiji Indians, who were brought as indentured labourers for the sugar industry under the British administration dating back to 1874 when Fiji was annexed to United Kingdom (see for example, Lal, 1990), form the second major ethnic group comprising of 38.0 percent of total population in 2004 (Fiji Islands Bureau of Statistics, 2006).

Fiji's demographic structure has changed as a result of the political crises eventuating in May 1987, where the democratically elected government was ousted by the Fiji Military (discussed in section 2.2.2 in Chapter 2). Emigration, largely of Fiji Indians, to high-income countries has been the major cause of Fiji's demographic shifts since then (Gani, 2000 and Reddy, Mohanty and Naidu, 2004). In 1987, Fiji Indians were the dominant ethnic group, making 48 percent of the total population while the ethnic Fijian population accounted for 46 percent of the total population (Gani, 2000). The ethnic Fijian population has increased significantly since 1987 and now accounts for just over half of total population. The minority ethnic groups include Europeans, part-Europeans, Chinese and Rotumans. High levels of emigration has withdrawn population of reproductive age from the Fiji Indian community and is one factor that has contributed to a reduction in their birth rates that declined from 26 per 1,000 in 1986 to 14.5 per 1,000 in 2002 (see Gani, 2000 and Fiji Islands Bureau of Statistics, 2006). On the other hand, the ethnic Fijian population increased with their growth rates averaging 2.5 percent per annum during 1987-03 period (Fiji Islands Bureau of Statistics, 2006). One contributing factor has been high birth rates among the ethnic Fijians (25.6 per 1,000 in 2002, Fiji Islands Bureau of Statistics, 2006).

The productive capacity of the economy is considered satisfactory for a country of this size. It has fertile agricultural land, large expanse of sea area (with fisheries and water sports as the major marine resource) educated population with low illiteracy levels, English as the official language, established commercial policies, a version of the British Westminster system of government and judiciary, and a good communications infrastructure; all well able to meet the private sectors and society's basic commercial needs. Fiji has for long relied on its agricultural sector that mainly focused on the exports of cane sugar both for foreign exchange as well as meeting domestic consumer demand. Its well-established tourism industry has also been a major player in its post independence development and now the largest foreign exchange earner. Several light manufacturing industries have also been established. Fiji's good human capital base, reasonably well established physical infrastructure and commercial policies of international standards have been important ingredients of its economic advancement since its independence in 1970.

1.3. Economic Structure

Fiji's economic performance can be examined by looking at its gross domestic product (GDP) – the value of goods and services produced within a country during a particular time period. However, a country's GDP is depended on its underlying production structure and in particular its ability to produce goods and services. The size of GDP ultimately determines the standard of living of a nation. Nations aiming for higher economic progress should aim to increase their productive ability (Dalziel and Lattimore, 1996). Fiji's production structure can be best analysed by examining its income and expenditure.

Table 1.1 shows Fiji's GDP by production and expenditure category for year 2004 and compares this with 1995. On the production side, other than public administration, the rest of the items indicate total market production of goods and services. In the market economy, wholesale and retail trade, restaurants and hotels is the largest production group followed by transport and communications in the second place and manufacturing in the third place. These sectors combine to produce close to 42 percent of Fiji's GDP. Agriculture, the dominant production sector in 1995 now contributes to just over 12 percent of GDP. Public administration, a non-market group, largely involves the provision of public goods where the final product is not directly purchased by the consumers such as education, health care, defence, justice and police. This group contributes to about 15 percent of GDP. There are also non-governmental organisations, community groups and in particular several of the community funded schools which contribute to the GDP and it seems their services are unaccounted for in the national statistics.

Looking at data in Table 1.1, GDP shows the measures of two things at once: the total income for everyone in Fiji and total expenditure on Fiji's output of goods and services. Thus, for an economy as whole, its income must equal its expenditure and this is confirmed by data in Table 1.1.

Table 1.1 also shows Fiji's GDP by expenditure. Close to two thirds of the expenditure is on private consumption, which is basically the spending by the households and the private sector on goods and services. Almost 18 percent of GDP is government consumption meaning spending on goods and services by the national government. Just over 11 percent are spent on capital goods such as roads, buildings, machinery and equipment. Net exports (exports less imports) amount to just over 6 percent of the GDP.

Table 1.2 presents data on Fiji's sectoral production and its contribution to GDP. The pattern noted in the data is typical for a country passing through various stages of economic development. Over the 30-year period, agricultural contribution to GDP has declined (see Reddy and Duncan, 2006) while the rest of the sectoral contribution to GDP has increased. The pattern noted for agricultural contribution is consistent with the theoretical propositions in the economic development literature where in the early stages of a countries development a large proportion of a country's production activity is concentrated with primary production. A thorough exposition of this process is provided by Jones (1998). As a country's economic development progresses, the country goes through structural shifts in production with secondary sectors like manufacturing and services tending to become large contributors to GDP and at times surpassing primary production. The data in Table 1.2 provides evidence of Fiji progressing through this structural shift in production.

Table 1.1. Fiji's GDP by Production and Expenditure

Category	Percent contribution to total GDP 1995	Percent contribution to total GDP in 2004
GDP by income		
Agriculture	16.3	12.4
Mining	1.4	1.0
Manufacturing	11.0	12.8
Electricity, gas and water	2.8	2.4
Construction	4.0	3.6
Wholesale and retail trade, hotels and restaurants	12.0	16.6
Transport and communications	10.0	13.4
Finance	14.0	9.0
Public Administration	15.5	15.0
Net indirect taxes	13.0	13.8
Total	100	100
GDP by expenditure		
Private consumption	63.0	62.0
Government consumption	15.4	17.9
Gross fixed capital formation	12.5	11.2
Increase in stocks	1.0	1.2
Net exports	7.0	6.6
Statistical discrepancy	1.1	1.1
Total	100	100

Source: The Asian Development Bank (2005) and Fiji Islands Bureau of Statistics (2006).

Table 1.2. Sectoral Value Added (% GDP)

Period Averages	Agriculture	All Industry	Manufacturing	Services
1970-79	24.7	21.9	11.8	53.4
1980-89	20.1	20.6	10.4	59.3
1990-99	19.7	25.3	13.3	55.0
2004	15.9	22.8	13.9	64.6

Source: The World Bank (2004) and Asian Development Bank (2005) for 2004 statistics.

The contribution of the primary sector to Fiji's gross income has been relatively large since independence showing the economic importance of this sector in the economy. However, its contribution in recent times has been in the downward trend with manufacturing and services gaining prominence (Table 1.2). Much of Fiji's primary agricultural production has been dominated by the sugarcane while paddy rice; fish and chicken have been other primary products followed by fisheries, copra, cocoa, ginger and rice. Other smaller crops like kava; taro and vegetables have contributed increasingly to export earnings in the post 1987 period.

In terms of foreign exchange earnings, tourism is the largest earner followed by sugar exports. Earnings from garments surpassed sugar earnings in 1997 and between 1997 and 2000; it has been the major export earner for Fiji (Table 1.3). Following the 2000 political crisis (an armed civilian overthrowing of the democratically elected government), the garment industry suffered a major production setback resulting from market uncertainties as foreign firms relocated their operations to other destinations. In recent times, the exports of mineral water have become an important foreign exchange earner, contributing some 8 percent of the total export earning (Table 1.3).

Table 1.3. Principal Foreign Exchange Earners (Percent of Total Export Earnings)

Commodity	1985	1990	1995	2000	2005
Tourism	...	24.3	26.1	36.8	60.1
Sugar	41.2	30.6	31.7	19.1	25.9
Garment	...	15.8	21.3	26.8	14.3
Gold	8.0	10.4	6.7	6.0	7.0
Fish	4.3	6.7	7.3	7.1	9.8
Timber and Wood Manufactures	2.1	6.2	5.2	4.4	5.4
Mineral Water	..	..	..	1.5	8.0

.. Indicates no exports.

... Indicates data not available.

Source: The Asian Development Bank (2005) and Fiji Islands Bureau of Statistics (2006).

The manufacturing sector has also been developed concentrated mainly on manufacture and processing of gold, silver, sugar, cement, flour, canned fish, soap and coconut oil. The boost to manufacturing sector was a result of shift of focus towards export-oriented production that began in 1981 with favourable commitment from Australia and New Zealand that provided long-term access to their markets. The manufacturing sector gained additional boost in 1987 with the establishment of tax free zones that attracted several foreign investors.

The services sector is the largest contributor to GDP dominated mainly by tourism followed by trading, finance, insurance and government administration. The tourism sector received 507,000 visitors in 2004 with visitors arriving mainly from Australia, Japan, New Zealand, Europe and the United States of America (South Pacific Tourism Organisation, 2006).

Given the overall production structure of the Fiji economy, its long–term pattern of economic progress can be tracked by looking at output per person or the real per capita gross domestic product. As such quantifying the behaviour of the GDP statistics will give deeper insights into economic progress. Although the per capita gross domestic product is a narrow measure of economic advancement, it is nevertheless a reasonable indicator of a country's economic performance over time (Krugman, 1996).

1.4. The Pattern of Fiji's Real per Capita Gross Domestic Product

Figure 1.1 depicts Fiji's real per capita GDP for the period 1970 to 2004. There are some important patterns to be noted. While the overall trend is on the rise over the 30-year period, in some years Fiji experienced a decline in its GDP per capita. Following strong growth soon after independence, the economy experienced almost zero growth from 1973 to 1976, rising sharply in 1979 and then contracting in 1980. While it recovered in 1981, the economy fell into recession in 1982-83. The economy experienced a rise and fall pattern of growth from 1983-86. The year 1987 experienced the largest contraction in growth since 1970. This is when Fiji's political crisis eventuated and much of the contraction is attributed to the years continued political instability (see for example, Chand and Duncan, 2002). The economy recovered sharply for the next four years followed by slight contraction in 1991. Between 1992 to 1996, the economy experienced continued positive growth while contracting in 1997 and 1998 followed by a positive recovery in 1999. Per capita GDP stood slightly above the 1999 level in 2000 followed by a continued increase in 2001 and 2002. It dipped dramatically in 2004 as a result of weakening of the economy.

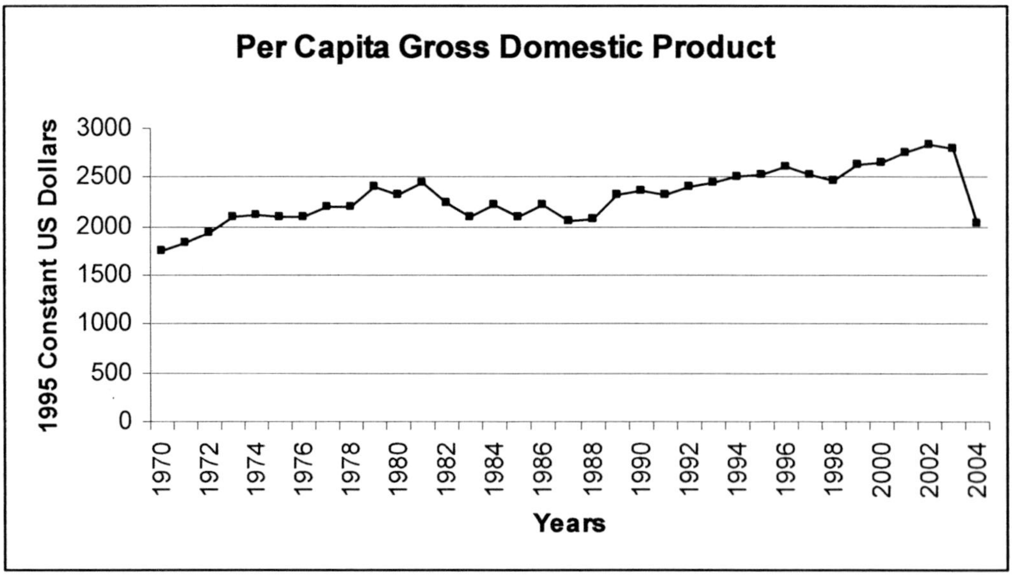

Source of data in Figure 1: The World Bank (2004) and Asian Development Bank (2005).

Figure 1.1.

The reasons for contractions noted above are attributable to both domestic and international events. The second oil shock seems to have hit Fiji hard leading to contractions in 1980. The world economic recession in early eighties seem to have negatively affected Fiji. Fiji was also subjected to adverse weather conditions in 1983, largely tropical cyclones that caused extensive damage to the agricultural sector, tourism industry, physical infrastructure and loss of lives. The political crisis of 1987 led the economy into severe recession. However, economic reform programmes that included major push for industrialisation, privatisation of government owned enterprises and labour market reforms led to solid growth in the first half of 1990's. A severe drought compounded by the secondary effects of East Asian financial crisis led to recession of 1998 (see Gani, 1998 and Garnaut, 1998). The political crisis of 2000 did not allow any marked improvements while growth recovery in 2001-03 led to an increase in the per capita GDP.

In short, the long-term trend shows that at independence, Fiji's per capita GDP was just over US$1,700 measured in 1995 prices and in 2003 it reached just over US$2,000. If the GDP per capita is taken as a rough measure of Fiji's economic advancement, then the pattern depicted in Figure 1.1 suggests that the country is at a slightly better stage of development now then three decades ago.

Fiji's economy is considered to be most robust among the neighbouring island countries in the South Pacific region and comparatively more advanced despite all its economic setbacks. Much of Fiji's long term progress can be attributed to its sugar industry which has been efficient up until mid-1990s while now it's on the verge of collapse as a result of unresolved land tenure issues (see Prasad, 2003). A profitable tourism sector and the development of the light manufacturing sector in the past twelve years have also contributed strongly to Fiji's long-term growth and development. Other than this, Fiji also made some right investments particularly investments in its physical infrastructure soon after independence. The country also has good transport and communication links both domestically and internationally as well as a good human capital base with an entrepreneurial society and both of these are much better than several countries in similar levels of development. All this has positively contributed to Fiji's long-term development.

1.5. Regressive Effects on Economic Growth and Development

While Fiji's long-term achievements in its economic growth and development are noteworthy, the country has been subject to several shocks; some beyond its control that has also negatively affected its long-term growth and development path (see Duncan, 1994). One such negative force has been the effect of developments outside Fiji or external economic shocks. For small island economies, the external shocks generally include sudden changes in commodity prices, reduction in overall world demand, changes in world interest rates and volatility of capital flows (Briguglio, 1995). The international arena has always been a fertile source of crises seriously impacting on the workings of the world economy. Fiji has been no exception.

Fiji's geographical setting is perhaps an important factor subjecting it to a number of disadvantages and making it vulnerable to several forces beyond its control. The lack of land-based resources (minerals, oil, gas and fertile arable land) means dependence on external sources for raw materials and industrial supplies. Apart from trading within Oceania (Australia, New Zealand and the Pacific Islands), Fiji trades with countries in Western Europe, United States of America and Asia. Reliance on foreign transactions has made Fiji vulnerable to foreign sector induced fluctuations in income and levels of economic activity. Fluctuations derive principally from variations in terms of trade, which are wide because of Fiji's concentration of exports in a narrow range of agricultural, mineral, services and manufactured exports. Changes in external economic conditions, particularly to that of its trading partners, are eventually transmitted into its economy.

Fiji's trading regime has little immunity to adverse impacts of internationally generated crises largely through trading partner's business cycles. A recession in trading partners can cause a reduction in demand for Fiji's goods. Over the years, Fiji has experienced the effects of several external crises: the two oil price hikes (1973-1975) and (1978-1979), the industrial country recessions (1975 and 1980) and the subsequent decline in commodity prices, the share market crash of 1987; the financial crisis of Southeast Asia around mid-1997; the 9/11 terrorism crises in the United States of America affecting its tourism industry; and the oil price hike of 2004-06 period.

At the same time, Fiji experienced the effects of shocks beyond its control, for example, adverse weather conditions mainly tropical cyclones and drought that has almost annually hit Fiji causing millions of dollars of agricultural crop and infrastructural damage and loss of lives. Fiji's location in the tropical latitudes makes it highly prone to natural disasters such as droughts, cyclones, hurricanes and floods. Costs per capita inflicted by natural disasters are relatively high due to Fiji's small size and low levels of output. While large developing and developed economies are also prone to natural disaster induced losses, the severity of this is considered much greater in Fiji. A sharper focus on factors threatening the economic viability of Fiji is presented using the composite index of vulnerability developed by Briguglio (1995). Fiji is found to be many times more vulnerable than the average for all developing countries and some of its neighbouring trading partners (Figure 1.2) and is ranked as the 24th most vulnerable country of the 114 countries noted in an earlier study in terms of exposure to foreign economic conditions and proneness to natural disasters (see Briguglio, 1995). According to Briguglio's (1995) measurements, Fiji is highly prone to natural disasters and ranked at twenty-seventh among the fifty-six high disaster prone countries in the world.

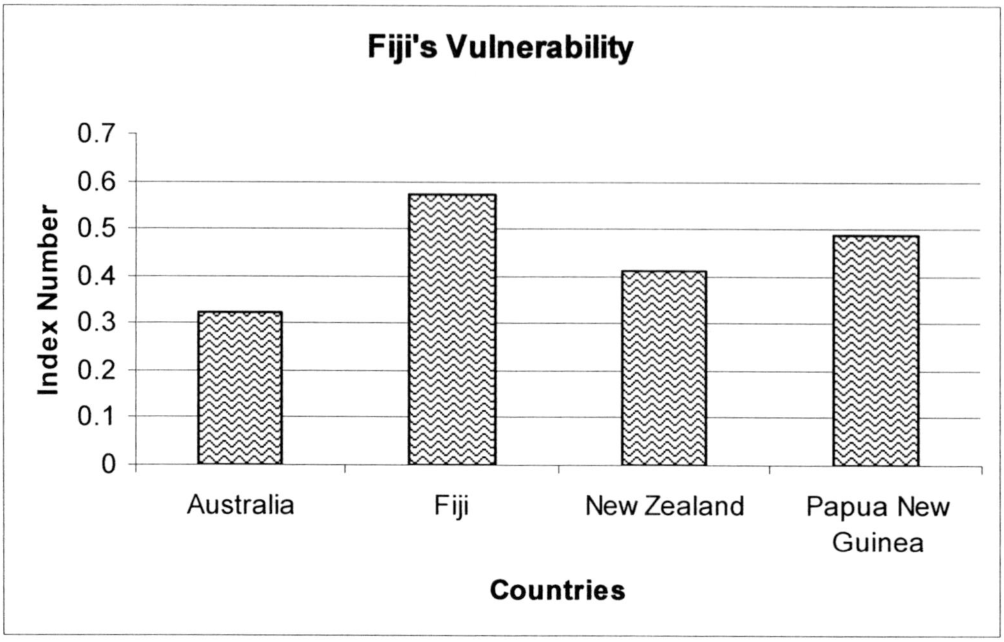

Source of data in Figure 1.2: Briguglio (1995).

Figure 1.2.

Fiji's political crises that first eventuated with two military coups in 1987 followed by another civilian armed seizure and overthrowing of elected government in year 2000 has been a major internal shock to the economy (for example, Kumar and Prasad, 2004). The country has largely remained politically unstable since 1987 and economic growth facing regressive effects as a result of falling investment, brain drain, corruption, financial scams, unresolved land tenure issues and the deterioration in law, order and public safety. In general, it has been argued that Fiji has largely backslided into a spiral of political conflicts and low economic growth (Prasad, 2006). The series of political crises has led Fiji to slip down in its international rankings of political rights as revealed by the Freedom House measures of political rankings (Figure 1.3). Higher scores in Figure 1.3 indicate worsening political environment. According to Figure 1.3, since 1997, Fiji's political standing has been rated between not so free to partly free as opposed to being free for pre-1987 period.

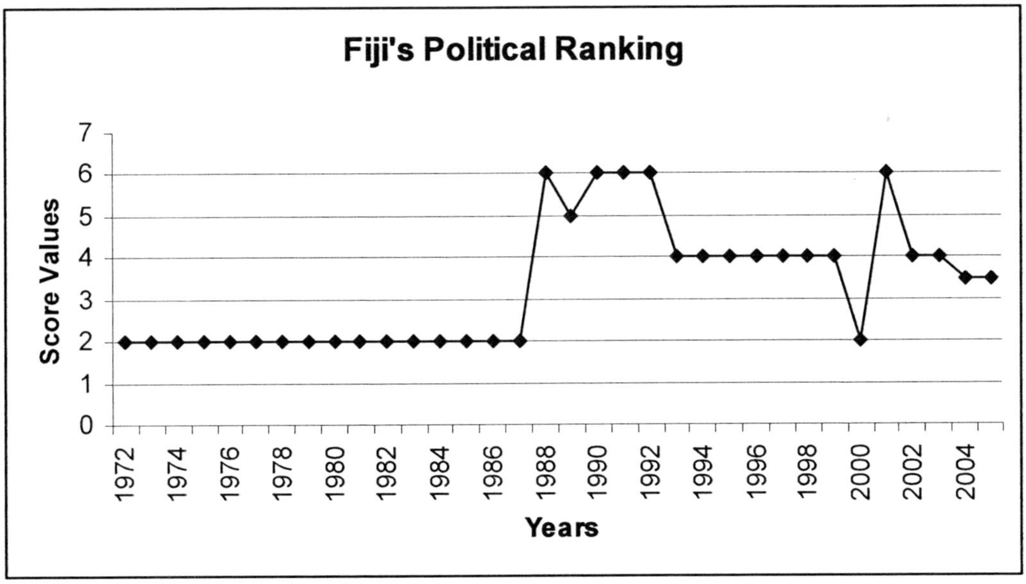

Source of data in Figure 1.3: Freedom House (2005).

Figure 1.3.

1.6. Fiji and the Global Economy

Fiji has a history of political and economic links with the outside world starting with United Kingdom with official contacts and relationship established in 1874. Other than its historic economic, political and sporting ties with neighbouring high-income countries of Australia and New Zealand, it has earned a well-established position with other countries such as the United States of America, Canada, several of the European Union member countries, Japan and India. In recent times, it has also established economic relationship with China and several countries in the Asia Pacific region.

As discussed earlier, the Fiji economy is vulnerable to the changes in the global economy that tend to have an important bearing on the domestic economy. The effect of such changes on the economy can be analysed by examining the statistics on Fiji's international trading environment. Fiji is heavily reliant on high-income countries for its exports as well as imports. Tables 1.4 and 1.5 present data on Fiji's direction of trade for 1990 and 2004. Fiji's main market for its export item is USA followed by Australia and United Kingdom. Fiji's main import country is Australia followed by Singapore with New Zealand at the third place.

Overall, Fiji is heavily reliant on Australia for both its exports and imports and developments in the Australian economy do translate into changes in the domestic economy.

Table 1.4. Fiji's Direction of Exports

Country	Percentage share of exports in total in 1990	Percentage share of exports in total in 2004
Australia	17.7	19.2
United Kingdom	22.9	12.8
United States of America	8.4	23.6
New Zealand	11.7	3.7
Japan	5.9	4.1

Source: The Asian Development Bank (2005).

Table 1.5. Fiji's Direction of Imports

Country	Percentage share of imports in total in 1990	Percentage share of imports in total in 2004
Australia	27.8	27.7
New Zealand	16.3	17.8
Singapore	5.8	24.8
Japan	11.0	4.2
China	2.8	2.8

Source: The Asian Development Bank (2005).

The value of Fiji's terms of trade becomes important when it comes to measuring its prosperity. The terms of trade is the average price of exported goods and services, divided by the average price of imported goods and services. If the terms of trade value increases, it means that the prices of its exported goods have risen quicker than the prices of its imported goods. The end result is that Fiji is likely to face an improvement in its economic prosperity. If the value of the terms of trade declines, it signals that the country should export a greater quantity of goods and services to pay for the same quantity of imports, and the domestic economy faces a decline in its prosperity.

Published data on Fiji's terms of trade is not available. Fiji's trade orientation is thus examined in terms of its exports and imports. Available statistics show a clear pattern: that since Fiji's independence, the value of imports has exceeded the value of exports thus making Fiji remain in trade deficits (discussed in detail in chapter three). Despite the progress made on the export side, Fiji's lack of resources, raw materials and technology for production has meant that it had to depend on other countries for its much-needed imports. On the basis of Standard Industrial Trade Classification (SITC), Fiji has spent significantly on imports of basic manufactures, machines and transport equipment, mineral fuels and other manufactured goods (Figure 1.4). These have chewed up much of Fiji's income leaving the country into continued path of trade deficits. Given the large and continued trade deficits over long-term it can be concluded that Fiji's economic prosperity has been constrained as a result of heavy import spending.

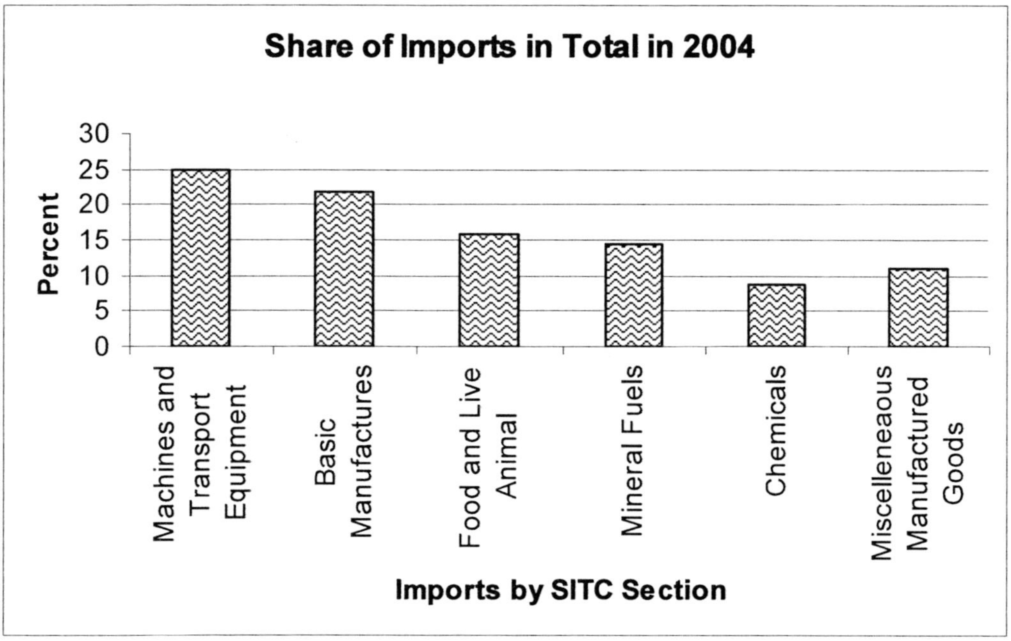

Source of data in Figure 1.4: Asian Development Bank (2005).

Figure 1.4.

1.7. Developmental Achievements

Fiji's level of development can be gauged with different measures. When judging whether a country is prospering or not, it is natural to look at the total income that the economy is earning. This is the function of the GNP and also a commonly used measure of national well being. Figure 1.5 depicts the trends in Fiji's per capita GNP. It has been on a steady rise since Fiji's independence. One way to gauge the usefulness of this measure of national well being is to examine other country cases too. It is common sense to ascertain that a large GNP can lead to a high level of national well being (Dalziel and Lattimore, 1996). Figure 1.5 also shows the average per capita GNP for the lower-middle-income countries and the East Asia and the Pacific region. If per capita GNP is taken as a broad indicator of level of development, than Fiji's development achievement have been better than the average achievement for the lower-middle-income countries as well as the average for the countries in the East Asia and the Pacific region.

It is worth pointing out that the validity of the per capita GNP as a measure of national well being can be disputed. The per capita income is considered to be too narrow a measure to gauge a country's socio-economic progress. For example, the per capita GNP does not represent the broadest dimension of human welfare such as health, literacy and access to public goods, among others. Nobel Laureate, Amartya Sen (see Sen, 1998), has argued "that the *per capita* GNP may be a good indicator of the average real income of a nation, but the quality of life of an individual depends not merely on personal income, but also on various physical and societal conditions: the epidemiological atmosphere, the availability of health care, education, orderliness of urban living and access to modern medical knowledge." While per capita income may not capture several aspects that determine individual well being, prominent economist, Paul Krugman (see Krugman, 1996) has extended his support of this measure arguing "that although the per capita GNP is generally considered to be a one-dimensional measure of economic development, it does not seriously distort the level of that development." Thus, it is useful to look at other measures, which more closely reflect the quality of national well being.

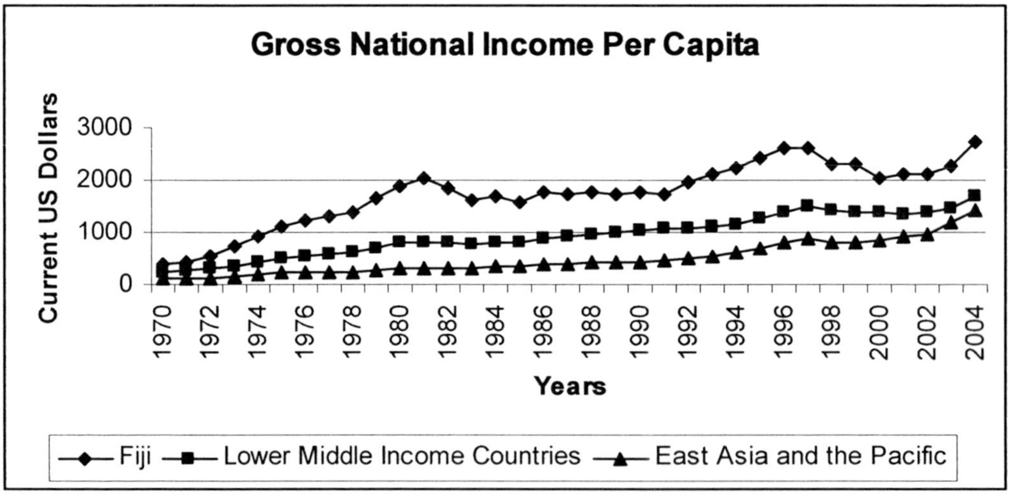

Source of data in Figure 1.5: The World Bank (2004) and the World Bank (2006).

Figure 1.5.

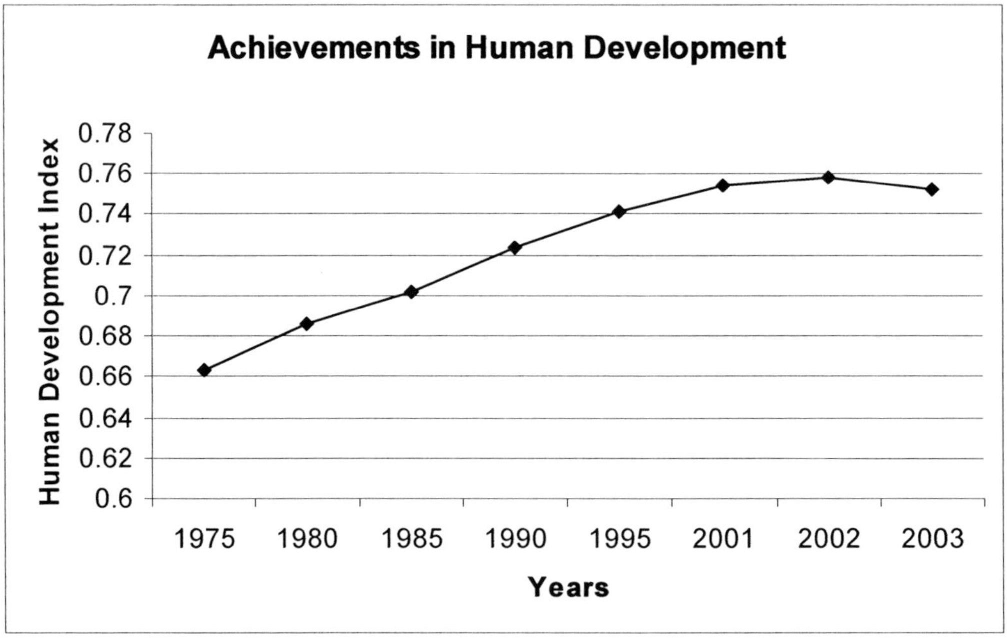

Source of data in Figure 1.6: United Nations Development Program (various issues).

Figure 1.6.

The human development index (HDI) developed by the United Nations Development Program has its own appeal. The HDI is a composite index comprising four variables: educational attainment, income, literacy and life expectancy (United Nations Development Program, 2005). Figure 1.6 depicts the HDI for Fiji revealing a steady improvement in human development from 1975 to 2002. Fiji's achievements in human development fell in 2003 and remained below the average HDI of 0.768 for countries in the East Asia and the Pacific region as a result of deteriorating economic growth and rising poverty. Fiji's continued political instability and poor economic growth has contributed to rising poverty and social deprivation in recent times (see for example, Kumar and Prasad, 2004).

Although the HDI seems to have elements of a desirable appeal among government policymakers (see for example, Streetan, 1999), some researchers have questioned its conceptual underpinnings in terms of the arbitrary selection of weights in the construction of HDI (for example, Basu, 2001 and Kanbur and Squire, 2001).

Noting the drawbacks of *per capita* GNP and HDI, another indicator that gives a more focused reflection of quality of life as proposed by the Nobel Laureate Amartya Sen is the infant mortality rate (Sen, 1998). The Nobel Laureates argument in support of this is that "it is epistemically rich, practically important, and mortality data also moves fast enough to provide guidance on a rapidly changing economic and social situation." Figure 1.7 presents the trend on Fiji's infant mortality rates against the average for lower-middle-income countries and East Asia and the Pacific region. Using infant mortality rate as an indicator of societal progress, Fiji fares well. Its infant mortality rate is far below the average for the countries in the lower-middle-income category as well as the average for the East Asia and the Pacific.

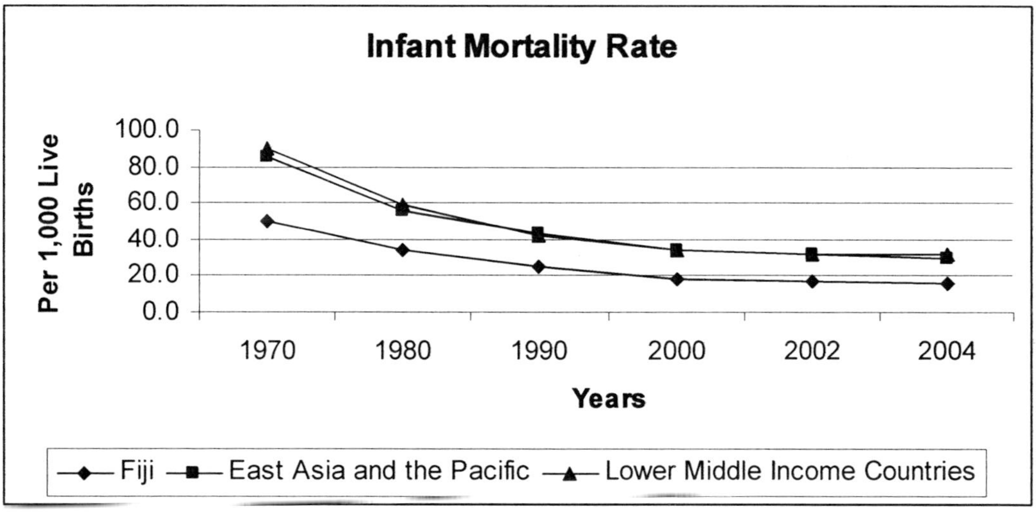

Source of data in Figure 1.7: The World Bank (2004 and 2006).

Figure 1.7.

1.8. Conclusion

Fiji is a very small highly open lower-middle-income country with a per capita income of US$3280 in 2005. Wholesale and retail trade, restaurants and hotels, manufacturing and transport and communications combine to produce close to 42 percent of Fiji's GDP. Over the 30-year period, agricultural contribution to GDP has declined while the rest of the sectoral contribution to GDP has increased providing evidence of Fiji progressing through this structural shift in production. Sugarcane production, which for long has dominated the Fiji economy in terms of its contribution to GDP shows signs that it is less likely to hold its dominant position as a major income earner to the country. Tourism earnings dominate Fiji's GDP. The manufacturing sector has also been developed as a result favourable commitment from Australia and New Zealand in providing long-term access to their markets together with the establishment of tax free zones that attracted several foreign investors. The services sector is the largest contributor to GDP dominated mainly by tourism. The tourism sector received over 500,000 visitors in 2004 and is the largest foreign exchange earner. Much of Fiji's long term progress can be attributed to its sugar industry; a profitable tourism sector and the development of the light manufacturing sector in the post-1987 period.

Despite Fiji's economic progress over the long-term, economic growth has been less than satisfactory (Prasad, 2003). Lack of land-based resources; vulnerability to foreign sector induced fluctuations in income and levels of economic activity; proneness to natural disasters; long periods of political instability; falling investment, brain drain, corruption, financial scams, unresolved land tenure issues and the deterioration in law, order and public safety had major regressive effects on its long-term economic growth.

Fiji's long-term social progress and achievements is considered to be good in comparison with countries in similar per capita income categories with several indicators of quality of life ranking higher than the average for countries in similar stages of development. Fiji's development achievement have been better than the average achievement for the lower-middle-income countries as well as the average for the countries in the East Asia and the Pacific region on the per capita GNP basis as well as HDI that revealed a steady improvement in human development from 1975 to 2003 with the HDI remaining below the average HDI of 0.768 for countries in the East Asia and the Pacific region as a result of deteriorating economic growth and rising poverty. Using infant mortality rate as an indicator of societal progress, Fiji fares well. Its infant mortality rate is far below the average for the countries in the lower-middle-income category as well as the average for the East Asia and the Pacific. Despite all the political developments and changing international economic events, Fiji still has potentials to achieve greater economic prosperity with appropriate policies. The remainder of the book will examine several aspects of the macroeconomy.

References

Asian Development Bank. (2005). *Key Indicators 2004*. Manila.

Basu, K. (2001). On the Goals of Development, in Meier, G. M. and Stiglitz, J. E, (Ed.), *Frontiers of Development Economics*, Washington. D.C.: The World Bank and Oxford University Press.

Briguglio, L. (1995). Small Island developing states and their economic vulnerabilities, *World Development*, Vol. 23, pp. 1615-32.

Chand, S. and Duncan, R. (2002). Arc of instability, *Asia Pacific Economic Literature*, Vol. 16, No. 1, pp. 1-11.

Dalziel, P. and R. Lattimore. (1996). *The New Zealand Macroeconomy: A Briefing on Reforms,* Oxford University Press: Auckland.

Duncan, R. (1994). On achieving and stable economic policies in the Pacific Islands, *Pacific Economic Bulletin*, Vol. 9, pp. 21-25.

Fiji Islands Bureau of Statistics. (March 2006). *Key Statistics*. Government Printer. Suva.

Freedom House. (2006). Freedom House Rankings. Available on line at: http://www.freedomhouse.org. Date of extraction: 7 July 2006.

Gani, A. (2000). Some dimensions of Fiji's recent emigration, *Pacific Economic Bulletin*, Vol. 15, No. 1, pp. 94-103.

Gani, A. (1999). Drought, the Asian crisis and Fiji's monetary policy response, *Pacific Economic Bulletin*, Vol.14, No.2, pp. 110-122.

Garnaut, R. (1998). The financial crisis, *Asia Pacific Economic Literature*, Vol. 12 No. (1), pp. 1-11.

Jones, C. I. (1998). *Introduction to Economic Growth*, New York: W. W. Norton and Co.

Kanbur, R. and Squire, L. (2001). The Evolution of Thinking About Poverty, in Meier, G. M. and Stiglitz, J. E. (Ed.), *Frontiers of Development Economics*, Washington. D.C.: The World Bank and Oxford University Press.

Krugman, P. (1996). Cycles of conventional wisdom on economic development, *International Affairs*, Vol. 72, pp. 717-732.

Kumar, S. and Prasad, B. (2004). Politics of race and poverty in Fiji: a case of Indo-Fijian community, *International Journal of Social Economics*, Vol. 31, No. 5/6, pp. 469- 486.

Lal, V. (1990). *Fiji Coups in Paradise*. Zed Books Ltd: London.

Prasad, B.C. (2006). Resolving the agricultural land lease impasse in Fiji, *Pacific Economic Bulletin*, Vol. 21, No. 2, pp. 177-193.

Prasad, B. C. (2003). Merging interests in Fiji: essential ingredients for better economic performance, *Pacific Economic Bulletin*, Vol. 18, No.1, pp. 121-130.

Prasad, B.C. (1998). The woes of economic reform: poverty and income inequality in Fiji, *International Journal of Social Economics*, Vol. 25, No. 6/7/8, pp. 1073-1094.

Reddy, M. and Duncan, R. (2006). Agricultural productivity in Pacific Island countries: issues and challenges, *The ICFAI Journal of Agricultural Economics*, Vol. 111, No, 2, pp. 16-31.

Reddy, M., Mohanty, M. and Naidu, V. (2004). Economic cost of human capital loss from Fiji: implications for sustainable development, *The International Migration Review*, Vol. 38, No.4, pp. 1447-1461.

Sen, A. (1998). Mortality as an indicator of economic success and failure, *The Economic Journal*, Vol. 108, pp. 1-25.

South Pacific Tourism Organisation. (2006). Table A3. South and Central Pacific Visitor Arrivals: 2000 – 2004. Available on line at: http://www.spto.org/investment/tableA3.shtml.

Srinivasan, T.N. (1986). The costs and benefits of being a small remote island landlocked or ministate economy, *World Bank Research Observer*, Vol. 1, No. 2, pp. 205-218.

Streeten, P. (1999). Components of a future development strategy: the importance of human development, *Finance and Development*, Vol. 36, pp. 30-33.

Streeten, P. (1997). The special problems of small countries, *World Development*, Vol. 21, No. 2, pp. 197-202.

The World Bank. (2004). *World Development Indicators CD ROM*. The World Bank: Washington, D.C.

The World Bank. (2006). Key Development Data and Statistics. Washington, D.C. Available on line at http://web.worldbank.org/website/external/datastatistics. Date of extraction: 10 July 2006.

United Nations Development Program. (Various Issues). *Human Development Report*. Oxford University Press, New York.

Chapter 2

MACROECONOMIC ACHIEVEMENTS SINCE INDEPENDENCE

2.1. INTRODUCTION

Chapter 1 introduced some of the long-term economic and social indicators so as to give an overview of Fiji's economic and social achievements in the post independence period. Two important indicators commonly used in analysis of economies performance – the real per capita gross domestic product and the structure of trade orientation were also analysed. This chapter takes a look at Fiji's macroeconomic achievements in core periods: from independence in 1970 to 1986; 1987, the year of Fiji's first political crisis; the developments in post crisis period,1988-1999; the political crisis of year 2000; and the post-2000 achievement. In doing so, the chapter focuses on some of the key macroeconomic aspects: real economic growth rate, the rate of inflation, the rate of unemployment and the current account of the balance of payments.

2.2. ECONOMIC GROWTH

This section focuses on the long-term GDP and identifies the short-run fluctuations of real GDP and its long-run trend. The previous chapter showed two aspects of Fiji's GDP: the total income earned and total expenditures on the economy are output of goods and services. The level of Fiji's GDP is a good gauge of its economic achievement and the growth of real GDP is an appropriate indicator of its economic progress.

2.2.1. Growth: Independence to 1986

The period under review starts with 1970 when Britain gave full independence to Fiji after it first annexed it in 1874 (see Lal, 1990). Prior to independence, agriculture was the predominant economic activity with coconut products and the introduced crop, sugarcane, forming the greatest source of revenue (Garnaut, 1972). The commercial production of sugar was the major economic activity where the Australian Colonial Sugar Refinery Company conducted processing, management and marketing operations with the economy remaining closely linked to United Kingdom mainly through the preferential prices it received for its sugar sales (Brown and Scott, 1989). The economy was performing well prior to independence. Evaluations of the postcolonial economy highlighted country's favourable "initial conditions" with average GDP growth rate of just over 7 percent recorded for the 1965-70 period (see Garnaut, 1972).

Figure 2.1 depicts the trends in Fiji's real economic growth since its independence together with the average real economic growth for the lower-middle-income and the East Asia and the Pacific categories. A major trend that stands out is that while growth for the average of the lower-middle-income and East Asia and the Pacific countries has remained positive throughout the 1970-86 periods, Fiji's economic growth has gyrated with several years experiencing very low or negative growth rates. Fiji has not been able maintain the trend noted for the lower-middle- income and the East Asia and the Pacific group of countries. A number of factors have contributed to Fiji's poor long term growth are discussed below.

At independence, Fiji's real GDP growth rates of close to 13 percent were much higher than the average for the lower-middle-income and the East Asia and the Pacific region. This trend was maintained up until 1973 and during these four years real GDP growth averaged just over 9.5 percent. The main contributors to this higher performance were robust growth in tourism and construction sectors and lucrative export prices for its main export commodity, sugar (Elek, Hill and Tabor, 1993).

The year 1973 was unfortunate for most economies around the globe as the Organisation of Petroleum Exporting Countries (OPEC) oil cartel increased oil prices that led to recessionary conditions. Large industrialised countries as well as developing nations suffered severely. Fiji was no exception as the lagged effects of oil price rise constrained growth in years that followed. For example, almost no growth was recorded in 1975 and economic growth remained below the average for the lower-middle-income and East Asia and the Pacific region from 1974-76 (Figure 2.1). Recessionary conditions in industrialised countries as a result of the oil price hike also acted negatively for Fiji as would be visitors faced lower purchasing power. It meant low visitor arrivals and tourist activity slowed (Brown and Scott, 1989). Fiji, however, was lucky in the sense that it avoided zero economic growth as a result of a rise in world sugar prices during this period (Figure 2.1). The *El Nino* weather patterns in Latin America and the Caribbean meant falling sugar production among other crops led to commodity price booms in 1973 and 74 (see The World Bank, 1996). Fiji's benefit of higher sugar prices meant a countervailing effect on falling tourist numbers and rising fuel prices and this provided some buffer to the looming recessionary conditions (Figure 2.1).

In the late 1970s Fiji experienced positive economic growth rates with just over 12 percent growth recorded in 1979 (Figure 2.1). Much is to do with government's economic strategy in expanding the economic output through the expansion of area under sugar cultivation and public investment in physical infrastructure particularly hydroelectric and piped water supply (Elek, Hill and Tabor, 1993). The tourism industry also recovered with increases in visitor arrivals (Brown and Scott, 1989). While high economic growth rate was recorded in 1979 (Figure 2.1), the effects of the second oil price shock in 1979 were counteracted by the rise in sugar prices. It is also likely that the effects of second oil shock appeared in early 1980s as a result of time lag (Figure 2.1).

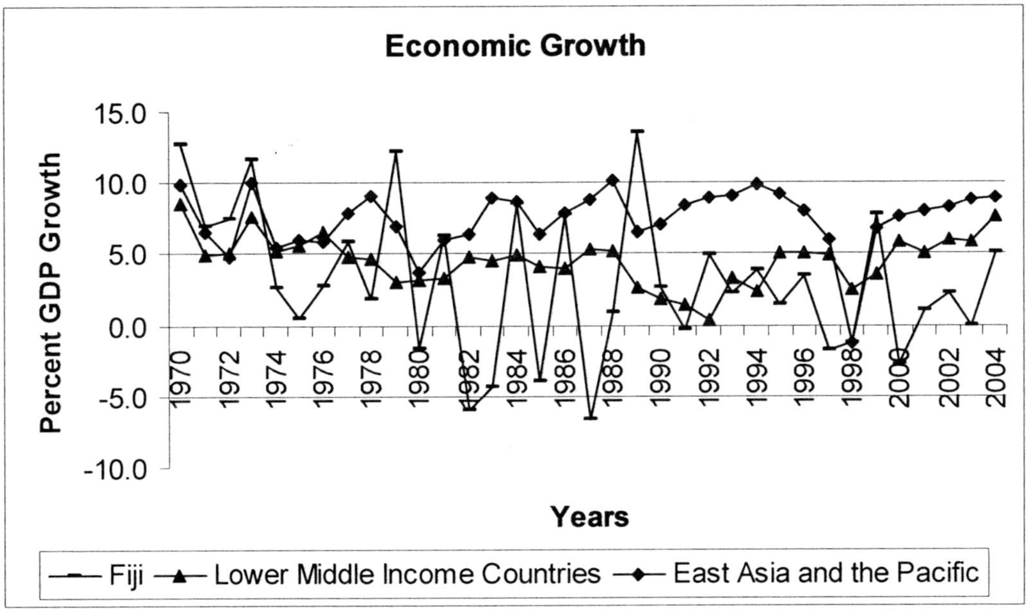

Source of data for Figure 2.1: The World Bank (2004 and 2006) and the Fiji Islands Bureau of Statistics (2006).

Figure 2.1.

Fiji's economic growth has remained less than satisfactory in the early 1980s with negative real GDP growth rates recorded in 1980, 1982, 1983 and 1985 (Figure 2.1). The economy rebounded in 1986 recording growth of close to 8 percent (Figure 2.1) largely as a result of increased investment, falling consumer prices and drop in prices of petroleum products (Cameron, 1993 and Elek, Hill and Tabor, 1993). Other than 1981 and 1984, Fiji's economic growth remained below the average growth achieved by the lower-middle-income and the East Asia and the Pacific economies (Figure 2.1). Fiji's economic growth averaged 1.2 percent annually during 1980-86, well below the 4-5 percent average achieved in the 1970s.

The poor economic performance during the first half of 1980s is largely a result of three broad categories of factors. First, external economic shock (oil price hikes, industrial country recession, falling visitor arrivals and commodity prices), a factor beyond Fiji's control has adversely affected economic growth. Second, poor domestic economic policies dealing with labour market and private sector development had a significant regressive effect (Elek, Hill and Tabor, 1993). For example, continued real wage increases contributed to weakening of fiscal accounts. Closely allied to this is that trade policies have been inward oriented (Brown and Scott, 1989 and Elek, Hill and Tabor, 1993) and seems to have fallen short of directing Fiji into a faster growing economy. The government has played a major role as a producer and distributor of goods and services rather than involving the private sector and encouraging production for domestic market and exports (Cameron, 1995 and The World Bank, 1996). Third, natural disasters have adversely affected economic growth as economic activity has been continuously affected by some of the worse cyclones that have hit Fiji annually. For example, in 1980 cyclones *Tia* and *Wally*; in 1982 cyclone *Hettie*; in 1983 cyclone *Oscar*; in 1985 cyclones *Eric* and *Nigel*; and in 1986 flooding (Gani, 1998). The natural disasters have caused millions of dollars of damage to the agricultural sector, to physical infrastructure; disruption to economic activity and loss of lives.

2.2.2. Growth and the 1987 Military Takeover of the Democratically Elected Government

Since independence, Fiji has been effectively governed by the Alliance Party, predominantly ethnic Fijian, and in coalition with the General Electors Party, non-Fijian and non-Fiji Indian, (see for example, Chand and Naidu, 1997). The Fiji Labour Party (FLP), representing largely the Fiji Indians and the underprivileged ethnic Fijians was formed in 1984 and launched in 1985 with the aim to establish itself as a major political force against the existing Fiji Indian dominated National Federation Party (NFP) and to challenge the Alliance government that has been in power since independence. The NFP since its inception has been a voice for Fiji Indians. Over time, its electoral responsibility tended to weaken with regard to the under privileged Fiji Indians who showed increasing levels of discontent towards this party. The January 1987 elections brought a victory to the FLP which in coalition with the NFP formed the government.

Resentment toward the FLP-NFP coalition government started to build up as ethnic Fijian community feared that they have lost control of their country to the Fiji Indians (Sharpham, 2000). Some indigenous Fijians were not prepared to accept the outcome of the general elections as well as the formation of the coalition government (Chand and Naidu, 1997). Conspired by the elements of the defeated Alliance Party, senior civil servants, high ranking police and military personnel's and external influence including the Central Intelligence Authority of United States of America (see Blum, 2002), third in the Fiji Military Forces command – Lieutenant Colonel Sitiveni Ligamamada Rabuka together with 10 of his soldiers launched the first military coup against the government on 14 May 1987. Dissatisfied with an arrangement of the interim government following the takeover in May 1987, Rabuka executed a second coup on 25 September 1987 and took the responsibility of the executive authority and formed an interim government.

The coups had a detrimental effect on the economy with serious social consequences. Growth in GDP fell drastically in 1987 to -7.0 percent from a high of 8 percent a year before (Figure 2.1). This was the worst growth recorded since Fiji's independence. The effect on GDP came from several fronts but the prominent ones were from falling sugar production, tourism, aid and investment and massive emigration of skilled workers (Cole and Hughes, 1988). Fiji's problem was further compounded by mismanagement of public funds, falling investor confidence, corruption, nepotism, institutional weaknesses, deteriorating law and order and rising misery and deprivation (Prasad and Tisdell, 1996).

Sugar output fell as predominantly Indian cane farmers protested against the loss of democracy thus interrupting and delaying sugarcane harvesting and processing (Brown and Scott, 1989). As a result of this sugarcane harvested was just over 2.9 million tonnes in 1987 compared to just over 4.1 million tonnes in 1986 (Fiji Islands Bureau of Statistics, December 1988). A severe drought in this year also had an impact on sugarcane as well as other agricultural crops. The tourism industry, also a major income earner, got hard hit with dramatic declines in tourist arrivals (Cole and Hughes, 1988). In response to military rule and fear of safety and security tourist arrivals which was rising since 1980 contracted by 36 percent in 1987 (Table 2.1).

Foreign investment suffered as a result of prevailing risky business environment and worsened further by boycotts from the Australian and New Zealand trade unions on Fiji's imports and exports (Elek, Hill and Tabor, 1993). Aid donors also responded by drastically reducing development assistance programmes while domestic investment rose in 1987, it fell in 1988 (Table 2.1). Emigration of Fiji Indians rose who feared of safety and security and saw no future for themselves in the country. Emigration was concentrated on highly skilled and educated Fiji Indian (Gani and Ward, 1995). Emigration rose from just over 3,000 in 1986 to almost 5,400 in 1987 and caused major skill shortages in both the private sector and public administration (Gani, 2000 and Reddy, Mohanty and Naidu, 2004). Emigrants also caused a further bottle neck to the economy as they started remitting their personal savings abroad (Cole and Hughes, 1988). Large businesses also engaged heavily on remitting their funds abroad all contributing to a squeeze in domestic investment (Gani, 2005).

Table 2.1. Some Macroeconomic Indicators

Variable	1986	1987	1988
GDP growth (annual %)	7.7	-6.6	1.0
Current account balance (% of GDP)	1.3	2.3	6.4
Inflation, consumer prices (annual %)	1.8	5.7	11.8
Unemployment, total (% of total labour force)	7.5	9.3	9.4
Gross fixed capital formation (% of GDP)	14.7	15.6	14.0
Gross domestic savings (% of GDP)	20.4	19.2	18.0
International tourism, number of arrivals	258,000	190,000	208,000
International tourism, receipts (% of total exports)	29.9	19.0	21.5
Official development assistance and aid (current US$)	42,480,000	35,870,000	54,320,000
Overall budget deficit (% of GDP)	-4.8	-5.0	-0.7
Gross international reserves in months of imports	3.6	2.9	4.4

Source: The World Bank (2004).

Following the coups of 1987 and ongoing economic crises, the country went through some of the major liberalisation programmes that were not seen since its independence (Elek, Hill and Tabor, 1993 and Cameron, 1993). The on slaught of the economic crises gave way to some rigorous overhaul of economic policies that in fact was the hallmark of Fiji's reform initiatives in the post-independent era. Given the small nature of the country, the reform initiatives that were taken are commendable that certainly did produce positive results for the economy in a very short time. Further the reforms have continued to show their positive lagged effects in several years following the crises. Reform initiatives focused in four main areas: exchange rate, investment, trade, labour market and tourism.

On the exchange rate front, the Reserve Bank of Fiji *devalued* the Fiji dollar by a total of 33 percent in two steps: 17 percent in June 1987 and 15 percent in October 1987 (Reserve Bank of Fiji, December 1988). It also imposed stringent measures to curb outflow of funds. The government's reform initiative on the investment front included a campaign on *attracting foreign* as well as domestic investors. In doing so, it designed a range of investment incentive packages. The most important aspect of the investment incentive was the 13 year tax holiday to foreign investors (see Elek, Hill and Tabor, 1993 and Cameron, 1993). On the trade side, the government vigorously focused on directing the economy towards being more outward oriented rather than inward looking by reducing tariffs on imports and eliminating majority of licensing requirements for imports (Elek, Hill and Tabor, 1993). Further, firms exporting over 95 percent of their final product were exempt from import duty payments (Fiji Islands Bureau of Statistics, December 1994). The government moved boldly and quickly to dismantle the import licensing system, putting in place initially high tariffs, which has been subsequently reduced to a maximum of 50 percent (Fiji Islands Bureau of Statistics, December 1994). Labour market reforms were introduced to allow for more *flexibility on wage rates* and employment conditions and to curb the power of trade unions. The government invested in marketing of Fiji tourism and developed *promotional packages* to attract tourists from major source countries: Australia, New Zealand, Japan and United States of America.

2.2.3. Growth: 1988-1999

Despite the political chaos of Rabuka's actions, the economic policies implemented under his leadership seem to have an important bearing for the way in which the economy performed during post-1987 period.

Figure 2.1 also depicts the pattern of Fiji's real GDP growth rate for the post 1987 period. The pattern of growth noted for Fiji in comparison with the average for East Asia and the Pacific and the lower-middle-income group is clear. With the exception of 1989, Fiji's economic growth has remained far below that experienced by the East Asia and the Pacific group of countries. During 1995-99, Fiji's growth has remained lower than the average growth for the lower-middle-income group (Figure 2.1).

Following the massive decline in growth of 1987, growth in 1988 reversed, although marginally but positive. An exceptional performance was noted in 1989 with a growth rate of just over 13 percent, the highest growth achieved for the 1988-99 period (Figure 2.1). This achievement was aided by an excellent sugar crop and the benefits of reforms that took place in 1987 (Elek, Hill and Tabor, 1993). Although the growth rate fell in 1990, it was still satisfactory recorded at close to 3 percent (Figure 2.1). A bumper sugarcane crop, rising tourist numbers and effects of reforms of 1987 were again contributory factors (Fiji Islands Bureau of Statistics, December 1988).

Despite the slump in 1991, the economy held up relatively well between 1992 and 1996 with real GDP growth rate averaging 3.9 percent per annum (Figure 2.1). The year 1997 faced recessionary conditions. At the beginning of 1997, the country suffered from two cyclones - *Gavin* in March and *June* in May (Gani, 1998). Together, they had an impact on agricultural production. One immediate effect was a rise in food prices earlier in the year as a result of destruction of agricultural food crops (Gani, 1999).

While the country healed from cyclone damage, the sugar industry faced disruptions from industrial disputes and frequent mill stoppages (Gani, 1999). As a result, sugar output suffered. The mining sector, an important contributor to national income was adversely affected by the slump in gold prices and the country went through a period of weak domestic demand and the lagged effects of sluggish investment (Gani, 1999). Of importance is investment spending, falling since 1980; now it is many times below the average for the lower-middle-income and East Asia and the Pacific countries (Figure 2.2). Together, all these events contributed to a 1.6 percent contraction in economic activity in 1997 (Figure 2.1).

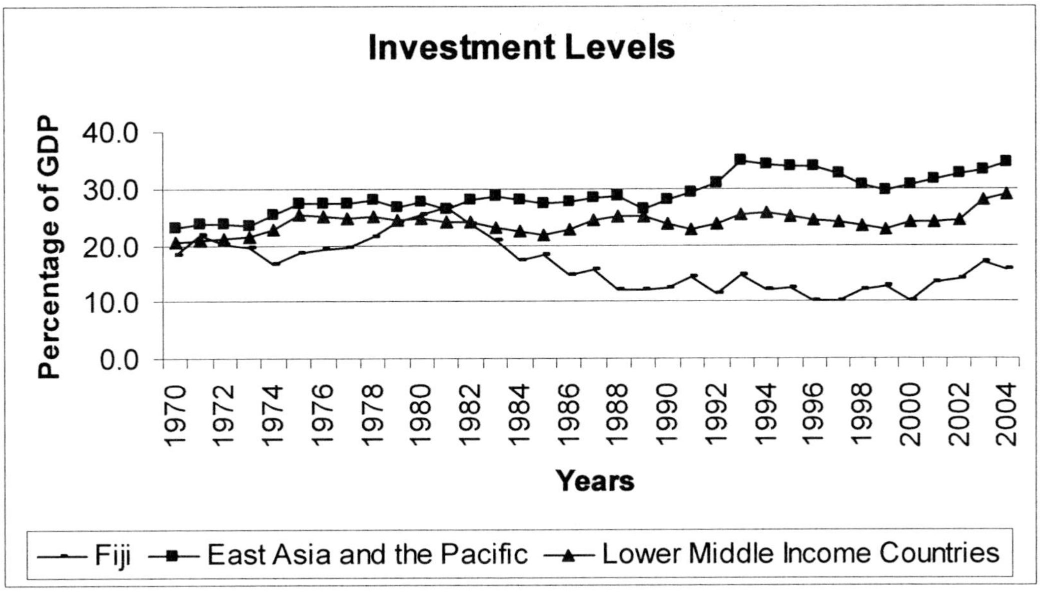

Source of data for Figure 2.2: The World Bank (2004 and 2006).

Figure 2.2.

The effects of *El Nino* weather patterns became evident in most parts of the country from September 1997 (Gani, 1999). The drought reduced agricultural production to an unprecedented level. The most immediate consequence was a fall in crop production (both subsistence and commercial), due to inadequate and poorly distributed rainfall. Sugarcane together with food crops (vegetables and rice) were the worst affected. Sugar production fell by around 23 percent in 1998 from an already low base in 1997 while the total sugar cane crushed in 1998 was 2.1 million tonnes, producing around 256,000 tonnes of sugar - the lowest in more than thirty years (Gani, 1999).

The slowdown in economic activity was largely attributable to domestic factors that threatened the growth prospects for 1998. The year 1997 was also when the East Asian Financial Crises eventuated (see Garnaut, 1998) and again this development in Fiji's external environment posed a threat to the Fiji economy (Chand, 1998). However, the effects of the Asian crisis were not impacting on the country at this stage. Nevertheless, the contraction in economic growth of 1997 threatened growth prospects for 1998

Available evidence indicates that Fiji's economy started experiencing trouble even before the onset of the Asian crisis and drought (see Gani, 1999). As 1998 approached, the economy continued to look weak. The lagged effects of the deterioration in economic conditions in 1997 seem to have continued into 1998 (Figure 2.1). Growth forecasts in the first quarter of 1998 by the Reserve Bank of Fiji revealed deterioration in the immediate economic outlook (Reserve Bank of Fiji, March 1998).

It also became evident that, over the past couple of years, the Fiji dollar appreciated against the currencies of Australia and New Zealand, two of Fiji's important trading partners

(Gani, 1997). One of the effects shows that Fiji's exports were considerably more expensive in those markets compared with exports from Fiji's Southeast Asian competitors. The sharp deterioration of Asian currencies beginning mid-1997 and 1998, and the related falls in the Australian and New Zealand currencies, reduced the competitiveness of Fiji's goods in these markets (see Chand, 1998 and Gani, 1997). These changes in trading partner countries meant weakness in Fiji's export competitiveness as a result of Fiji's appreciating currency.

While for Fiji the effects of Asia's problems were mostly indirect, they were nonetheless important. Although Fiji had very limited direct trade and investment linkages with the Asian region, it was at risk because of potential contagion effects of the crisis on its main export markets, such as Australia and New Zealand, and through competitiveness effects on the tourism and garment industries (Gani, 1999). Because Fiji exports close to 70 percent of production, a weaker global economy, particularly in trading partner countries such as Australia and New Zealand as they faced economic slowdown could have had a flow on effect to Fiji.

Prior to the Asian episode, both the Australian and the New Zealand economies were expected to strengthen in 1998, following policy adjustments in 1997 (see Garnaut, 1998). This expectation was not realised, particularly in the case of New Zealand, as it fell into recession. New Zealand although the third largest trading partner, it is quite likely that some of the effects of the Asian problem would have had a flow on effect in Fiji. However, Australia on the other hand, Fiji's largest trading partner, continued to show positive growth rate and this momentum is likely to have helped moderate the effects of the Asian problems and reduce any flow on effects to Fiji.

While the Asian crisis worsened during 1998, the *El Nino* driven weather pattern also worsened. Low levels of rainfall were recorded in late 1997 and early 1998 (see Gani, 1999). The rainfall pattern set in the early months of 1998 continued. Low rains during the late months of 1997 and early months of 1998 threatened the 1998 sugar cane crop. The effect of drought became clearer in the middle of the year when rainfall was low and ground crops remained stunted. The sugar crop largely in the West, and the rice crop in the West and the North were severely affected and a sharp drop in the production was recorded for 1998 (Fiji Islands Bureau of Statistics, December 1999). While the Asian crisis was becoming a major external threat, the *El Nino* driven drought of 1998 caused a major internal shock and one of the worst in Fiji's history. Because these two major shocks coincided, Fiji was rather unfortunate, slipping into recession in 1997 and contracting further in 1998 (Figure 2.1). During this period growth rates were well below the average for the developing countries (Figure 2.1). It had dire social consequences with approximately 50,000 families or some 240,000 people were directly affected by the drought and received food rations (see Gani, 1999).

The tourism industry is Fiji's largest foreign exchange earner got severely affected. The Asian crisis had some effect on tourism numbers and in particular, Asian tourist arrivals (Chand, 1998). Tourists from Asia represented 12.8 percent of Fiji's total tourist arrivals in 1998 compared with 20.9 percent in 1997 (Fiji Islands Bureau of Statistics, December 1999). Visitors from Japan and South Korea dropped as a result of the economic weakness experienced by these countries.

Fiji did respond to the Asian crisis through an expenditure-switching policy. This involved the 20 percent devaluation of the currency in January 1998 (Reserve Bank of Fiji, March 1998). The competitive exchange rate cushioned the economy from the weak global environment and reduced the vulnerability of exports to any further deterioration in global economic and financial conditions.

The Fiji economy also benefited through a major political development in 1998: the adoption of the revised constitution. In 1990, a new constitution was drafted and promulgated that provided additional safeguards to indigenous Fijian interests (Sharpham, 2000). Leaving his military career, Rabuka entered politics, remained in power until elections in 1992. He led the *Sogosogo ni Vakavulew ni Taukei* (SVT) party into 1992 election but failed to secure enough support from ethnic Fijian members. In a subsequent election, he received majority ethnic Fijian support and became the Prime Minister; winning elections in 1994 with convincing win (see Sharpham, 2000). Rabuka's political thinking changed with his belief that multi-ethnicity can be workable with long-term beneficial effects to the country. He initiated the revision of the constitution that eventually came into being in July 1998. In coalition with the opposition NFP party, Rabuka campaigned in the general elections of 1999 based on the principle of unity and multi-racial co-operation. Apparently he lost the 1999 general elections with the FLP coming back as winners and formed the government under the 1998 constitution, appointing Mahendra Pal Chaudhary as Fiji's first Fiji Indian Prime Minister.

2.2.4. Parliamentary Siege of Year 2000, the Macroeconomy and its Aftermath

After eleven years of political instability, the year 1998 brought about a new twist in Fiji's politics with the implementation of a revised constitution that was regarded as acceptable by a large cross-section of Fiji's multiethnic population. Despite earlier expectations amongst the Fiji Indians of their possible marginalisation in political and economic participation following the events of 1987, the revised constitution had more to offer, both to the indigenous Fijians as well as Fiji Indians. While strengthening indigenous Fijian interests, it did not deprive the political and economic rights of the Fiji Indians. The revised constitution received a wide and favourable acceptance by all of Fiji's communities as well as the international community. This development opened a new era of hope for Fiji's multicultural community and the economy.

In May 1999, general elections took place, on the basis of the revised constitution, the campaign in itself considered to be fair and open. The FLP won majority of the seats across the nation. In coalition with two minor parties, the FLP formed the government in which, Mahendra Chaudhary, a Fiji Indian became the Prime Minister. The NFP did not win a single seat while the SVT which came into existence after the 1987 coups won few seats but did not become part of the government in 1999. However, exactly one year later, on 19 May 2000, at 10.35 a.m., the events of 1987 were repeated - the parliament was seized at gunpoint, this time by armed civilians with several members of the Labour Government held hostage for fifty-six days. It again provoked economic slowdown and social distress.

The hostage taking of the government marked Fiji's first major political and economic crisis for this century and its political instability still precipitates as of November 2006. Several indicators provided evidence that the economy went through some very rough times (Table 2.2); the severity of this crisis was considered to be worse than the crisis in 1987. The crisis was further compounded by a major cyclone (cyclone *Ami*) in January 2003 that led to millions of dollars of infrastructural damage and loss of agricultural produce and human lives. Economic growth contracted sharply; current account deficits rose; unemployment rate worsened; investment fell and tourist arrivals declined (Table 2.2).

Table 2.2. Some Macroeconomic Indicators

Variable	1999	2000	2001	2002	2003	2004
GDP growth constant 1995 prices (annual %)	8.8	-1.4	1.7	2.9	-0.1	5.0
Current account balance (% of GDP)	0.7	-5.5	-3.4	-3.0	-7.2	-15.6
Inflation, consumer prices (annual %)	2.0	1.1	4.3	1.6	4.2	3.3
Unemployment rate (annual %)	7.6	12.1	...	...	...	...
Gross fixed capital formation (% of GDP)	12.7	10.0	13.5	14.0	17.0	15.6
Gross domestic savings (% of GDP)	10.4	6.8	19.9	...	...	...
International tourism, number of visitor arrivals	410,000	294,000	348,000	397,859	430,800	498,518
International tourism, receipts (% of total exports)	26.5	36.8	48.3	50.3	50.4	59.8
Overall budget deficit (% of GDP)	0.7	3.2	6.6	5.6	6.0	6.8
Gross international reserves in months of imports	4.5	4.6	4.3	4.4	4.2	5.7

... indicates data unavailable.

Source: The World Bank (2004 and 2006), the Reserve Bank of Fiji (September 2006) and Fiji Islands Bureau of Statistics (March 2004 and 2006).

While the previous sections give a comprehensive account of Fiji's macroeconomic achievements since independence, it is also useful to look at the achievements in some of the core macroeconomic aggregates: current account balance; the unemployment rate and the rate of inflation. The next three sections discuss these.

2. 3. Current Account Balance

Fiji like other countries keeps balance of payments accounts where Fiji's international transactions including outward payments (imports, gifts and investments abroad) and inward payments (exports, gifts and investment by foreigners) are recorded. The current account of the balance of payments account is important as it reflects the sources and uses of country's total income (Dalziel and Lattimore, 1996). For example, exports of goods and services generate income while purchases of imports mean uses of country's income. When current account falls into deficits or surplus, it signals the economy in regard to its overall performance. For example, a current account deficit for a country means that the country is spending more than its income.

Figure 2.3 depicts the pattern of Fiji's current account balance for 1979-04. A number of aspects of Fiji's current account balance are worth highlighting.

Deteriorating economic growth led to worsening current account balance in 1980 and in 1981, the current account deficit rose to just over 13 percent of GDP compared to just over 1 percent in 1980. Rising consumer demand for imported products and imports of capital equipment for investment projects led to the unsustainable levels of current account deficits (Asian Development Bank, 2004). The current account position remained in deficits up until 1985.

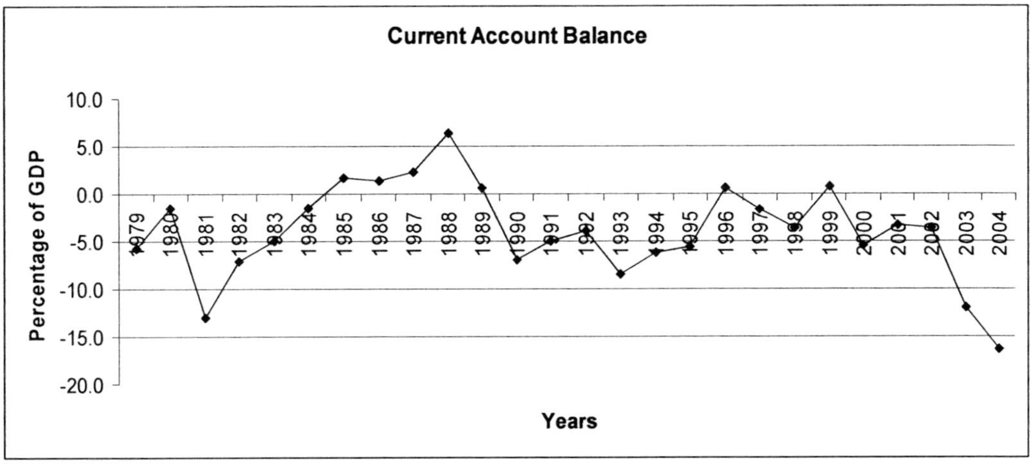

Source of data for Figure 2.3: The World Bank (2004) and the Reserve Bank of Fiji (2006).

Figure 2.3.

The economic rebound of 1986, recording growth of close to 8 percent (Figure 2.1), largely as a result of increased investment, falling consumer prices, drop in prices of petroleum products, and flexible exchange rate management led to the current account recording surplus (Elek, Hill and Tabor, 1993). The current account recording surplus that stood at just over 2 percent of the GDP (Figure 2.3). Two factors contributed to this surplus. First, despite the decline in sugar production, sugar prices were attractive (Brown and Scott, 1989 and Prasad and Tisdell, 1996). In additions, gold output rose so as its price. Second as a result of trade embargoes imposed by the trade unions in Fiji (Elek, Hill and Tabor, 1993), Australia and New Zealand, imports got restricted and fell by approximately 21 percent from the previous year.

Following the events of 1987, a healthy current account surplus was recorded in 1988 while the surplus for 1989 was just marginal (Figure 2.3). The large surplus is largely a result of foreign capital inflows attracted by reforms in domestic investment policies and a push for industrial expansion (Cole and Hughes, 1998). Foreign interest in this area strengthened. Also, the tourism industry regained its momentum with gradual rise in tourist arrivals.

Between 1990 and 1995, the current account remained in deficits averaging close to 6 percent of GDP despite positive real growth rate during this period (Figure 2.3). Much of the position of the current account for this period can be explained by the significant rise in imports of machines, transport equipment, basic manufactures and mineral fuel. The rise in tourist numbers and sugar receipts triggered the current account surplus in 1996 (Fiji Islands Bureau of Statistics, December 1997).

Current account recorded a deficit of 1.6 and 3.8 percent of GDP respectively for 1997 and 1998 (Figure 2.3). The impact of drought was severe on the 1998 sugar crop while the financial crisis of Asia meant falling tourist numbers from Asia (South Korea and Japan) as Australia, New Zealand and USA. As a result of the drought in late 1997, Fiji's exports fell from around US$583 million in 1996 to US$486 million in 1997 (The World Bank, 2004). Falling world sugar prices together with a fall in the volume of sugar aggravated the problem. Lumber exports also fell in 1998 due to contraction in demand in Asian markets (Fiji Islands Bureau of Statistics, December 1999). The value of gold exports also declined, largely due to falling gold prices. While the devaluation of the dollar in 1998 helped export income, the effect of drought on the sugar industry resulted in exports falling further. The effect of devaluation resulted in a rise in value of imports in 1998 (Fiji Islands Bureau of Statistics, December 1999). Imports of machinery and equipment recorded major declines. Current account balance worsened in the post-2000 period following the crisis of 2000 (Figure 2.3). Rising imports and falling export receipts have contributed to the deteriorating current account position in post-2000 period. In 2004, current account deficit stood at just over 16 percent of GDP (Figure 2.3), the worse in last 25 years.

2.4. Unemployment

In the previous discussions on economic performance, some of the forces that determined Fiji's growth since its independence were highlighted. Periods of strong growth are likely to have led to a better standard of living while periods of recessionary conditions are likely to have led to deterioration in the standard of living. A more obvious determinant of the standard of living is the amount of unemployment a country typically experiences. The fact is simple: people who want to work but cannot find a job are not contributing to the economy's production of goods and services. On the other hand when a country keeps its workers employed as fully as possible, it is likely to achieve a higher level of gross output than if those workers were unemployed. Higher levels of output contribute to higher standards of living. This section looks at Fiji's natural rate of unemployment as it is directly related to economic growth. Because of lack of data, further analysis in terms of cyclical unemployment cannot be made.

While official published statistics on unemployment is unavailable for the 1970-73 periods, it is quite likely that high growth experienced during this time meant that employment opportunities would have expanded and living standards would have risen. However, the slowdown in economic activity around mid-1970s and even in late 70s would have led to an increase in unemployment.

Available statistics on labour market between 1980-85, a period of economic slowdown verifies the labour market outcomes. Figure 2.4 depicts the unemployment rate for years 1982-2000. Tracing the trend, it is clear that the economic slowdown between 1983-2000 would have negatively affected labour market with less job creation and more of unemployment. According to Figure 2.4 the official unemployment rate increased from just around 7 percent in 1983 to 7.5 percent in 1986. Labour market got seriously hit with rising unemployment in 1987 and 1988 (Figure 2.4). The crisis of 1987 not only translated in reduction in job creation but massive job loses. Although unemployment statistics are understated, it certainly rose from the previous year.

While unemployment remained high in 1988 largely attributable to previous year's deterioration in the economy and more so in the private sector in which many workers lost jobs, the rise in economic activity during most of 1990s meant employment creation. Much of the employment creation took place in the garment industry which halted a rise in unemployment rate as it has been a major absorber of domestic labour force. Unemployment rate remained low between much of 1989-97 period and seems to be consistent with the economy's positive performance in a number of years during this period. Deteriorating domestic economic conditions in 1997 and 1998 saw a rise in unemployment rate. Unemployment rate worsened further in 2000 due to the closer of several garment factories as a result of the political crisis. The garment industry suffered the most with many factories shutting their operations and relocating to other countries.

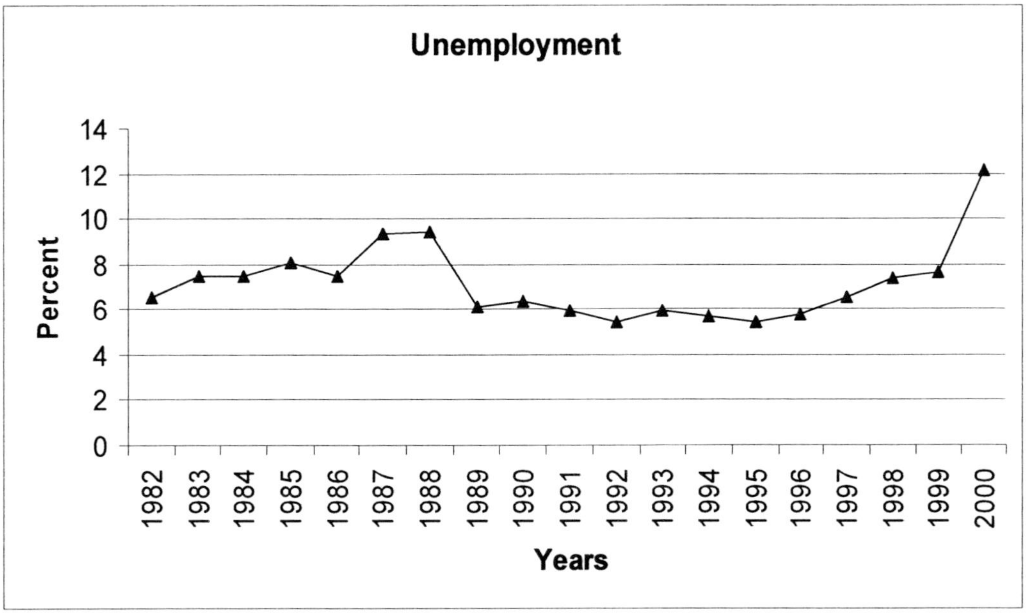

Source of data for Figure 2.4: Asian Development Bank (2005).

Figure 2.4.

A point that deserves much attention about Fiji's unemployment rate is that the official unemployment rate for Fiji as depicted in Figure 2.4 has to be interpreted with great caution. In fact, anecdotal evidence suggests that the rate could have been many times more than that represented in Figure 2.4 due to three reasons. First, Fiji's unemployment rate is insufficiently and incorrectly measured. The Fiji Islands Bureau of Statistics, which is responsible for collecting data on unemployment, does not seem to have a comprehensive and accessible way to gather data on those unemployed. Much of the labour market data is fed through the Ministry of Labour that keeps a record of those looking for work. However, their records are only official reported cases and only those unemployed workers who get access to the offices of this Ministry where those unemployed get registered. Many workers out in remote areas and outer islands who cannot report their cases of being unemployed are unaccounted for. Second, there are thousands of discouraged workers – individuals who prefer to work but have given up looking for work. This comprises of those who are illiterate, lack sufficient education, school leavers and rural women. This group is left out of the national unemployment statistics largely due to their inability to communicate their employment status. Third, Fiji unlike other high-income countries does not have any public unemployment insurance program. Therefore, there is no such incentive for people to respond and get counted as unemployed. Hence, Fiji's official unemployment rate is not a reliable indicator of conditions of unemployment and is best viewed as an imperfect measure of unemployment.

Its unemployment rate is much worse than revealed by the official published data and on most accounts it is likely to be double than those shown by officially published statistics.

2.5. Inflation

Inflation is a term used to describe a situation in which an economy's overall price level is rising. Inflation is a closely monitored aspect of a country's macroeconomic performance and one of the key macroeconomic variables in setting macroeconomic policy. The analysis here traces the trends in Fiji's consumer price inflation and is a starting point only. A detailed examination of the causes and effects of inflation and how it relates with Fiji's other macroeconomic variables is given further insight in Chapter five.

Fiji's pattern of consumer price inflation for the 1970-04 period is depicted in Figure 2.5. Inflation was low at around 4 percent in 1970, rising to a high of 22 percent in 1972 and then falling to about 11 percent in 1973 (Figure 2.5). High inflationary outcome in 1972 is likely to be from large wage increases in the public sector (Brown and Scott, 1989). Although inflation was halved in 1973 to that of 1972 levels, it is considered to be still high. The OPEC oil price rises affected Fiji like other oil dependent countries. Fiji's heavy reliance on imported oil meant inflationary pressure from import prices.

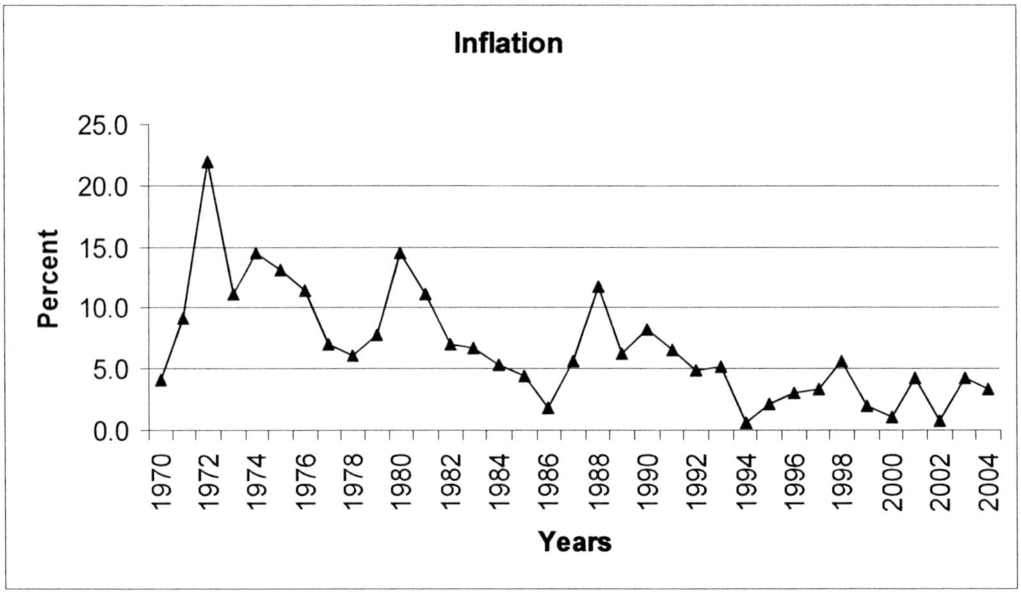

Source of data for Figure 2.5: The World Bank (2004) and the Reserve Bank of Fiji (2006).

Figure 2.5.

Inflation remained in double digits from 1972 to 1976 although falling into single digits in 1977 to 1979 but still up the initial low of 1970 (Figure 2.5). One reason for this was wage rises in latter part of 1970s as Fiji's strong labour unions successfully negotiated wage increases despite a period of economic slowdown (see Chapter 7). The Central Monetary Authority (now the Reserve Bank of Fiji) also interfered by influencing bank liquidity that included specified minimum ratios of cash and holdings of government securities to deposit liabilities (Brown and Scott, 1989). Such a policy seems to have limited further rises in prices.

Inflation was recorded at a high of 14.5 percent in 1980, which fell to 7 percent in 1982 (Figure 2.5). The rise was fuelled largely through imported inflation (again rising fuel prices) and rise in demand for consumer goods in response to wage and salary increases. Further, domestic pressures on inflation also came across as a result of rising prices from cyclone damage during the first half of the 1980s. Falling prices of oil led to a drop in inflation in 1986 and the economy during this year recorded a healthy growth of close to 8 percent.

In the post-1987 period, inflationary pressures got built up from the domestic demand side as a result of panic among consumers for basic food items in response to Fiji's deteriorating political climate (Elek, Hill and Tabor, 1993). Retailers also exaggerated the situation in face of trade embargoes that saw consumers rushing to stockpile food items. Inflation went up to close to 6 percent following a low of just under 2 percent in 1986 (Figure 2.5).

With the exception of 1988, inflation remained in single digits in all other years. In fact there has been a continuous decline in inflation from the high of 1988 reaching a low of just close to 1 percent in 1994 (Figure 2.5). Much of this trend in inflation is largely due to policy changes of 1987 with lag effects showing up in the later years. Also during this period, Fiji did not share much of imported inflation. Further domestic demand pressures weakened with lesser spending as many Fiji Indians started saving and emigrating.

Between 1994 and 1998, inflation rose gradually, still in single digits and remaining below 6 percent (Figure 2.5). Deteriorating domestic economic conditions including expansionary fiscal stance (see for example, Narayan, Narayan and Prasad, 2006) as well as the ongoing external crises (Asian Financial Crises) saw inflation heading close to the 6 percent mark in 1998. In the late 1990s, wages also played an important role in influencing inflation. An agreement between the government and the unions in late 1997 allowed a 6 percent wage increase for public sector workers (Reserve Bank of Fiji, March 1998). In 1998, private sector wage increases were generally around 3 to 4 percent, a good outcome and consistent with low inflation (Reserve Bank of Fiji, March 1999). However, some large private firms and industries also indicated wage increases of 6 to 10 percent, certainly out of line with labour productivity growth. It is worth noting that Fiji's relative labour productivity levels have been below relative wages (Duncan, 1996). This is most likely associated with Fiji's inward looking industrial policies.

In 1998, the devaluation of the Fiji dollar also influenced the inflationary outcome. A one-off effect of the 1998 devaluation was the hike in the price level. The year-on-year percent change in Fiji's consumer price index was close to 6.0 for 1998 compared to 2.9 for 1997 (Figure 2.5). Devaluation, together with the drought, contributed to this effect. Food prices increased more than the non-food items and this contributed to a rise in Fiji's inflation rate. A significant proportion of edibles in Fiji are imported and devaluation contributed to increases in prices of imported items. During 2000-04, inflation averaged 2.9 percent per annum largely as a result of better labour market conditions and low inflation in Fiji's major trading partners.

2.6. CONCLUSION

The overall growth pattern noted for Fiji during 1970-04 period indicates that economic growth has been unsatisfactory; unemployment has been twice high of that been recorded and current account remaining in deficits. Fiji's economic growth has been on a gradual decline and below the average for the countries in the lower-middle- income and East Asia and the Pacific group of countries. While good growth results were achieved in the early years following Fiji's independence, this trend could not be maintained. Although external economic shocks and natural disasters had some serious negative effects on the economy during some years of the 1970-04 periods, Fiji could have performed much better. Much of the blame on less than satisfactory level of achievements can be directed towards Fiji's economic policies which seem to have been rather short-sighted and didn't direct the country in terms of setting the right pre-conditions to economic growth and broadening its economic base. Much has to do with policies that did not enhance the degree of Fiji's market orientation with lack of focus on private ownership, domestic market liberalisation, and domestic investment.

Given the analysis presented above on macroeconomic variables, it is possible to pass a judgment whether or not Fiji achieved a satisfactory level of growth since its independence. It can be concluded that Fiji's growth achievement has been unsatisfactory while countries in the Asia Pacific region have achieved superior growth rates. Current account balance has largely remained in deficits and unemployment rates were much higher than those reported.

It looks as if Fiji throughout the post independence period has dwelled on a thin economic line. Economic policy makers were heavily relied on sugar as the prime economic mover for Fiji. This mono crop agriculture has been taken as a guaranteed stance towards Fiji's economic sustenance without much thought of expanding the private sector and moving the economy more broadly through diversifying the economic base.

Much of the economic thinking among policy makers seems to have remained locked to few economic issues. Fiji seems to have fallen short of its broad economic thinking and also its ignorance on setting the right pre-conditions to economic growth. Much effort seems to have been placed on the political process both from ruling and opposition political parties. During this period Fiji has remained highly inward oriented and lost grounds in capitalising on frugal opportunities such as the expansion of the private sector, reducing the role of state in market activities and strengthening of institutions.

Fiji's unsatisfactory economic performance is not a huge mystery. The available empirical evidence on growth suggests that low growth can be explained by standard economic variables that have practical policy implications. Several country-specific and cross-country growth studies involving other countries show that growth is related to the degree of market orientation, including openness to trade, private rather than state ownership, domestic market liberalisation and protection of private property rights; increased investment and good governance. Despite Fiji's vulnerability to external economic shocks and adverse weather patterns, several of the above factors account broadly for Fiji's long-term growth.

REFERENCES

Asian Development Bank. (2004 and 2005). *Key Indicators*. Manila.

Blum, W. (2002). *Rogue State*, Zed Books, London.

Browne, C. and Scott, D.A. (1989). *Economic Development in Seven Pacific Island Countries,* International Monetary Fund, Washington, D.C.

Cameron. J. (1993). A political economy of market-led structural adjustment. A case study of Fiji, *Journal of International Development,* Vol. 5, pp. 123-133.

Chand, S. (1998). Flow-on effects from the East Asian financial crisis on Pacific Island economies, *Pacific Economic Bulletin*, Vol. 13, No. 2, pp. 147-157.

Chand, G and Naidu, V. (1997). *Fiji: Coups, Crises and Reconciliation, 1987 – 1997*, Fiji Institute of Applied Studies, Suva.

Cole, R. and Hughes, H. (1988). *The Fiji Economy, May 1987: Problems and Prospects,* Pacific Policy Papers No.4, National Centre for Development Studies, Australian National University, Canberra.

Dalziel, P. and R. Lattimore. (1996). *The New Zealand Macroeconomy: A Briefing on Reforms,* Oxford University Press: Auckland.

Duncan, R. (1996). Unit labour costs in manufacturing in Fiji and Papua New Guinea, *Pacific Economic Bulletin*, Vol. 11, No. 2, pp. 39-47.

Elek, A., Hill, H., and Tabor, S. R. (1993). Liberalisation and diversification in a small economy: Fiji since the 1987 coups, *World Development*, Vol. 21, No. 5, pp. 749-769.

Fiji Islands Bureau of Statistics. (December 1988, 1994, 1997, 1999 and 2000 and March 2006). *Key Statistics*. Government Printer, Suva.

Gani, A. (2005). Fiji's emigrant transfers and potential macroeconomic effects, *Pacific Economic Bulletin*, Vol. 20, No.2, pp. 117-128.

Gani, A. (2000). Some dimensions of Fiji's recent emigration, *Pacific Economic Bulletin*, Vol. 15, No.2, pp. 63-76.

Gani, A. (1999). Drought, the Asian crisis and Fiji's monetary policy response, *Pacific Economic Bulletin*, Vol. 14, No. 2, pp. 36-48.

Gani, A. (1998). Macroeconomic determinants of growth in the South Pacific Island economies, *Applied Economics Letters*, Vol. 5, pp. 747-749.

Gani, A. (1997). The relationship between Fiji's exchange rate and trade balance: some policy implications, *Pacific Economic Bulletin*, Vol. 12, No. 1, pp. 41-52.

Gani, A. and Ward, B.D. (1995). Migration of professionals from Fiji to New Zealand: a reduced from supply-demand model, *World Development*, Vol. 23, No. 9, pp. 1247-63.

Garnaut, R. (1998). The financial crisis, *Asia Pacific Economic Literature*, Vol. 12, No. 1, pp. 1- 11.

Garnaut, R. (1972). Independent Fiji in a world economy, *Economic Record*, Vol. 48, No. 121, pp. 103-115.

Grynberg, R., Munro, D., and White, M., (2002). *Crisis: The Collapse of the National Bank of Fiji*, Crawford House, Adelaide.

Lal, V. (1990). *Fiji Coups in Paradise*, Zed Books Ltd, London.

Narayan, P. K., Narayan, S. and Prasad, A. (2006). Modeling the relationship between budget deficits, money supply and inflation in Fiji, *Pacific Economic Bulletin*, Vol. 21, No.2, pp. 103-116.

Prasad, B.C. and Tisdell, C. (1996) Institutional constraints to economic development: the case of native land rights in Fiji", *Asia Pacific Development Journal,* Vol.3, No.2, pp.49-71.

Reddy, M., Mohanty, M. and Naidu, V. (2004). Economic cost of human capital loss from Fiji: implications for sustainable development, *The International Migration Review*, Vol. 38, No.4, pp. 1447-1461.

Reserve Bank of Fiji. (March 1998, 1999 and 2006 and December 1988). *Quarterly Economic Bulletin*, Suva.

Sharpham, J. (2000). *Rabuka of Fiji*, Central Queensland University Press, Rockhampton, Queensland.

The World Bank. (1996). *Pacific Island Economies - Building a Resilient Economic Base for the Twenty First Century*, World Bank: Washington, DC.

The World Bank. (2004). *World Development Indicators CD ROM*. Washington, D.C.

The World Bank. (2006). *World Development Indicators Database*, Washington, D.C. Available online at: http://devdata.worldbank.org/external/CPProfile.asp?PTYPE=CP&CCODE=FJI. Date of extraction: 7 July 2006.

Chapter 3

TRADE PERFORMANCE AND POLICY

3.1. INTRODUCTION

Trade has been Fiji's major economic component. Following independence, Fiji's trade policy started with an inward looking import substitution orientation. It has imposed severe regressive effects on the competitiveness of the domestic economy. This together with small domestic market, narrow range of exports, limited natural resources and distant trading partners constrained its developmental prospects. The political crisis of 1987 forced the country into recession and made a compelling need to reform its trading environment so as to allow the economy to be more outward oriented. Despite reform initiatives following the 1987 crises, the economy's performance has been less than impressive; economic growth over the 1987-2004 periods has averaged a meager 1.2 per cent per annum. Part of the explanation for low economic growth has been a sustained period of political instability, the non-resolution of land leases since 1987 and high production costs. As a result, Fiji has neither succeeded in diversifying its export base nor has it been able to attract significant foreign investments in its export sectors. In view of these developments, this chapter discusses the key issues regarding Fiji's trade sector: exports, imports, comparative advantage, markets, trade policy and current trade policy regimes.

3.2. STRUCTURE OF PRODUCTION

Fiji's trade performance has been largely dictated by its production structure. Sectoral production data indicates that Fiji has gone through structural transformation. Figure 3.1 depicts Fiji's sectoral production with the decline of the agricultural sector accompanied by the strong expansion of the services sectors. Based on Hecksher-Ohlin trade theory (see for example, Balassa, 1965; Chenery and Syrquin, 1975; and Kuznets, 1966) we would expect that changing economic structure and, therefore, changing factor endowments would result in shifts in the structure of trade. Fiji has experienced the dynamic processes of changing comparative advantage over the last three decades as depicted in Figure 3.1.

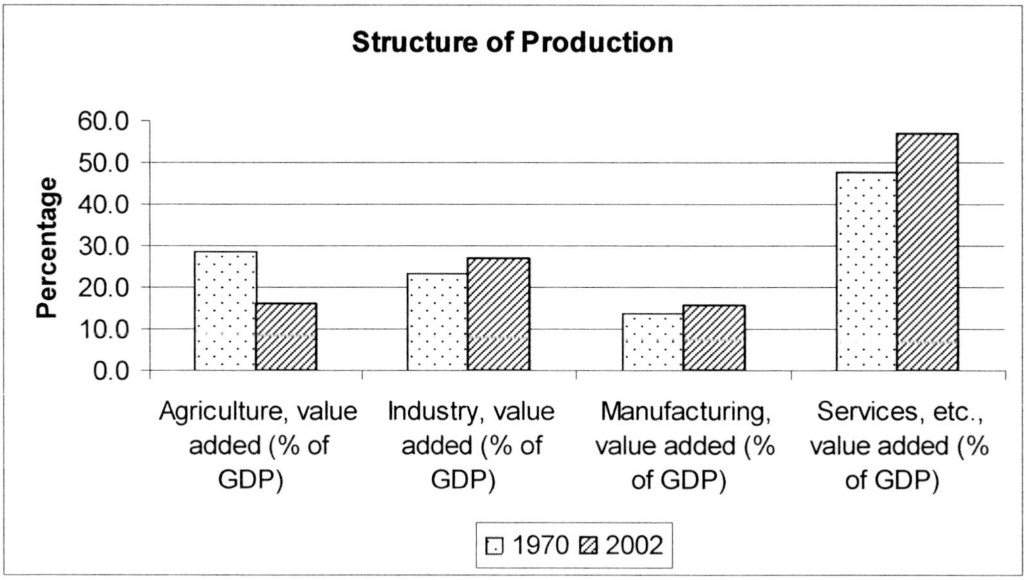

Source of data for Figure 3.1: The World Bank (2004).

Figure 3.1.

According to the trends depicted in Figure 3.1, the agricultural sector has declined gradually over time. The change in this sector is most visible of all where its proportion fell steadily from 29 percent of GDP in 1970 to 16 percent of GDP in 2002 (Figure 3.1). In contrast the share of industry rose from 23 percent of GDP in 1970 to 27 percent of GDP in 2002 (Figure 3.1). Manufacturing sector also expanded. Since 1970, services have been the largest sector and currently accounts for just over 57 percent of GDP. The progress noted in terms of the contribution of the industry, manufacturing and services to GDP particularly since late 1980s is largely attributable to major reforms undertaken by the interim government in 1987 following the political crises as mentioned in the previous chapter. These reforms led to a more outward looking economy.

3.3. The Pattern of Exports and Imports

A look at some basic trade statistics gives a first hand view of the growing importance of international trade to Fiji. Figure 3.2 depicts the trends in Fiji's exports and imports of goods and services as shares of gross domestic product from 1970 to 2002.

Two points are apparent from Figure 3.2. First, between 1970 and 2001, Fiji has been importing more than exporting except for some years in late 1980s. Second, Fiji's trade has not gone through sharp fluctuations except for small periods in mid-1970s, 1987, and 1990. While these fluctuations are noted, the gap between exports and imports of goods and services has narrowed in the post 1987 period as compared to pre-1987 period (Figure 3.2).

Source of data for Figure 3.2: The World Bank (2004).

Figure 3.2.

The importance of international trade to Fiji is put into perspective with some of its neighbouring countries in the South Pacific. Figure 3.3 shows the 2003 shares of exports and imports in GDP for Fiji together with Australia and New Zealand. The evidence from Figure 3.3 is clear: that international trade is more important to Fiji than countries like Australia and New Zealand which by virtue of the diversity of their resource endowments and size actually rely less on international trade than Fiji.

Source of data for Figure 3.3: The World Bank (2006) and Fiji Islands Bureau of Statistics (2006).

Figure 3.3.

3.4. Export Patterns and Performance

At independence, Fiji's total exports amounted to US$107 million (The World Bank, 2004). Exports as a share of GDP took a dive during the first half of the 1970s confirming Fiji's inward orientation of its trading structure (Figure 3.4). While exports rose in the second half of the 1970s, the first half of 1980s shows exports remaining almost constant (Figure 3.4). Stagnant exports during this period are largely attributable to recessionary conditions prevailing in the economy. Following the first political crisis in 1987, Fiji's exports of goods and services as a share of GDP rose dramatically to just over 60 percent of GDP in 1989 (Figure 3.4). Trade reforms initiated a year before together with a rise in garment exports accounted for much of this improvement (see Elek, Hill and Tabor, 1993). Fiji's total export earnings rose significantly from US$329 million in 1987 to US$606 million in 2001 (Figure 3.4). As a share of GDP the export of goods and services also increased from 48 percent in 1970 to just over 71 percent in 2001 (Figure 3.4). This export boom has generally supported Fiji's economic growth (see also Narayan and Narayan, 2004). Fiji's economic growth over the last two decades as revealed by the scatter plot in Figure 3.5, depicting a positive association: an increase in export growth is associated with an increase in GDP growth.

Source of data for Figure 3.4: The World Bank (2004).

Figure 3.4.

During the post crisis period, the dollar value of exports grew at an average annual rate of 6 percent. The year 1997 marked an unprecedented export earnings downfall largely as a result of the Asian financial crisis. Compounded by the drought in late 1997, Fiji's merchandise exports fell from around US$583 million in 1996 to US$486 million in 1998. Falling world sugar prices together with a fall in the volume of sugar aggravated the problem. Lumber exports also fell in 1998 as a result of the contraction in demand in Asian markets.

The value of gold exports also declined as a result of falling gold prices. While the devaluation of the dollar in 1998 helped export income, the effect of drought on the sugar industry resulted in exports falling further (Gani, 1997). During that year export earnings from sugar, molasses, canned and fresh fish and wood chips fell. Export earnings in 2000 remained stagnant as a result of the political crisis (Figure 3.4).

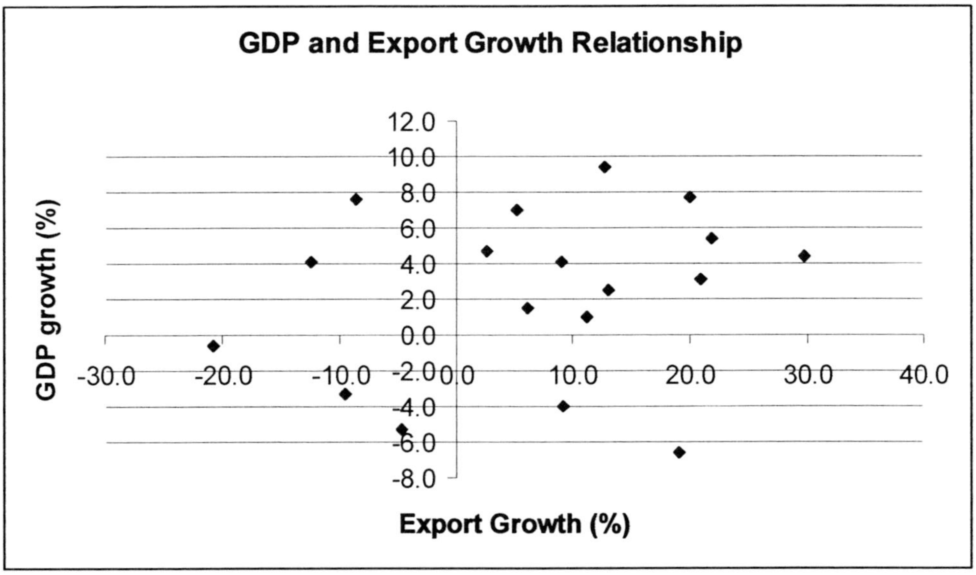

Source of data for Figure 3.5: The World Bank (2004).

Figure 3.5.

3.5. Export Composition

Fiji's export structure is largely based on land and sea resources and thus falls under the primary commodity exporting country category. Fiji is predominantly exporting products from these two natural resources bases. Figures 3.6 and 3.7 depict Fiji's export composition for the 1988-04 period. The main export commodities following independence include sugar and molasses. It started exporting other commodities: canned fish, fresh fish, coconut oil and gold as its industrial sector started to grow. Tourism has also been a major income earner with earnings amounting to almost 60 percent of total exports in 2004 compared to 24 percent of total exports in 1990 (Figure 3.8). Today, tourism is Fiji's top most export income earner with the industry experiencing healthy growth since 2000 (see Figure 3.8).

Following the crisis of 1987, Fiji moved into trade liberalisation and its export composition began to change. A major industrial expansion was the establishment of light manufacturing industry, in particular garments (see Cole and Hughes, 1988). Since then further diversification of the export mix has taken place with newer export products being developed such as woodchips, textiles and footwear. After the mid-1990s, the export composition expanded to include additional commodities: mineral water, yaqona, vegetables and chemicals.

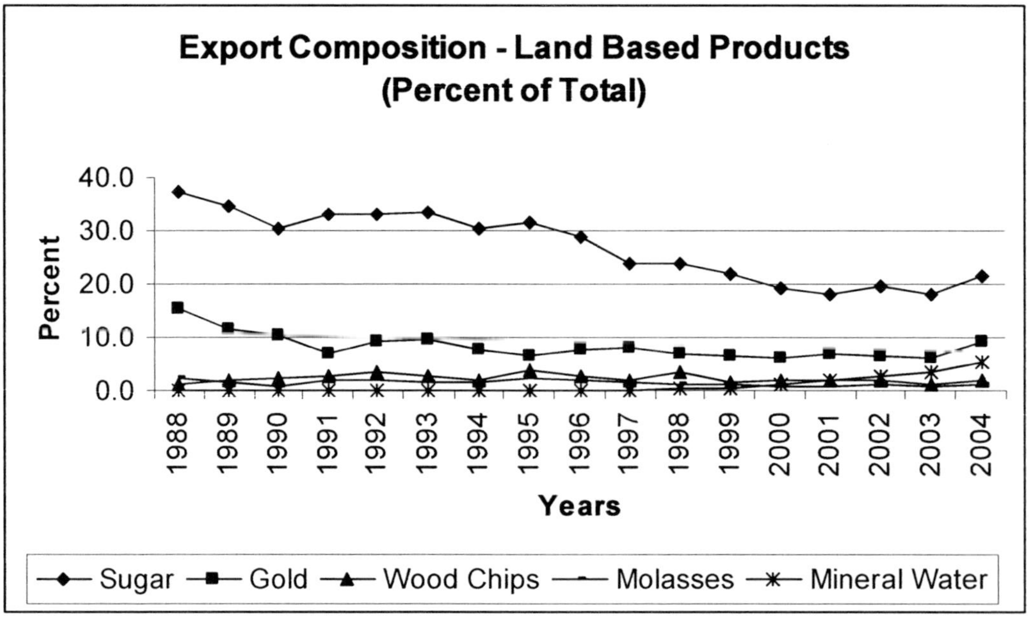

Source of data for Figure 3.6: Asian Development Bank (2004 and 2005) and Fiji Islands Bureau of Statistics (2006).

Figure 3.6.

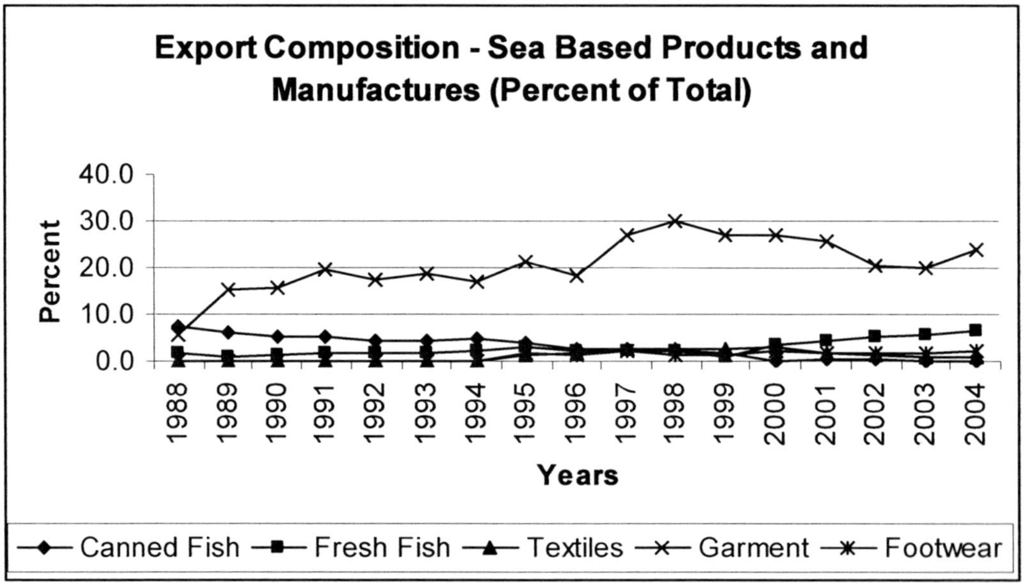

Source of data for Figure 3.7: Asian Development Bank (2004) and Fiji Islands Bureau of Statistics (2006).

Figure 3.7.

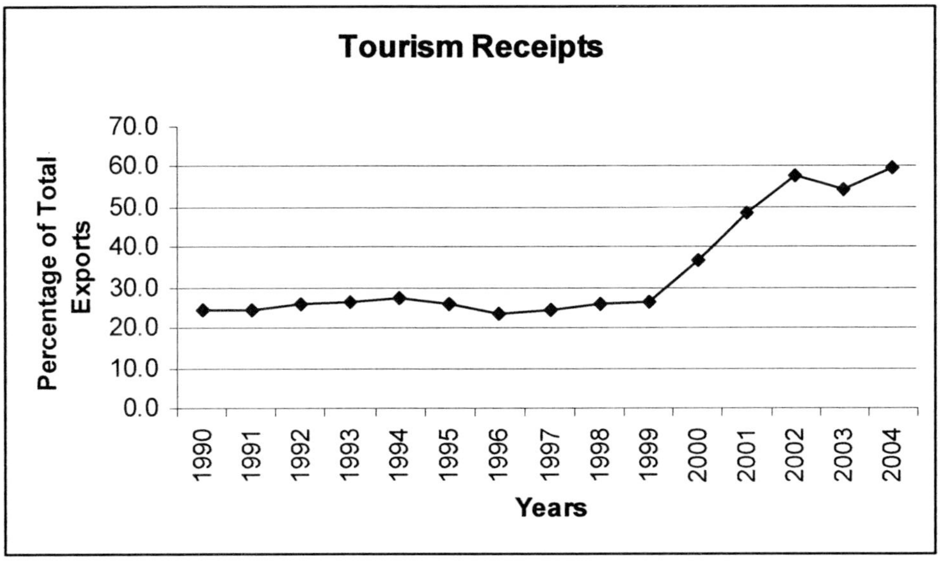

Source of data for Figure 3.8: The World Bank (2004) and Fiji Islands Bureau of Statistics (2006).

Figure 3.8.

Figures 3.6 and 3.7 also reveal an interesting pattern regarding commodity export composition. The composition of resource based products such as sugar, molasses, canned fish, coconut oil and gold has been gradually eroding. On the other hand, export composition mineral water, textiles, garment and footwear has expanded gradually. One notable feature in terms of Fiji's export composition is that during the post crisis period, sugar and garments have moved in opposite directions. As a share of total exports, sugar declined from a high of 37 percent in 1988 to 18 percent in 2003 while garments rose from around 6 percent in 1988 to 24 percent in 2004 (Figures 3.6 and 3.7). Of all the commodities exported in the last five years, mineral water recorded the largest growth in terms of export earnings.

While Fiji's export structure has diversified in the post coup years, it is useful to know if Fiji's export products have the comparative advantage. Fiji's comparative advantage has been numerically measured and this provides a better understanding of its export competitiveness (see Gani and Prasad, 2005). According to Balassa (1965) and Hoekman, Mattoo and English (2002), an appropriate measure of a country's comparative advantage is the index of revealed comparative advantage (RCA). The RCA with a value of less than unity implies that the country has revealed comparative disadvantage in the product and if the index exceeds unity that country is said to have a revealed comparative advantage in the product. The RCA of Fiji is computed by Gani and Prasad (2005) presented in Table 3.1 for 1988-2001 for twelve major export products at the three-digit Standard Industrial Trade Classification (SITC) level.

Fiji's RCA confirms that nine export products are in the RCA achievers group, that is, RCA values of greater than one. These are largely resource-based products and include sugar, canned fish, fresh fish, dalo, wood chips, textiles, garments, footwear and gold. In this group, the data confirm that during the post coup period, the RCA has strengthened for sugar, dalo, textiles, garments and footwear providing strong evidence that Fiji's competitiveness in the world trade of these products has continued to remain strong. The data in Table 3.1 also confirms that the comparative advantage position weakened for canned fish and gold over time. The RCA scores for sugar, fresh fish, wood chips and garments increased over the post 1987 period. This not only reveals strong comparative advantage but also the strengthening of comparative advantage position. The RCA scores revealed that yaqona, copra and coconut oil do not have any comparative advantage, as the RCA scores remained less than one.

Table 3.1. Index of Revealed Comparative Advantage

Years	Years	Canned Fish	Fresh Fish	Dalo	Wood Chips	Yaqona	Copra	Coconut Oil	Textiles	Garment	Foot-wear	Gold
1988	93.9	107.3	3.6	0.2	23.8	0.0	0.0	0.1	0.0	2.15	0.0	39.9
1989	88.4	101.6	2.0	0.3	38.9	0.0	0.0	0.1	0.0	64.3	0.0	29.0
1990	79.6	84.3	3.5	0.8	50.5	0.0	0.0	0.1	0.0	65.3	0.0	26.1
1991	110.0	81.1	3.8	0.3	74.6	0.0	0.0	0.0	0.0	76.0	0.0	18.0
1992	116.8	67.8	4.0	0.6	106.9	0.0	0.0	0.1	0.0	64.7	0.0	21.1
1993	118.8	78.1	4.5	0.2	72.9	0.0	0.0	0.1	0.0	70.0	0.0	21.5
1994	110.8	78.8	5.5	1.4	52.9	0.0	0.0	0.0	0.0	66.7	0.0	16.6
1995	115.5	72.5	9.2	2.0	91.9	0.2	0.0	0.0	1.8	85.4	2.2	16.4
1996	98.0	53.3	6.4	2.0	67.2	0.2	0.0	0.0	3.1	71.9	1.5	20.4
1997	89.9	56.4	6.8	2.4	56.5	0.2	0.0	0.1	4.2	104.2	2.5	21.2
1998	98.8	42.9	6.1	1.9	100.9	2.0	1.5	0.1	4.1	108.4	2.0	16.6
1990	110.3	40.6	2.4	1.7	53.7	0.3	1.2	0.1	4.6	95.2	1.6	16.4
2000	120.0	3.1	11.2	3.1	66.7	0.3	0.8	0.1	5.9	100.5	3.0	16.4
2001	935.4	14.3	12.0	2.9	64.6	0.2	0.5	0.0	3.5	91.0	2.7	17.9

Source: Gani and Prasad (2005).

Table 3.2. Direction of Exports (%)

	1980-84	1985-89	1990-94	1995-99	2000-04
Australia	25.1	18.0	17.4	30.4	20.1
United States of America	9.5	4.7	12.5	12.3	24.1
United Kingdom	10.9	30.6	24.2	16.8	12.6
Japan	3.6	3.9	6.3	5.3	4.6
New Zealand	6.7	7.3	7.4	6.3	3.7
Samoa	...	1.5	0.4	2.7	5.6
Portugal	0.0	2.5	0.7	1.8	1.5
Tonga	3.7	0.2	0.0	2.1	2.4
Hong Kong	...	0.6	0.7	0.9	2.0
Kiribati	...	0.6	0.3	1.0	1.7

... indicates data unavailable.

Source: Asian Development Bank (2005).

3.6. Export Markets and Opportunities

Fiji began to diversify its export base following the crisis in 1987. Being a major trading nation among the Pacific Island countries, there has been a growing concern in Fiji in terms of seeking more markets. In 1980-84, Australia was the main export market for Fiji followed by United Kingdom, USA and New Zealand (Table 3.2). However, since 1990, exports to United Kingdom have declined. Exports to the USA gained increasing momentum, rising from 9.5 percent in 1980–84 to 24.1 percent in 2000–04 (Table 3.2). Exports to New Zealand have been gradually declining since 1990. Fiji, nevertheless has gained increasing market share in some of the neighbouring Pacific Island countries: Samoa, Tonga and Kiribati. While the Pacific Island markets are positive developments, they are however, very small. Fiji certainly needs to break into more large country markets so as to maintain a viable export structure.

3.7. Import: Pattern, Performance and Composition

Imports form a major component of Fiji's trade structure. Since independence, Fiji's imports rose significantly from US$114 million in 1970 to US$1,092 million in 2001, a ten fold increase (Figure 3.2). The year 1987 noticed a decline in imports where imports were US$495 million, the lowest during the period 1980 to 2001 (Figure 3.2). Following the crisis of 1987 and up until 1994, Fiji's total import spending more than doubled, rising from US$495 million in 1987 to US$1,085 million in 1994. As a share of GDP the imports of goods and services also increased from 52 percent in 1970 to just over 65 percent in 2001. Fiji's major imports are machines and transport equipment. This together with imports of mineral fuels, crude materials and chemicals are vital inputs to the production process. The scatter plot in Figure 3.9 depicts rising imports having a positive association with higher economic growth confirming that imported inputs are vital for its growth.

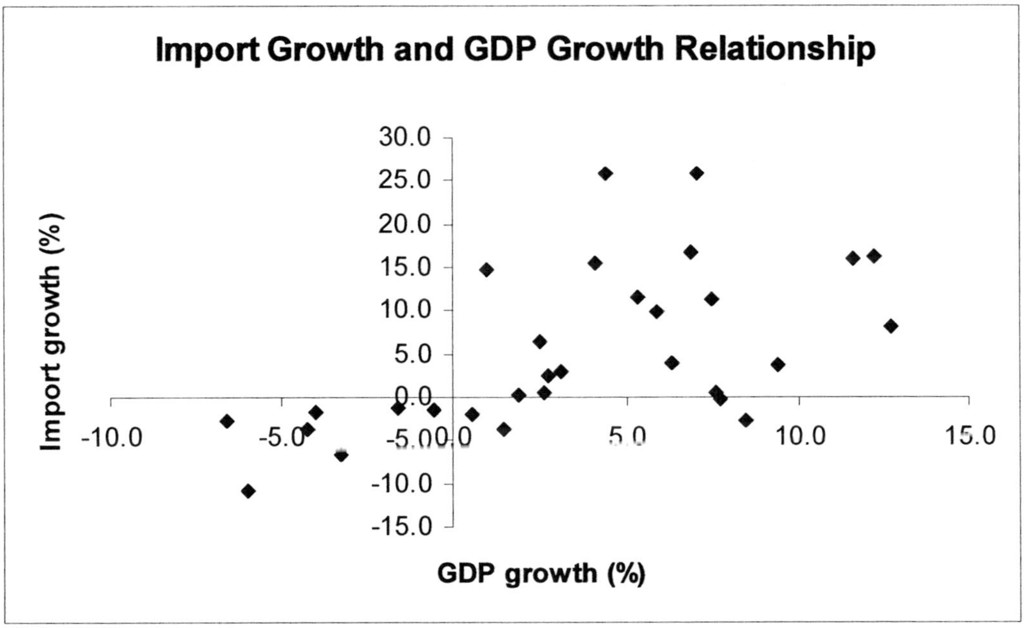

Source of data for Figure 3.9: The World Bank (2004).

Figure 3.9.

Fiji's import pattern seems to be determined by its import composition and prices (see also Narayan and Narayan, 2004). Table 3.3 presents data on Fiji's imports by SITC section. Fiji's foremost import spending in 2004 has been on mineral fuels and machines and transport equipment (Table 3.3). Imports of basic manufactures have ranked second followed by food and live animals.

Table 3.3. Imports by SITC section (Percent of Total)

SITC Section	1980	1990	2004
Food and live animals	14.2	12.8	14.1
Beverage and tobacco	0.8	0.7	0.8
Crude materials excluding fuels	0.1	0.7	0.8
Mineral fuels etc	25.6	14.1	23.5
Animal, vegetable oils and fats	1.1	1.0	0.6
Chemicals	6.9	7.3	7.9
Basic manufactures	16.5	21.9	19.4
Machines and transport equipment	21.8	30.7	22.4
Miscellaneous manufactured goods	8.8	9.6	10.1
Unclassified goods	3.3	0.1	0.5

Source: Asian Development Bank (1985 and 2005).

3.8. Import Markets and Opportunities

For long Fiji's main import markets have been high income countries: Australia, New Zealand, Japan and the United States. During 1985-89, Australia, New Zealand and Japan have been the major markets (Table 3.4). Even today, Australia continues to remain the major import market. However, Fiji's imports from New Zealand and Japan have been dwindling since 1990 as a result of high import prices. While Australia continues to remain the major import market, Fiji at the same time has been seeking newer markets particularly in Asia that are cheaper than the traditional high-income country markets.

Table 3.4. Direction of Imports (Percentage in Total)

Country	1985-89	1990-94	1995-99	2000-04
Australia	30.8	31.3	42.7	41.3
New Zealand	17.5	17.4	14.7	15.5
Singapore	6.2	6.2	5.6	12.9
United States	5.0	9.6	8.6	2.7
Japan	12.7	10.3	5.8	4.1
China	2.7	3.1	2.5	3.3
Hong Kong	2.5	3.0	2.4	2.9
Thailand	1.1	1.9	2.1	2.1
India	0.6	0.5	1.3	1.9
Indonesia	0.3	0.4	1.5	1.9

Source: Asian Development Bank (2005) and Fiji Islands Bureau of Statistics (2006).

There has been a growing concern in Fiji in terms of seeking cheaper markets. Hence, Fiji turned its direction of imports towards Asia. Fiji now imports from several Asian countries: Singapore, China, Hong Kong, Thailand, India and Indonesia. The trend of imports from Asia is clear: over the period 1985-2004, imports from the six of the Asian markets have increased (Table 3.4). Fiji, also imports from neighbouring Pacific Island countries. However, their market share still remains small. The direction of imports from Asia holds greater growth and developmental potential as Fiji is able to tap in low cost imports. It is highly likely that in the medium term some Asian countries will become Fiji's main source of imports.

3.9. TRADE POLICY SINCE INDEPENDENCE

Fiji enjoyed preferential market access to the European Community (now the European Union, EU) for its sale of sugar following its independence. At the same time, it remained closely attached to United Kingdom, again enjoying preferential prices for its sugar as well as a major market for its imports. In the face of guaranteed market for sugar, Fiji failed to diversify its export base to enhance its merchandise and service exports (see Prasad and Asafu-Adjaye, 2003). As such, it continued with a narrow export base. At the same time it adopted a comprehensive and costly trading regime with import substitution in order to develop its sectors (see Chand, 2004). This discriminated its exports with significant parts of its domestic manufacturing being protected by non-tariff barriers, largely in the form of licences. High tariffs were compounded with higher effective rates of protection (Elek, Hill and Tabor, 1993).

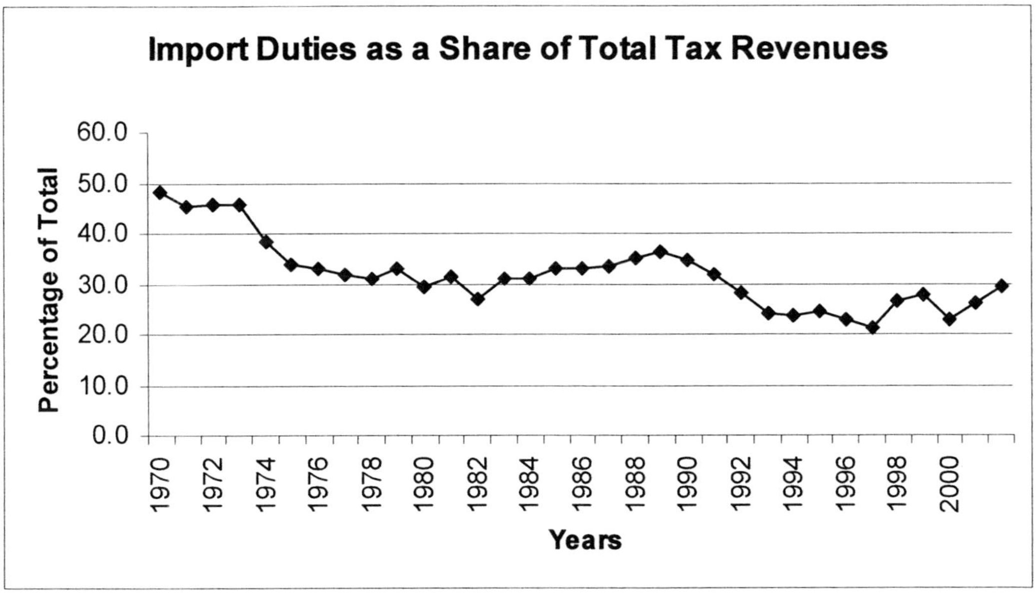

Source of data for Figure 3.10: The World Bank (2004)

Figure 3.10.

While data on effective rates of protection is unavailable, Figure 3.10 depicts import duties as a share of total revenues for the 1970-04 period so as to capture the extent of protection. The pattern depicted in Figure 3.10 shows that import duties as a share of tax revenue declined gradually over the 1970-02 period, it increased in the 2002-04 periods and reached a high of 61 in 2003. Import duties as a share of tax revenues averaged 39 percent during 1970-79; 32 percent during 1980-89 and 26.2 percent during 1990.

As a result of strong campaign to attract foreign investors following the 1987 crises, Fiji began liberalizing its trading environment (Cameron, 1993 and Prasad and Asafu-Adjaye, 2003). It embarked on dismantling the anti-export bias policy that it adopted since independence; eliminated majority of licensing requirements; and firms exporting more than 95 percent of their output were exempted from import duty payments (Elek, Hill and Tabor, 1993). At the same time, the government embarked on a program of import tariff reductions. The average applied tariff rates has been gradually falling over the last ten years (Figure 3.11).

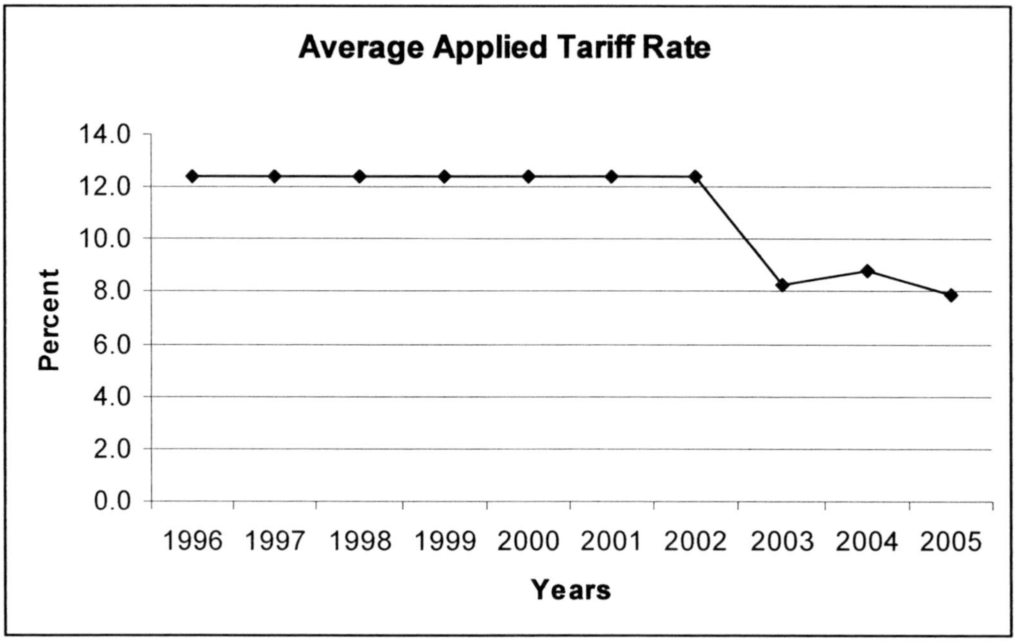

Source of data for Figure 3.11: The World Bank (2005).

Figure 3.11.

One of the reforms that had a positive spill over effect was the introduction of the tax-free factories (TFF) where firms were granted a 13 year tax free holiday (see Fiji Trade and Investment Board, 2005). Most of the TFF factories were in garment manufacturing. The South Pacific Regional Trade and Economic Cooperation Agreement (SPARTECA) with Australia and New Zealand was in place. The SPARTECA provided duty free access to Fijian goods in New Zealand and Australia (see Fiji Ministry of Foreign Affairs, 2005). Fiji exporters benefited from this. Other than Australia and New Zealand, Fiji enjoyed preferential access to United States (with entirely quota free entry for garments until 1990) and to European Community under the Lome provisions of the ACP group of countries (see Chand,

2004). Fiji's access to SPARTECA eroded in December 2004 as Multi Fibre Agreement (MFA) based restrictions are eliminated as textile and clothing trade is brought back under the General Agreement on Trade and Tariff (GATT) rules during the 1990s.

Fiji's high level of structural openness and the extent of its integration into the international economy especially in the Asia Pacific region make it a good candidate of significant beneficiary of the world trade reform. However, Fiji's narrow export base also means that it is vulnerable to reforms as it is likely to lead to the erosion of margins of preference as it is in case of EU sugar prices. While it's negative effect is likely to be detrimental in the short to medium term particularly on Fiji's agriculture, it is likely to be beneficial in the long-term if the likelihood of the diversification into alternative activities with greater growth potential are explored (see for example, Prasad and Asafu-Adjaye, 2003).

Trade reforms in agriculture have been a major battleground in global trade liberalization (see for example, Hoekman, Mattoo and English, 2002). One of the major initiatives of agricultural trade reform has been the EU's reduction of support for agriculture subsidy to the production of sugar beet. The detrimental externality is the impact on the world sugar market. Under the Sugar protocol, the EU guaranteed market access and prices of cane sugar exported from Fiji among other small states and the phased reduction in EU guaranteed prices for sugar is having a direct negative impact on income of Fiji sugar farmers (see for example, Chand, 2004).

Trade reform in manufactures has also affected Fiji. Trade reform in manufactures has been an important area of global trade reform with the key effect on textile manufacturing activities (see Hoekman, Mattoo and English, 2003). The gradual elimination of quotas under the Uruguay round as the multi fibre agreement is integrated into the MFN framework. This reform is likely to lead to a loss of relative preferential access to Fiji. Faced with greater threat of competiton in textile industry from China and other Asian nations, Fiji will have to improve its value added through upgrading its technology and human capital. In general the impact of trade reforms is likely on balance to be unfavorable for Fiji.

3.10. Current Trade Policy Regimes

Trade policy has become an increasingly important component of Fiji's international economic setting in the last two decades. Fiji has thus inclined itself towards an outward looking approach to trade in the last fifteen years. Import restrictions have been reduced with greater encouragement of the export sector. Fiji now has a more open trading environment that is contributing to increased prosperity. Fiji's trade regime is largely structured on three core trade policy regimes: the bilateral trade agreements (BTA), the regional trade agreement (RTA) and the multilateral trading system (MLS). A detailed account of these arrangements is available at Fiji Trade and Investment Board (2005), Fiji Ministry of Foreign Affairs (2005) and Narsey (2004). Various trade arrangements summarized from the above sources are presented below.

The Bilateral Trade Arrangement

Fiji is a signatory to a number of bilateral trade arrangements with small and large states. With small states of Tonga, Cook Islands and Tuvalu, it has a non-reciprocal agreement. Its agreement with Tonga has been in place since 1995 while with Cook Islands and Tuvalu, the agreements are recent. Fiji also has reciprocal BTAs with larger countries (Australia, China and Papua New Guinea). Negotiations have also started for reciprocal BTAs with the Solomon Islands, New Caledonia, Kiribati, Nauru and Samoa.

Fiji also has BTA's with high-income countries. With Australia, it signed the Fiji-Australia Trade and Economic Cooperation Agreement (FATERA) on 11 March 1999. The Fiji New Zealand BTA was suspended in 1999 but negotiations on this have started. The USA is a major market for Fiji's exports of garments and water. The two countries signed a BTA in 1995 in regard to exports of garments. Fiji also has a BTA with China since 1997 under which China offers Fiji's exports MFN treatment. Fiji also has cordial bilateral relations with Japan and South Korea and with its "Look North Policy"; this is likely to be strengthened.

The Regional Trade Agreements

Fiji's regional trade agreement includes the Melanesian Spearhead Group (MSG) and the SPARTECA.

The MSG came into effect in July 1993 and Fiji became a formal member in April 1998. Others include Papua New Guinea, Vanuatu and the Solomon Islands. The core focus of the MSG is to trade in products free of fiscal duty.

The SPARTECA was signed in 1981 between Australia and New Zealand and the Forum Island member countries allowing duty free access to their goods in Australia and New Zealand subject to rules of origin regulations. The aim is to readdress the unequal trade relationships between the two groups. Fiji's textiles, clothing and footwear (TCF) industry has been the major beneficiary of SPARTECA. The rapid expansion of the Fiji TCF industry (Figure 3.12) has been attributed to the removal of TCF quotas by the Australian Government in 1987 which allowed quota free and duty free access under SPARTECA, the introduction of the Tax Free Factory/Zone (TFF/TFZ) Scheme in 1988 and the Australian Import Credit Scheme (ICS). Under the SPARTECA arrangements, goods can enter Australia duty free where the allowable factory cost is greater than or equal to 50 percent of the total ex-factory cost of manufacturing the goods. These arrangements continue to stand. The SPARTECA TCF provisions enabled firms to utilize excess local area content (ELAC) from certain SPARTECA qualifying TCF goods to help meet the 50 percent content requirement in otherwise on-qualifying eligible goods. ELAC is derived where products local area content exceeds 70 percent. Similarly, ELAC can only be used where a products local area content is greater than 35 percent and where there is a last process of manufacture performed in forum island member countries. The duration of SPARTECA-TCF scheme was from 1 March 2001 to 31 December 2004.

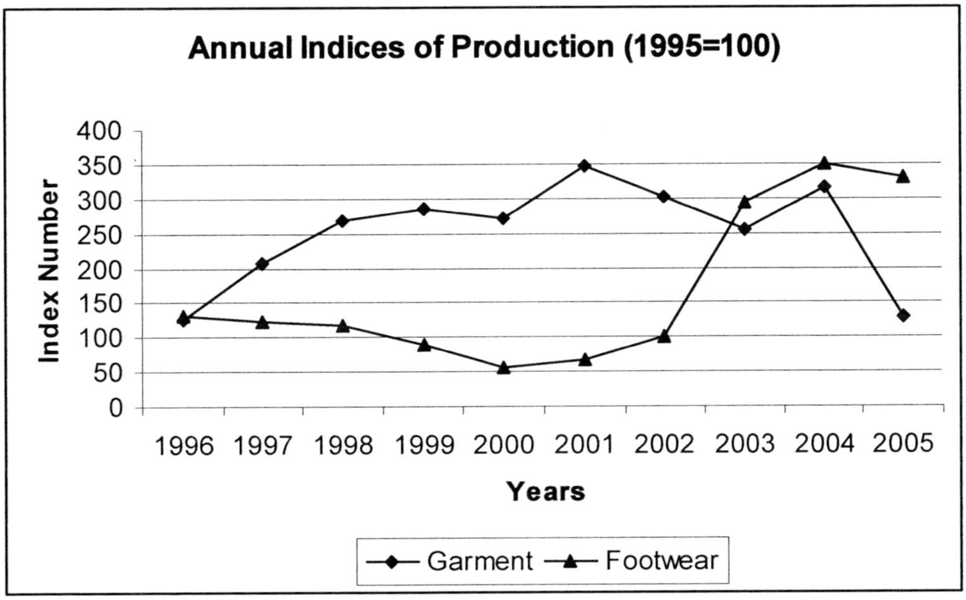

Source of data for Figure 3.12: Asian Development Bank (2005).

Figure 3.12.

Multilateral Trade Arrangements (MTAs)

The MTAs include a free trade area, the regional free trade area and the Cotonou agreement.

Free Trade Area

Fiji is a member of the World Trade Organisation (WTO). Multilateral negotiations through WTO combined with the Most Favoured Nation (MFN) principle, allows Fiji to benefit from the access concessions made to larger countries. This increases Fiji's market access which allows exporters to boost production and thus revenue and employment. However, freer global trade will lead to erosion of the preferences that Fiji enjoys with developed nations and thus will cause problems for traditional exports such as sugar, garment and fish.

The 1999 Forum Trade Ministers meeting endorsed a free trade area proposal.

Fiji is bound to abide by the WTO rules. Key concerns to Fiji are areas in which it has to negotiate for better trade deals. In agriculture, Fiji's concern is on market access. Along with African, Caribbean and the Pacific (ACP)-EU member countries, Fiji has to defend its sugar exports to foreign markets under ACP-EU preferential arrangements. Fiji's services sector has been expanding yet Fiji has no legal framework that is WTO consistent. The general agreement on trade in services (GATS) adopts a positive approach to providing rights to foreign investors. Countries are allowed to liberalise gradually and to specify during the trade negotiations the services sectors in which they would be willing to grant foreign suppliers the right to establish a commercial presence and invest. Fiji's schedule of commitments under GATS covers two sectors: hotels and restaurants.

The agreement on trade related aspects of intellectual property rights (TRIPS) allows for minimum standards for the protection of intellectual property, domestic enforcement procedures and intellectual dispute settlement are relevant to the legal environment affecting investment. Fiji has already established the copyright act. The trade marks bill, patents bills and designs bill are also completed.

Regional Free Trade Areas (PICTA/PACER)

Fiji's history of free trade agreement proposal dates back to 1971 through the South Pacific Bureau of Economic Cooperation (now the Forum Secretariat). On the 18th August 2001, the 32nd Pacific Islands Forum in Nauru, Forum leaders endorsed and signed the Pacific Agreement on Closer Economic Relations (PACER). PACER provides the framework for strengthening trade and economic cooperation among all Forum members (including Australia and New Zealand) at an appropriate 'pace' reflecting the differing development status of the matters. Fiji is also a signatory to the Pacific Island Countries Trade Agreement (PICTA). PICTA is a free trade agreement amongst the 14 Pacific Island countries. At the Nauru meeting the three compact countries as well as Papua New Guinea and the Solomon Islands did not sign the two agreements. This means that only 11 Forum countries signed PACER and 9 countries signed the PICTA agreement. PACER will enter force after 7 countries have ratified the agreement while PICTA on the other hand will come into force after the ratification by 6 Forum Island Countries.

Cotonou Agreement

In 1972, the European Union (EU) granted a preferential trade regime to ACP. Trade preferences, commodity protocols and instruments of trade cooperation were part of the four successive Lome Conventions (1975-2000). The Contonou Agreement (CA) signed in June 2000 addresses a loss of significant preferences. It extends trade preferences for eight years but defines the negotiating framework to enable ACP and EU to conclude new trade agreements compatible with WTO rules by 31 December 2007 at the latest. The CA is not a trade agreement but contains a commitment to agree at a later date (2008) on several new ACP-EU reciprocal trade agreements that are compatible with WTO rules and will replace the present non-reciprocal preferential trade agreement. For the first time, ACP countries will negotiate a reciprocal trade agreement with EU which had so far granted preferences.

Leading from ACP draft Action Plan, Fiji has derived its own national action plan which concentrates on capacity building, involving relevant government stakeholders, non-state actors and formulating a consultative and negotiating mechanism which adequately represents and involves all the major stakeholders in the negotiating process of a new partner-ship agreement with the EU under the Cotonou Structure.

3.11. Conclusion

International trade has been important to Fiji with its trading pattern dictated by its structural transformation. Its structural transformation and changing factor endowments led to decline in agriculture value added and increases in services value added. Trade data indicates that Fiji has lived with long periods of trade deficits, importing more than exporting. However, Fiji's trading environment experienced a major turning point following the political crisis in 1987 with total export earnings rising significantly from US$329 million in 1987 to US$606 million in 2001. Overtime, gradual trade reforms led to major improvements as export of goods and services as a share of GDP increased from 48 percent in 1970 to just over 71 percent in 2001.

Tourism is now the leading income earner with earnings amounting to almost 60 percent of total exports in 2004 compared to 24 percent of total exports in 1990. Other then the developments in the tourism sector, Fiji's industrial expansion including the establishment of light manufacturing industry, has led to newer export products such as woodchips, textiles and footwear. After the mid-1990s, the export composition expanded to include additional commodities: mineral water, yaqona, vegetables and chemicals. The performance of Fiji's predominant industry, sugar, is no longer the top income earner. Of all the commodities exported in the last five years, mineral water recorded the largest growth in terms of export earnings. Fiji, while maintaining stronger comparative advantage in its largely primary products, does face strong competition from other primary producers around the world.

Exports to the USA gained increasing momentum, rising from 9.5 percent in 1980–84 to 24.1 percent in 2000–04. Since independence, Fiji's imports rose significantly from US$114 million in 1970 to US$1,092 million in 2001, a ten fold increase. Fiji's major imports are machines and transport equipment. This together with imports of mineral fuels, crude materials and chemicals are vital inputs to the production process.

For long Fiji's main export and import markets have been high income countries: Australia, New Zealand, Japan and the United States. Today, Australia continues to remain the major import market while USA is the main export market. Fiji at the same time has been seeking newer markets particularly in Asia (Singapore, China, Hong Kong, Thailand, India and Indonesia) that are cheaper than the traditional high-income country markets.

Fiji certainly needs to diversify its export base so as to dampen the possibility of exogenous shocks. Fiji has a high level of structural openness as reflected in the share of its trade in GDP/GNP often close to and in some years over 100 percent. The developments in the global trading environment will continue to affect Fiji's trading pattern. The phased introduction of global trade reform within the principles of World Trade Organisation hold both opportunities (overcome any diseconomies of scale through the expansion of markets) and threats (income and employment) to its growth prospects. Therefore, Fiji certainly needs to diversify its export base perhaps into high value added products to reap the benefits of global freer trade regimes. Fiji also needs to engage into more bilateral trading relationships and in continued search for more export markets and cheaper import markets.

REFERENCES

Asian Development Bank. (2005). *Key Indicators*. Manila.

Balassa, B. (1965). Trade liberalisation and 'revealed' comparative advantage, *Manchester School*, Vol. 33, No. 2, pp. 99-123.

Cameron. J. (1993). A political economy of market-led structural adjustment. A case study of Fiji, *Journal of International Development,* Vol. 5, pp. 123-133.

Chand, S. (2004). Trade gains for small island economies, *World Trade Review*, Vol.3, No. 3, pp. 409-415.

Chenery, H. B. and M. Syrquin. (1975). *Patterns of Development, 1950-1970.* London, Oxford University Press for the World Bank.

Cole, R. and Hughes, H. (1988). *The Fiji Economy, May 1987: Problems and Prospects,* Pacific Policy Papers No.4, National Centre for Development Studies, Australian National University, Canberra.

Das, D. (1998). Changing comparative advantage and the changing composition of Asian exports, *The World Economy,* Vol. 21, No.1, pp. 121-140.

Elek, A., Hill, H., and Tabor, S.R. (1993). Liberalisation and diversification in a small economy: Fiji since the 1987 coups, *World Development*, Vol. 21, No. 5, pp.749-769.

Fiji Islands Bureau of Statistics. (Various issues). *Current Economic Statistics*. Government Printer, Suva.

Fiji Ministry of Foreign Affairs. (2005). Trade Policy. Available on line at: http://www.foreignaffairs.gov.fj/trade_policy.html. Date of extraction: 10 September 2005.

Fiji Trade and Investment Board. (2005). Bilateral Trade Agreement, available on line at: http://www.ftib.org.fj/show/contents/exporting_fiji/arrange_agree/bilateral.htm. Date of extraction: 10 September 2005.

Gani, A. and Prasad, B.C. (2005). Fiji's exports and comparative advantage, USPEC Working Paper No. 15/2005. School of Economics. The University of the South Pacific. Suva.

Gani, A. (1997). The relationship between Fiji's real exchange rate and trade balance, *Pacific Economic Bulletin*, Vol. 12, No. 1, pp. 126-130.

Hoekman, B., Mattoo, A., English, P. (2002). *Development, Trade and WTO – A Handbook*, The World Bank, Washington, D.C.

Kuznets, S. (1966). *Modern Economic Growth: Rate, Structure and Spread*, New Haven. CT: The Yale University Press.

Narayan, P.K., and Narayan, S. (2004). Determinants of demand for Fiji's exports: An empirical investigation, *The Developing Economies*, Vol. XLII, pp. 95-112.

Narayan, P.K., and Narayan, S. (2004) Estimating Income and Price Elasticities of Imports for Fiji in a Cointegration Framework, *Economic Modelling* (in press, available from www.sciencedirect.com).

Narsey, W. (2004). PICTA, PACER and EPAs: Where are we going? Tales of FAGS, BOOZE and RUGBY. USPEC Working Paper No. 6/2004. School of Economics, The University of the South Pacific. Suva.

Prasad, B.C. and Asafu-Adjaye, J. (2003). Trade liberalization and environment in Pacific Island countries: is it a case of "two gains for one?" *International Journal of Social Economics*, Vol. 30, No. 12, pp.1288-1305.

The World Bank. (2004). *World Development Indicators CD ROM.* Washington, D.C.

The World Bank. (2005). Available on line at http://siteresources.worldbank.org/intres/resources/tar2005.xls. Date of extraction 10 November 2006.

The World Bank. (2006). *Key Development Data and Statistics.* Washington, D.C. Available on line at: http://web.worldbank.org/website/external/datastatistics. Date of extraction: 10 July 2006.

Chapter 4

The Fiscal Environment

4.1. Introduction

This chapter describes Fiji's long term fiscal position and the fiscal policy reforms undertaken beginning mid-1990s. It presents government's financial statement and outlines the core areas of revenues and expenditure and consumption. It also describes the series of economic reform initiatives introduced since 1996 and provides evidence of the payoffs of economic reform using available data.

4.2. The Government's Financial Statement

Table 4.1 presents a stylized version of the government's financial statement for the fiscal years 1995 and 2005. The total revenue (the money collected by the government) in 2005 was F$1,214.4 million equating to 26 percent of GDP and the total expenditure (goods and services bought by the government) was F$1,535.5 million equating to 33 percent of GDP. The deficit (difference between revenues and expenditure) was F$321.1 million or 7 percent of GDP in 2005 compared to 5.4 percent of GDP in 1995.

The government's total revenue falls under two categories: taxes and other receipts. In 2005, taxation revenue made up approximately 89 percent of government income. Of this, almost 61.3 percent of tax receipts come from indirect taxes, with another 27.4 percent of tax receipts provided by direct taxes. In 1995, taxation revenues accounted for approximately 86.4 percent of government income. Other receipts include incomes from loans, capital and current transfers and fees, fines and penalties.

Table 4.1 also presents data on government's total expenditure in three categories: expenditure on transfers and subsidies; public services and debt servicing. The first major expenditure is public services as recorded by functional classification. In 2005, the three largest functional expenditures were education (F$191.5 million); general public services (F$191.2 million); and economic services (F$131.0 million). Other core areas include health and defence. The second major expenditure is on transfers which include transfers to private non-profit making institutions, social security and other current transfers.

Table 4.1. Fiji Government Financial Statement

Revenue	Millions of Fiji Dollars 1995	2005	Expenditure	Millions of Fiji Dollars 1995	2005
Taxation Revenue			*Public Services*		
Indirect taxes	382.7	744.6	General public services	94.2	191.2
Direct taxes	225.0	333.0	Defence	44.8	58.2
Other Receipts			Education	112.0	191.5
Property income	22.6	71.6	Health	56.9	109.9
Fees, fines and penalties	30.7	29.4	Social security	...	2.8
			Housing and amenities	...	8.5
Current transfers	28.1	26.0	Other social services	...	1.0
Capital transfers	9.9	8.8	Economic services	91.1	131.0
Loan payments	3.5	1.0	Property income	82.5	133.6
			Social security benefits	41.4	69.4
			Current transfers	41.8	95.7
			Other transfers	60.7	111.4
			Gross fixed capital formation	59.6	165.4
			Redemption of debt	77.4	204.3
			Capital transfers	28.1	61.7
Total	703.0	1,214.4	Total	796.6	1535.5
Balance	-127.9	-321.1			

... indicates data unavailable.

Source: Fiji Islands Bureau of Statistics (March 2004 and March 2006).

4.3. Fiscal Balance

Figure 4.1 depicts government's fiscal balance for the period 1970 to 2004. It measures the difference between total government revenue and total government expenditure. Total government revenue averaged 22.5 percent of GDP for the 1970-1992 periods. On 1st July 1992, the government introduced the value added tax (VAT) that led to an increase in tax revenues in the post-1993 period. In addition to the introduction of VAT, government also abolished the estate and gift duties with effect from 1992. This together with stringent controls on government spending by the new formed Labour government led to a near budget balance in 1999. This was the most significant improvement in governments' fiscal balance since 1990. Year 2000 was a turning point with the onset of the political crisis that worsened Fiji's fiscal balance.

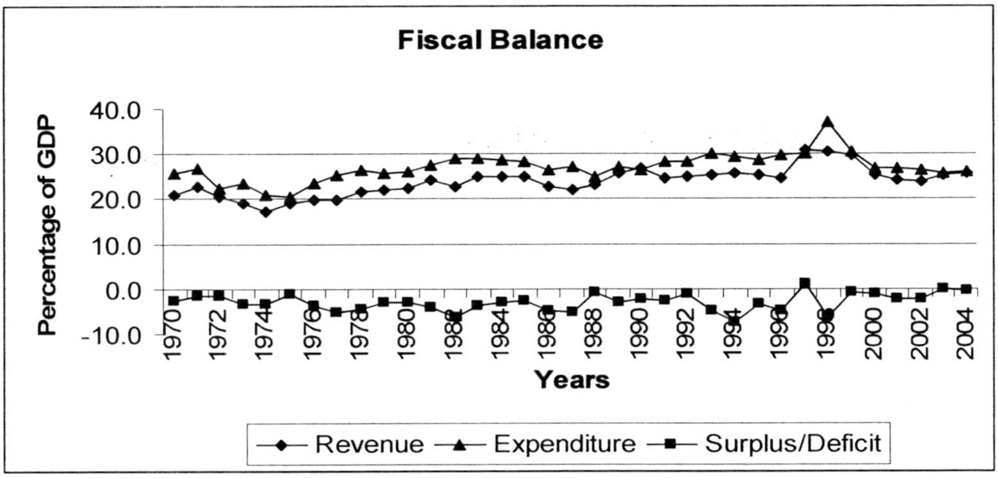

Source of data for Figure 4.1: The World Bank (2004) and Fiji Islands Bureau of Statistics (March 2006).

Figure 4.1.

Government deficit in year 2000 was 2.8 percent of GDP. This was a result of stronger than expected revenue collections, the fiscal austerity measures (stringent expenditure controls) of 2000 (Reserve of Fiji, March 2001). In 2001, government adopted an expansionary fiscal policy with government expenditure offsetting revenues. This included the reinstatement of the 12.5 percent pay cut for all civil servants introduced in 2000, a reduction in company tax rates (resident as well as non-resident) to 34 percent and a reduction in the top personal tax rate from 35 percent to 34 percent for both residents and non-residents (Reserve Bank of Fiji, March 2002). The government's expansionary fiscal stance continued in 2002 with deficit of 3.0 percent of GDP. Although fiscal revenue collections increased as a result of higher fiscal and excise duty collections (Reserve Bank of Fiji, March 2003), government expenditure continued to remain high.

In 2003, budget deficits rose to just over 6 percent of GDP. This was a result of an appropriation of F$30.2 million targeted to finance rehabilitation work after cyclone *Ami* and rising expenditures on the Suva-Nausori water supply project (Reserve Bank of Fiji, March 2004). The government in presenting its 2004 budget in late 2003 announced a contractionary fiscal stance for 2004. The government also introduced the Fiji Integrated Tax System (FITS) in November 2003 with the aim of improving the quality of revenue collection services and strengthens compliance (Reserve Bank of Fiji, March 2003). The Reserve Bank of Fiji (March 2005) notes that in announcing its 2004 budget, the government introduced three notable policy changes. First, it reduced the corporate and personnel taxes for the upper income category from 32 percent to 31 percent and the reduction in export tax for sugar from 10 percent to 3 percent. Second, it proposed a F$170 million capital expenditure for the Fiji Sugar Corporation (FSC) over a five year period beginning 2004 to improve productivity and efficiency as part of the reform of the sugar industry. Third, it announced the transition from the Cost of Living Adjustment (COLA) to the implementation of the Performance Management System, thus linking civil servants pay increases to performance. In 2004, governments budget deficits was 4.8 percent of GDP as a result of two additional appropriations by the government totaling F$50.9 million to meet costs related to floods in

April 2004 and additional requirements of the government ministries (Reserve Bank of Fiji, March 2005).

It is clear from the trends depicted in Figure 4.1 that successive governments since Fiji's independence have continuously produced a fiscal deficit that averaged 3 percent of GDP for the 1970-2004 period. The only exception is 1997 that produced a fiscal surplus of close to 1 percent of GDP. It is also confirmed by a recent study that government fiscal policy impacts Fiji's gross domestic product to a greater extent than its monetary policy (see Dahalan and Jayaraman, 2006).

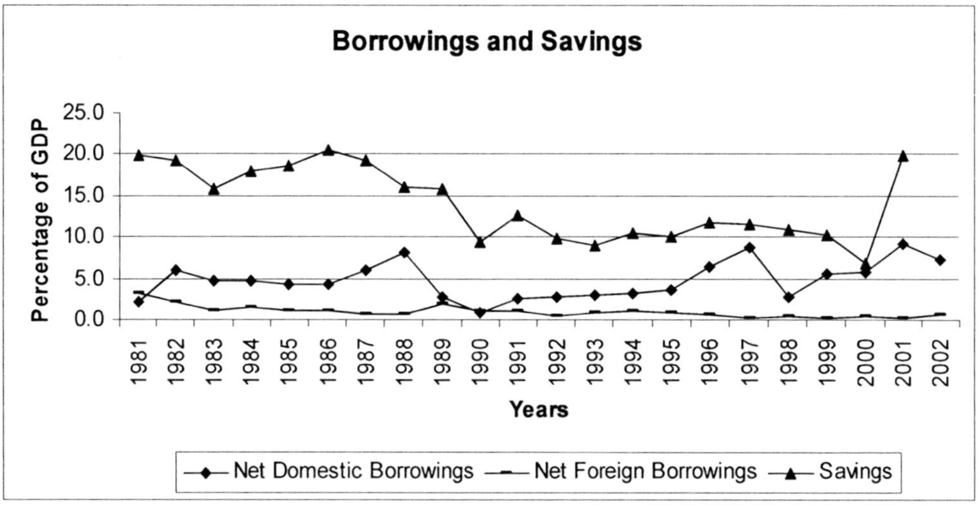

Source of data for Figure 4.2: Asian Development Bank (2004a and 2005).

Figure 4.2.

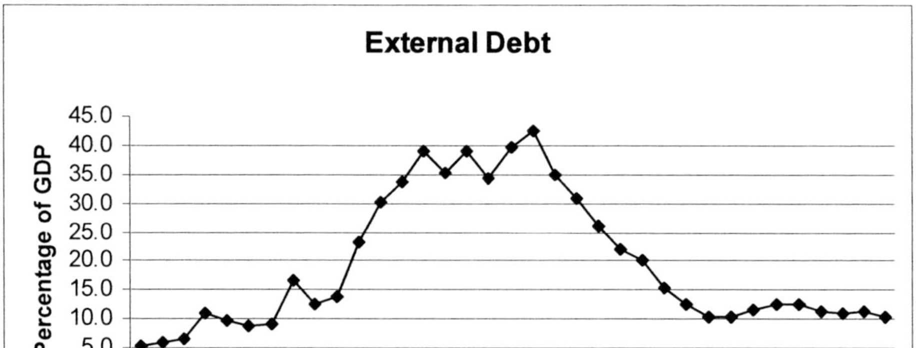

Source of data for Figure 4.3: The World Bank (2004) and Fiji Islands Bureau of Statistics (March 2006).

Figure 4.3.

The wide gaps between revenues and expenditure also led to mounting debt as domestic borrowings increased significantly in post 1990 period (Figure 4.2). As a result of declining foreign borrowings, foreign debt fell in the post 1990 period and this has been recorded as over 10 percent of GDP (Figure 4.3). Rising debt has also contributed to low levels of savings (Gani, 1999) as depicted by the trends in (Figure 4.2).

4.4. Government Revenues

Figure 4.4 depicts the main sources of government revenues. Income tax and estate and gift duties have been the dominant source of government's revenue up until 2000 followed by customs and port duties. Revenues from income tax took a sharp fall as a result of 2000 political crisis which led to the closure of several businesses and thousands of job losses (Narayan and Prasad, 2003). The Fiji Islands Bureau of Statistics (March 2006) data indicate that between 1992 and 2000, income tax revenues averaged just over 55 percent of total taxes while in 2000-2004 periods, it averaged 28 percent of total tax revenues. Governments reform of its ports and the reforms in its customs area led to significant increases in tax revenues from customs and port duties (Ministry of Public Enterprises and Public Sector Reforms, 2004). In 2004, this alone amounted for 60 percent of total tax revenues compared to just over 25 percent in 2000 (Fiji Islands Bureau of Statistics, March 2006).

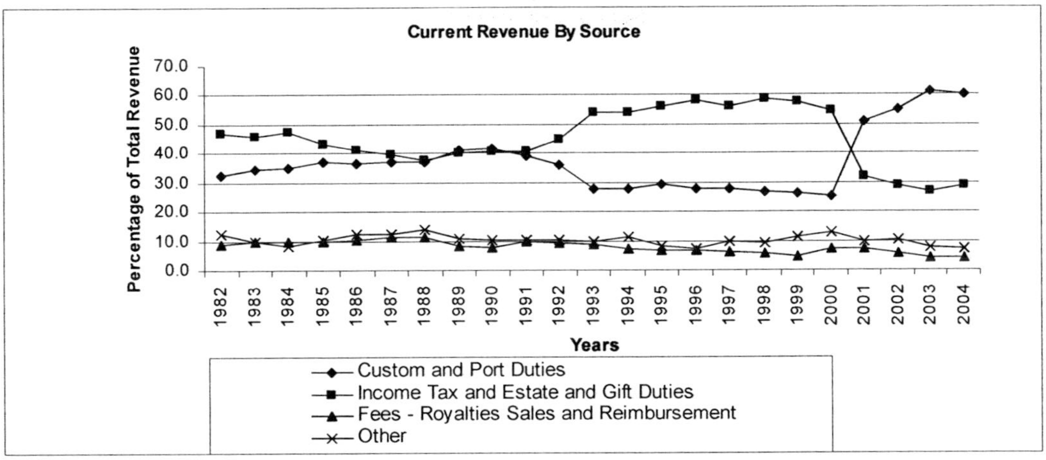

Source of data for Figure 4.4: Fiji Islands Bureau of Statistics (March 1992 and 2006).

Figure 4.4.

4.5. Government Expenditure

Consistent set of data on government expenditure is available for the years 1981-2004 (Figure 4.5). The bottom series in Figure 4.5 depict spending in core functional areas: general public services (general administration, external affairs and public order and safety); defence; education; health and economic services (agriculture, industry, electricity/gas/water, and transport and communication). It is clear those general public services, economic services and education has been the three priority areas of government spending. Following the political crises of 1987, government maintained a contractionary fiscal stance with the government expenditure falling to a low of 14.4 per cent of GDP in 1989 compared to 17.8 percent of GDP in 1987 (Figure 4.5). As depicted in Figure 4.5, the government increased its expenditure since 1990 so as to give a fiscal stimulus to aggregate demand. Government expenditure peaked to almost 20 percent of GDP in 1993 with increased spending in education as the main contributor (Figure 4.5). Government expenditure remained relatively stable between 1994 and 1997 (Figure 4.5). However, it rose to a high of 18.4 percent of GDP in 1998 largely as a result of increased spending in general public services. It declined since 1999 reaching a low of 15.6 percent of GDP in 2001 (Figure 4.5). Government's expansionary fiscal stance is reflected in 2003 and 2004 with government expenditure rising dramatically to 39 percent of GDP in 2004.

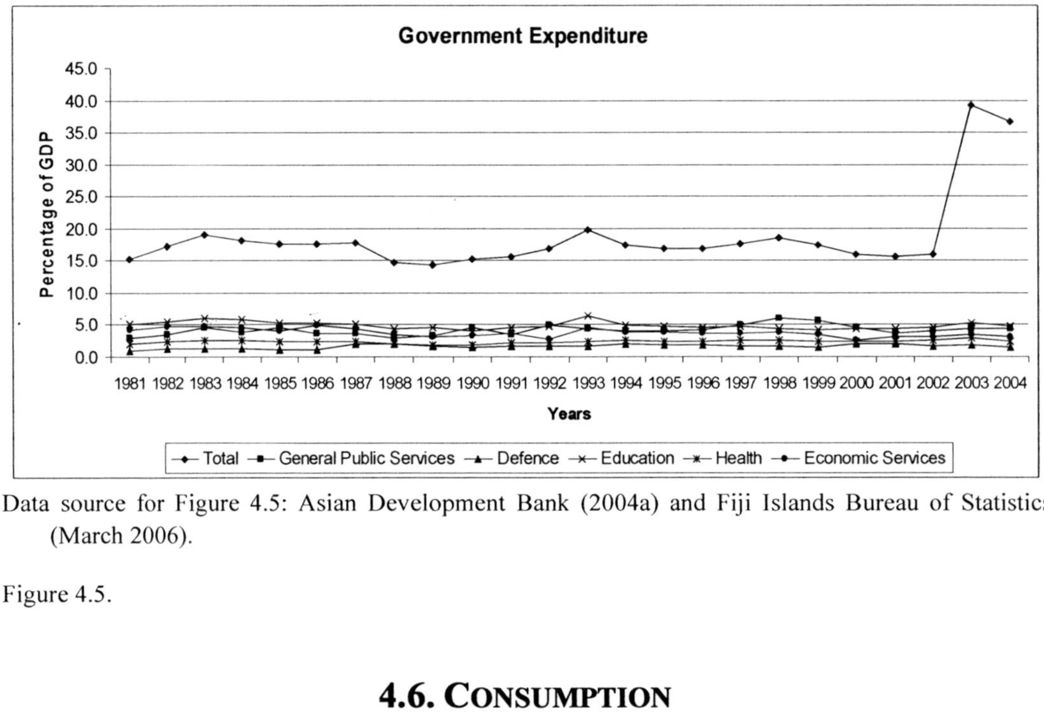

Data source for Figure 4.5: Asian Development Bank (2004a) and Fiji Islands Bureau of Statistics (March 2006).

Figure 4.5.

4.6. CONSUMPTION

Figure 4.6 depicts trends in private and public consumption. Private consumption is the total expenditure by the private sector on final goods and services. Public consumption is total expenditure by the government on final goods and services. Over the period 1981-2001, public consumption has been more stable than private consumption (Figure 4.6). According to trends in Figure 4.6, between 1981-2001, public consumption averaged 17 percent of GDP while private consumption averaged 66 percent of GDP. The pattern shown by public consumption reveals that government has not maintained a fiscal restraint in terms of scaling down its consumption (see also Reddy, 2005) and government sustaining its fiscal position remaining questionable (see Narayan and Narayan, 2003). It also indicates a sluggish pace of reforms initiated in early 1990s (see Duncan, Cuthbertson and Bosworth, 1999). Fiji's political crises that eventuated in 1987 seemed to have hit private consumption that has continued on a downward trend since 1991 (Figure 4.6). Figure 4.6 also indicates that private consumption fell from 78 percent of GDP in 1991 to 58 percent of GDP in 2001. This indicates regressive growth in Fiji's private sector brought in by the continued unstable political environment following the coups of 1987 (Asian Development bank, 2004b). While government has increased its expenditures in post 2000 period, much of this has been directed towards meeting current needs rather than productive investment. In fact government's fixed investment has remained less than 3 percent of GDP (Asian Development Bank, 2004a).

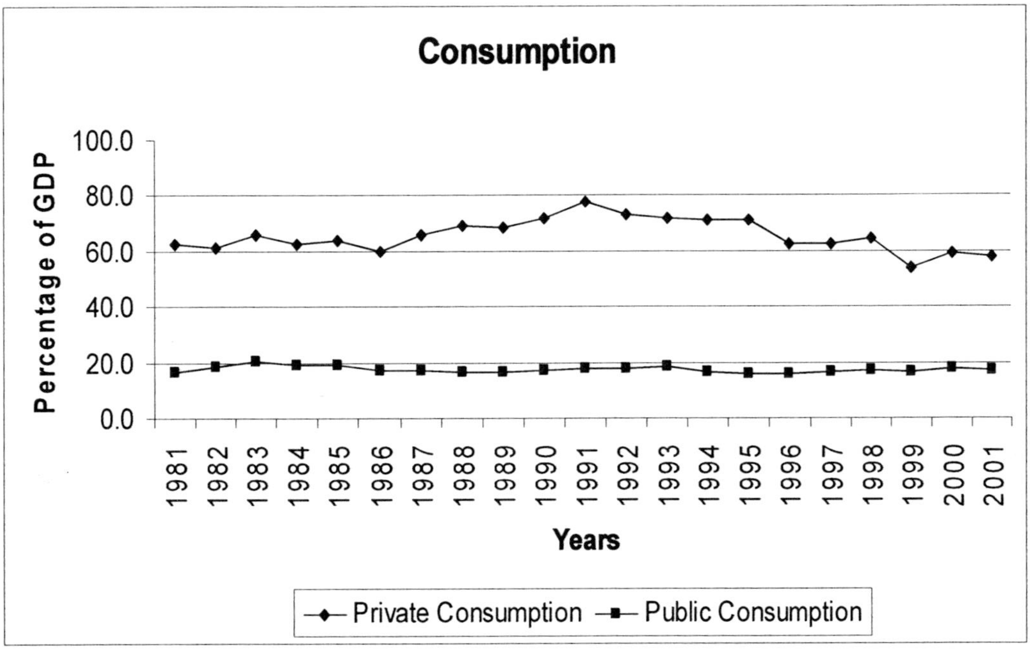

Source of data for Figure 4.6: Asian Development Bank (2004a and 2005).

Figure 4.6.

Other than the government fiscal position, economic reforms have been a key feature of governments' fiscal environment particularly in the post-1987 period (see for example, Asian Development Bank, 2004b). The continuing gap between revenues and expenditure since independence became a cause of concern to policy makers that inefficiency was ramanent in its public sector. In an attempt to improve governments fiscal position the crises of 1987 made the government realize to rethink its fiscal position (see Jayaraman, 2000). Hence, a key component of the post-1987 economic reform initiative has been the governments' commitment towards reform of public enterprises (see Ministry of Public Enterprises and Public Sector Reforms, 2004).

4.7. Public Enterprises Reform

Fiji is a mixed economy, that is, while many economic activities are undertaken by the private firms, others are undertaken by the government. For several years the government had involved itself in market activities in terms of producer and distributor of goods and services. Government's involvement in business activities includes power generation, management of ports (sea and air), agriculture production (sugar, rice, cattle, crop and aquaculture) and communications (significant shareholdings in telecommunications and newspaper). Government involvement in market led activities is further evident in terms of its shareholdings in 29 entities; the employment of some 32 percent of the labour force; and bearing a wage bill of the work force amounting to some 11.5 percent of GDP (see Asian Development Bank, 2004b).

However, since the government's impact on the private economy depends on its policies (regulatory and tax), there is no single indicator of the government's effect on the economy (Stiglitz, 2000). Nevertheless, a commonly used indicator to gauge government's effect on an economy is the size of public expenditures relative to the size of the aggregate economy (gross domestic product). For example, looking at the previous graph on public consumption, it is clear that government has maintained high levels of consumption that has remained on average more than 60 percent of GDP for the 1981-2001 periods (Figure 4.6).

Since 1980s most market economies around the globe realized that governments do not often succeed in correcting the failures of the market and that private markets should play the central role in the economy (see Stiglitz, 2000). Fiji has been no exception. The government realized the inefficiencies within its public sector and public enterprises: multiple and conflicting objectives, lack of accountability in performance, dependency on government for financial support and excessive protection from competition (see Ministry of Public Enterprises and Public Sector Reforms, 2004). Further evidence of the inefficiencies have been indicated in reviews done by the Asian Development Bank in year 2002 that showed that the combined return on assets of state owned enterprises was close to zero (Asian Development Bank, 2004b).

Elsewhere governmental role has been reflected in two core initiatives: deregulation (reducing the role of government in regulating the economy) and privatization (converting government enterprises into private firms). In view of these inefficiencies, the government has embarked with reforms in order to reduce the size of the government, improving efficiency and quality of services it provides. Fiji's regulatory environment has been overly burdensome to domestic and foreign investors alike (see Duncan, Cuthbertson and Bosworth, 1999). Realizing this, the government proceeded with public enterprises and public sector reforms in 1996 with the establishment of the Public Enterprises Act (Ministry of Public Enterprises and Public Sector Reform, 2004). The Act gives the government powers to reorganize state owned entity, appoint boards, monitor performance and ensure reporting compliance. Further, it makes provisions to place state owned enterprises on a more financially sound basis and ensure more efficient operation. This reform programme is administered by the Ministry of Public Enterprises and Public Sector Reforms. The two broad areas of focus are the reform of the public enterprises and the reorganization and restructuring of identified government ministries, departments and agencies. The Ministry of Finance owns the share holding in Government Commercial Corporations (GCCs) while the Ministry of Public Enterprises is responsible for performance.

4.7.1 Reform Initiatives

Fiji's reform options have ranged from privatization, to management contracts, to public private partnerships and to corporatisation. The reform initiatives discussed in this section are summarized from the Ministry of Public Enterprises and Public Sector Reforms (2004). Reform efforts in recent times have included three core areas: restructuring of non-performing enterprises; reforming entities and sectors that went through an initial phase of reforms and declaration of new entities for reorganization or restructuring.

The restructuring of non-performing enterprises include Rewa Rice Limited; Viti Corps Company Limited; Daily Post Limited; Fiji Ships and Heavy Industries and Yaqara Pastoral Company Limited.

Further reforms included aviation (separation of commercial functions); ports (reorganizing and rationalizing the corporate structure); electricity (separating and removing the licencing arm from the Fiji Electricity Authority); the Public Trust Office (corporatising of trust accounts and trust property worth F$70 million); the government handicraft centre (reorganizing for potential management contract); the Department of Immigration (transfer of frontline and border processing role at the airports to Fiji Islands Customs and Revenue Authority effective 1 July 2005). The benefits of this are likely to be immense: facilitate tourism; airport shopping; and profiling passengers in an integrated manner.

Reform initiatives in the Ministry of Agriculture, Sugar and Land Resettlement include the institutional strengthening of the Department of Quarantine so as to allow it to play a more dynamic role in Bio Security and Market Access issues. The government also has proposals to streamline the activities of the Fiji Meat Industry Board and Coconut Industry Development Authority.

The Public Enterprises Reform Programme have been targeting improvements in its Ministries as well as its commercial companies have targeted Ministry of Works, Ministry of Agriculture, Sugar and Land Resettlement, Department of Immigration, Ports, Forestry and government commercial companies.

The reforms in the Ministry of Works and Energy include the improved availability, quality and delivery of basic utilities such as water, sewerage and roads. This Ministry is to be reformed into autonomous Departments with Department of Water and Sewerage and Department of National Roads. This will allow these Departments to have their own accounting, management and support system necessary for better planning and decisions making. The Ministries Buildings, Architects, Electrical and Mechanical Sections will be reorgansied into Department of Asset Management and Procurement so as to ensure effective data base systems and accountabilities for better management.

Government has also commissioned the reforms of its ports (air and sea). The government is looking at introducing competition in the aviation sector particularly in the management and operation of commercial airports. On the sea port reforms, this is nearing completion with the new port company; Fiji Ports Corporation Limited is now established and fully operational. This company will take a lead role in development of Fiji as the "hub port" in the South Pacific. The Ports Terminal Limited has been positioned to operate as a wholly owned subsidiary of this company. There are also proposals to wind-up the Maritime Ports Authority of Fiji and to transfer its regulatory functions to Fiji Islands Maritime Safety Authority.

In the area of forestry, government has commercialsed the harvesting of mahogany with the establishment of 100 percent government owned company, Fiji Hardwood Corporation Limited. The government is also supporting private investment from investors in downstream processing of mahogany in various forms and magnitude.

The government is also pursuing reforms on government commercial companies to ensure good economic returns. The government is accelerating the pace of divesture of government from public enterprise in entities such as the Yaqara Pastoral Company, Fiji Broadcasting Corporation and Food Processors Limited and Fiji Ships and Heavy Industries Limited. There has been remarkable development at the Viti Corps Limited Dairy Farms Fiji which is a partnership of two entities from New Zealand, Highway Stabilizers and Marphona Farms. They have already invested approximately F$750,000 and employing some 61 people.

The government is also engaged in the right sizing of the public service. The government is targeting to reduce wages bill for the civil service from as high as 11 percent of GDP to 9 percent of GDP.

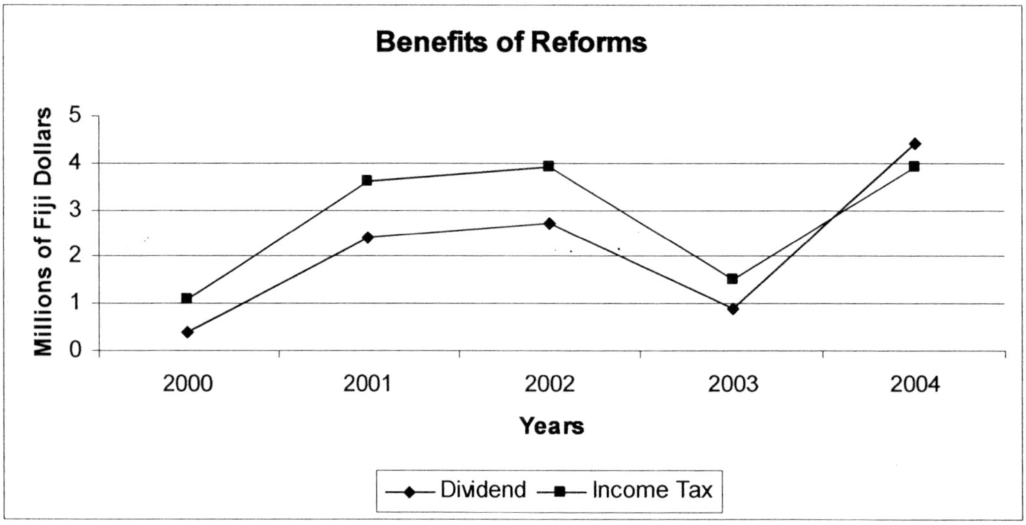

Source of data for Figure 4.7: Ministry of Public Enterprises and Public Sector Reforms (2004).

Figure 4.7.

4.7.2 Reform Payoffs

Available statistics confirm that the benefits of reforms are been gradually realized and in fact the benefits are on a rising trend. Figure 4.7 depicts the benefits accrued through dividends and income tax. Although data available is for a short time period, there are, however, significant increases in the dividends as well as income tax. The trend depicted by dividends and income tax is likely to continue on a rising scale given reform measures that are continuing as mentioned above. The government has also noted other non-monetary payoffs such as quality services, reduced costs, release of resources to health and education, creation of investor friendly environment, more competition in the market and the stimulation of the capital market development (Ministry of Public Enterprises and Public Sector Reforms, 2004).

While the government engaged in reform programs in view of the inherent inefficiencies so as to reduce the size of the government, improving efficiency and quality of services it provides, available data indicates that government involvement continues to expand (Figure 4.5). Nevertheless, a commonly used indicator to gauge government's effect on an economy is the size of public expenditures relative to the size of the aggregate economy (gross domestic product). For example, government consumption continues to remain high exceeding more than 60 percent of GDP, budget deficits continue to widen, and public sector wage bills keep increasing.

4.8. Conclusion

Fiji's fiscal position has been characterized with continued fiscal deficit that averaged 3 percent of GDP since its independence. In recent times budget deficits have been close to 7 percent of GDP. Government spending has largely been in areas of public services, economic services and education. While the government maintained a contractionary fiscal stance following the crises of 1987, an expansionary fiscal environment followed since 1990. Fiji's political crises that eventuated in 1987 had a regressive effect on the private sector. Although, a mixed economy, government involvement in private production remains extensive. This has reduced the prospects of a competitive market and new market participants. It has also crowded out potential private sector development. Its regulatory environment has been overly burdensome to domestic and foreign investors alike. In view of inefficiencies experienced as a producer of goods and services, the government has embarked with major reforms in order to reduce the size of the government, improving efficiency and quality of services it provides through the establishment of the Public Enterprises Act in 1996. Through this the government has to focus on the reform of the public enterprises and the reorganization and restructuring of identified government ministries, departments and agencies. Recent data confirm that the benefits of reforms are been realized with increases in dividends and income tax. The state should therefore concentrate on establishing the environment which facilitates the independent functioning and prosperity of the private enterprises while reducing its role in private production and distribution of goods and services.

References

Asian Development Bank. (2004a and 2005). *Key Indicators*. Manila.

Asian Development Bank. (2004b). *Fiji Private Sector Assessment*, Manila. (Available on line at http://www.adb.org/document/reports/psa/fij/fijiislands.pdf). Date of extraction: 10 September 2005.

Dahalan, J. and Jayaraman, T.K. (2006). Monetary and fiscal policies in Fiji: a test of effectiveness, *Pacific Economic Bulletin*, Vol. 21, No. 2, pp. 94-102.

Duncan, R.C., Cuthbertson, S., and Bosworth, M. (1999). Pursuing Economic Reform in the Pacific, Pacific Studies Series No. 18, Asian Development Bank, Manila.

Fiji Islands Bureau of Statistics. (March 1992 and 2006). *Key Statistics*. Government Printer. Suva.

Gani, A. (1999). The burden of external debt on South Pacific island countries, *Savings and Development*, Vol. XXIII, pp. 76-89.

Jayaraman, T.K. (2000). Fiscal and monetary policies in South Pacific Island countries, *Development Bulletin*, No. 52, pp. 78-80.

Ministry of Public Enterprises and Public Sector Reforms. (2004). Public Enterprises Reform – Towards a Better Fiji. Suva.

Narayan, P. K. and Narayan, S. (2003). The sustainability of Fiji's budget deficit: an econometric analysis, *Pacific Economic Bulletin*, Vol. 18, No.2, pp. 77-91.

Narayan, P.K. and Prasad, B.C. (2003). Fiji national budget 2003: building a resilient economy, *Pacific Economic Bulletin*, Vol. 18 (2), pp. 91-108.

Reddy, M. (2005). *Public Finance in Fiji – Theory and Practice*. Development Studies Program, The University of the South Pacific, Suva.

Reserve Bank of Fiji. (March issues 2001, 2002, 2003, 2004 and 2005). *Quarterly Economic Bulletin*. Suva.

Stiglitz, J. E. (2000). *Economics of Public Sector* (Third Edition), Norton, New York.

Chapter 5

THE MONETARY ENVIRONMENT

5.1. INTRODUCTION

This chapter seeks to provide a review of Fiji's monetary policy. It provides a brief historical account of monetary policy setting. Monetary policy objectives are outlined followed by a discussion of how the monetary policy is formulated and executed. It also seeks to evaluate monetary policy in terms of core monetary policy objectives: maintaining price stability and adequate foreign reserves. Finally, an analysis is presented on how Fiji's monetary policy has affected the broader macroeconomic goals and the effects on the economy.

5.2. THE MONETARY POLICY SETTING

The Reserve Bank of Fiji (RBF) manages the monetary policy conduct of Fiji. The RBF that came into being on 1 January 1984 is the forerunner of the Central Monetary Authority (CMA) that was established in early 1973 (Reserve Bank of Fiji, 1987). Since its inception, CMA and now the RBF have been tasked to manage Fiji's money. The RBF's major role today is to enable a stable growth path for the Fijian economy by ensuring low inflation, maintaining adequate foreign reserves and overseeing a well functioning financial system (Reserve Bank of Fiji, 2004). The overall mission of this institution is to facilitate the growth and development of the Fijian economy. In doing so, it has two major roles. First, to regulate banks to ensure the health of the banking system. Second, to control the quantity of the money that is made available in the economy. Decisions by the policy makers concerning the money supply constitute monetary policy. In additions, the RBF tends to provide sound economic advice to the government, is in charge of maintaining a reputable financing system, facilitate the dissemination of timely and quality information and train and retain a professional team of workers. The monetary policy framework adopted by RBF has largely been determined by its economic capacity and the extent of the development and the operational environment of its financial sector. Here, the key player has been the exchange rate system. Fiji has a trade weighted exchange rate system where the Fijian dollar is pegged to a basket of five currencies of its major trading partners: United States of America,

Australia, New Zealand, Japan and the European Union (see also Jayaraman, 2003). Thus, Fiji's monetary policy happens to be guided by not only by the developments in the domestic economic conditions but also the developments in these major trading partners.

5.3. The Objectives of Fiji's Monetary Policy

Following its transition from CMA to RBF, the RBF Act of 1983 formally launched the objectives of Fiji's monetary policy. The core objective is to maintain an appropriate environment for sustainable economic growth through price stability and ensuring adequate level of foreign reserves (Reserve Bank of Fiji, 1987 and 2004). Common to Central Banks elsewhere, the RBF has price stability as one of its main objectives. While having no inflation target as done in countries such as New Zealand, Australia and Canada, the RBF tends to favour an inflation rate of below 3 percent. The RBF takes this policy objective staidly given Fiji's high imports as well as domestic influences (effects of wage rises as well as natural disturbances like cyclones and drought on the agricultural sector and infrastructure). The RBF also places an equal emphasis on maintaining an adequate level of foreign reserves. While the appropriate level of foreign reserves depend on a country's economic circumstances, the RBF follows the international standards of maintaining foreign reserves equivalent to 3 months of its imports.

5.4. Monetary Policy Formulation and Implementation

Fiji's monetary policy formulation is directly linked to the developments in the domestic as well as external sector (trading partner economies). By monitoring the performance of several economic variables and their impact on inflation and foreign reserves on a continual basis by its own Policy Coordinating Committee, the RBF's board decides on the appropriate monetary policy stance at the end of each month (see Reserve Bank of Fiji, 2004). Hence, the RBF will use the appropriate instruments to work through the monetary policy objective decided by the board.

The instruments used to influence core monetary variables include interest rates, credit and money aggregates which then determine the inflationary and foreign reserve position so as to influence overall economic growth. The RBF up until 1989 implemented direct controls: controls on the amount of commercial bank lending and the interest rates at which loans were provided. The control on the quantity of money supplied was the hallmark of this approach. The RBF used the changes in the statutory reserve deposits (SRD) of commercial banks to influence broad money and credit aggregates in order to influence inflation. The financial system in pre-1989 period was heavily regulated and RBF had no choice but to resort to direct controls (Ali and Jayaraman, 2001).

Financial sector reforms triggered by the crises of 1987 led to major changes in RBF's monetary policy conduct - the adoption of market based approach of conducting monetary policy (Ali and Jayaraman, 2001). In 1989, the RBF introduced its own notes, and so a replacement of the direct controls policy. Since then, the open market operations (OMO) – the purchase and sale of bonds by the RBF, have become the primary instrument for conducting monetary policy (Reserve Bank of Fiji, 2004).

The main component of the OMO is the sale and purchase of securities to influence the liquidity position of the banking system in order to have a direct effect on the short term interest rates. The RBF uses its own securities, the RBF notes to conduct OMO. This is in contrast to central banks elsewhere that use government instruments. The RBF notes are sold through weekly auction and so by buying or selling RBF notes, the RBF adds or withdraws funds from the financial system. Market participants are informed via newspapers, emails and fax. The tenders open between 9.00 am and 11.00 a.m. on Tuesdays and Thursdays. Therefore, the changes in banks fund position affect the short term interest rate.

The short term interest rate that RBF uses is the 91-day RBF note rate as it is easily influenced through its OMO (Reserve Bank of Fiji, 2004). Once RBF configures that the 91 day rate is misaligned, it tends to sell or purchase small amounts of note in the market, thus maintaining a continuous pressure so as to move rates towards the equilibrium. Hence, through influencing the 91 day rate, it tends to influence other interest rates and thus exert the flow on effect on the broader economy. In particular, a change in the 91 day rates would directly affect commercial banks lending and deposit rates. This would have a direct effect on changes in commercial banks credits and the economic activity.

Based on the current and forecasted performance of the domestic economy, the policy indicator rate (91 day rate) may increase (contractionary monetary policy) or decrease (expansionary monetary policy). The RBF also keeps a close watch on the foreign reserve position where deterioration is overcome by a monetary policy tightening. On the other hand the RBF may reduce the indicator rate in absence of any threats of rising price of when foreign reserve position is frugal.

The success of the monetary policy is based on the achievement of the two objectives of low inflation and adequate levels of foreign reserves. The next section discusses the achievements in these two variables.

5.5. Achievements in Monetary Policy Objectives

The achievements in monetary policy objectives can be gauged by examining the key variables that the RBF includes as its policy targets, price stability (inflation rate) and reserves (foreign reserves).

Figure 5.1 depicts the trends in inflation measured by the changes in consumer price index (CPI) as well as the GDP deflator. Figure 5.1 makes it clear that Fiji went through a period of high inflation during most of 1970s and early eighties resulting largely from oil price shocks and high levels of imports. While inflation was high in the 1970s, Fiji was virtually free of hyper-inflation. Between 1972 and 1984, consumer price inflation remained above 5 percent and in some years during this period remaining above 10 percent. Between 1982 and 1986, CPI inflation gradually declined hitting a low of 1.8 in 1986. CPI as well as GDP deflator inflation rose in 1987 and both remained above the 5 percent mark for most periods between 1987 and 1993. While the RBF preferred a lower inflation of 3 percent or below, this was possible in few years in the post 1994 period. Over the long period, the RBF does not seem to have comfortably realised its ultimate objective of price stability as maintaining inflation below the 3 percent target mark has been a rare achievement.

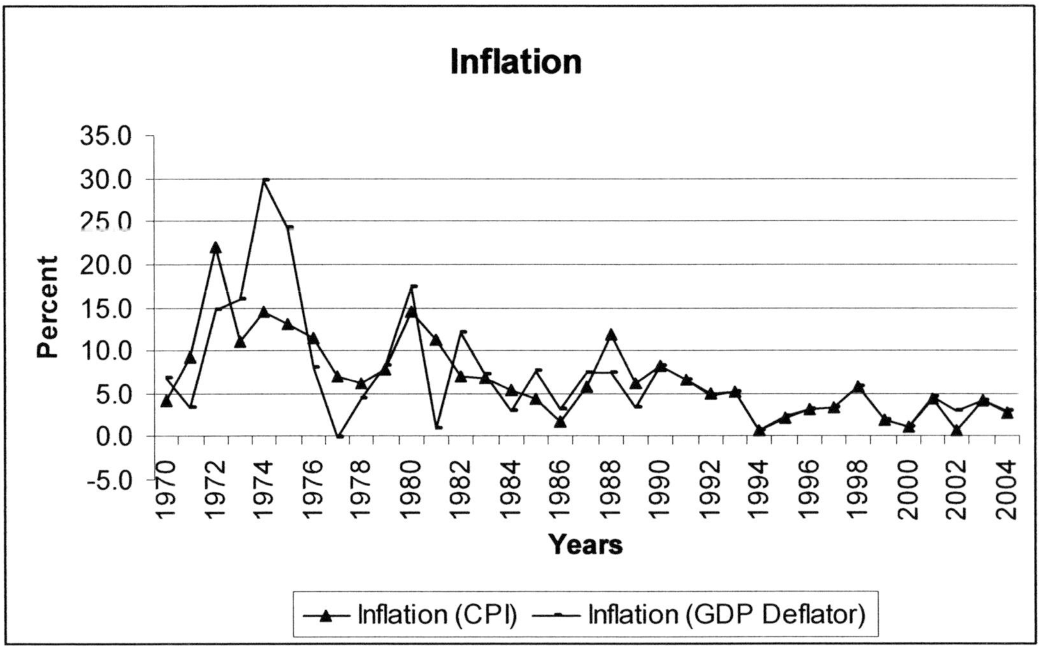

Source of data for Figure 5.1: The World Bank (2004) and Fiji Islands Bureau of Statistics (March 2006).

Figure 5.1.

The second important objective of Fiji's monetary policy has been to maintain an adequate level of foreign reserves. While data is inadequate for years following independence, Fiji's foreign reserve position for the period 1979-2004 is depicted in Figure 5.2. According to Figure 5.2, the foreign reserves deteriorated in the first half of 1980s remaining below the required level of three months of imports. Deterioration in domestic economic conditions together with high import costs contributed to the worsening of the foreign reserve position in the first half of 1980s. While the foreign reserve position improved in 1986, it deteriorated in 1987 falling below the target rate. However, between 1988 and 1993, Fiji was well able to maintain its required foreign reserve position in light of improved economic position compared to the crises led recession of 1987 followed by its banking crisis that involved the collapse of the National Bank of Fiji (see Grynberg, Munro and White, 2002). Since 1995, as a result of improved economic performance, Fiji has noted a significant improvement in its foreign reserves position that has remained between 4 to 6 months of imports. Thus, RBF has managed to comfortably realise its objective with regard to maintaining adequate levels of foreign reserves mostly in the last decade.

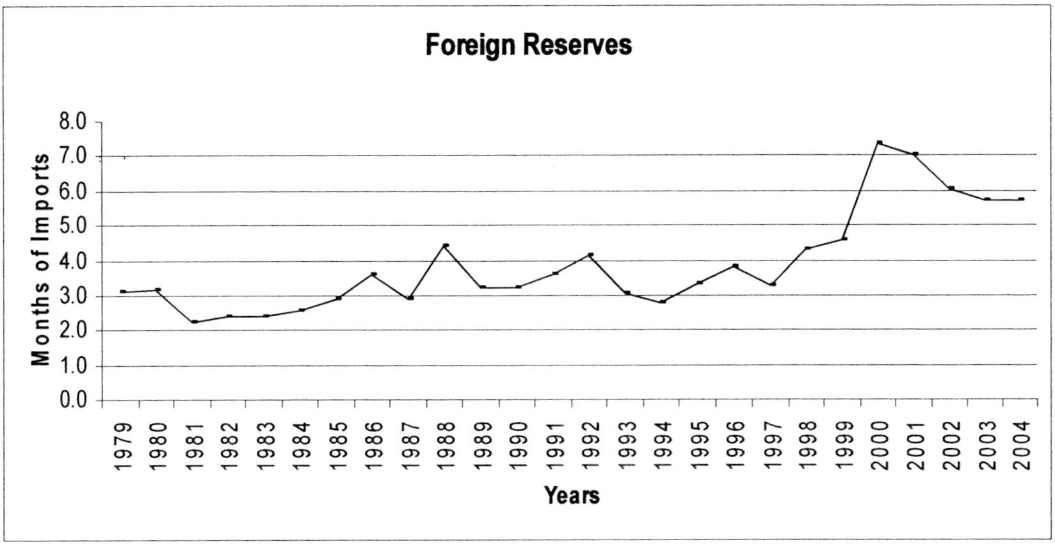

Source of data for Figure 5.2: The World Bank (2004) and Fiji Islands Bureau of Statistics (March 2006).

Figure 5.2.

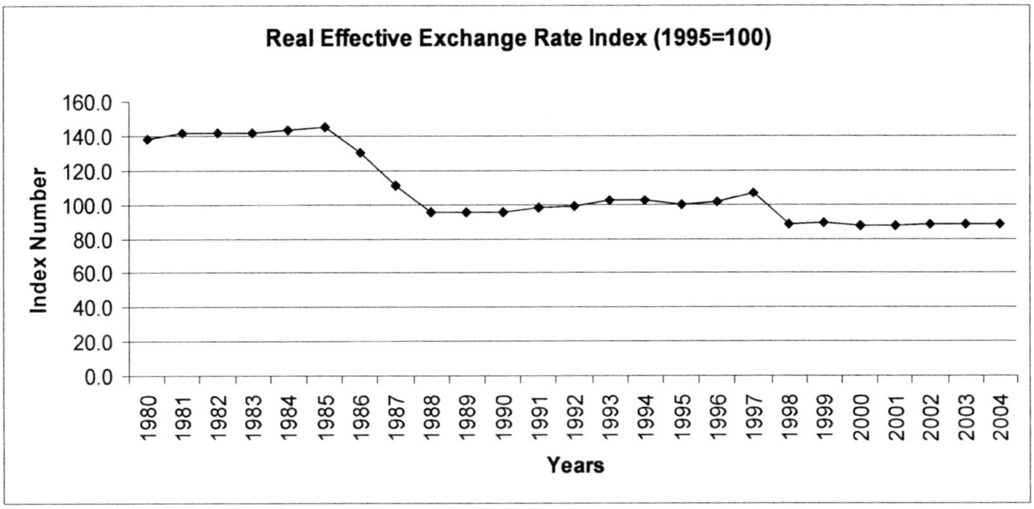

Source of data for Figure 5.3: The World Bank (2004) and Fiji Islands Bureau of Statistics (March 2006).

Figure 5.3.

The RBF has managed to maintain stability in its exchange rate. The exchange rate for the Fiji dollar is determined daily on the basis of a weighted average of currencies of Fiji's major trading partners. Given the nature of the regime in place (a trade weighted exchange rate) not much intervention in the exchange rate was required other than those led by the crises of 1987 that resulted in the devaluation of the Fiji dollar by 17.75 percent on 29 June 1987 and 15.25 percent on 7 October 1987 (Figure 5.3). A further devaluation of 20 percent was instituted on 20 January 1998 in light of deteriorating domestic economic conditions where Fiji was losing its export competitiveness (Reserve Bank of Fiji, 2004). Fiji's devaluation during these times did facilitate the adjustment in the trade balance as it enhanced Fiji's export competitiveness while making imports, in domestic terms, more expensive. Supported by the favourable investment climate (tax free zones), the share of manufacturing value added in national output expanded that aided in greater foreign exchange earnings.

5.6. Money Supply Growth and Interest Rates

Money is the set of assets in the economy that people regularly use to buy goods and services from other people. It is a medium of exchange, a unit of account, and a store of value. The medium of exchange includes the paper bills and coins in the hands of the public (currency issued by the Reserve Bank) plus demand deposits (balances in bank account that depositors can get on demand). Demand deposits make the greatest portion of the money supply. Generally there are two definitions of nominal money supply: M1 (currency and demand deposits) and M3, the broad money supply (everything in M1, savings and small time deposits and all the other financial institution deposits). Figure 5.4 depicts the growth rate of Fiji's M3.

Prior to 1989, Fiji's financial system was highly regulated where the monetary authorities directly regulated the level of credit (Jayaraman, 2003). Figure 5.4 reveals the evidence of periods of monetary policy easing (1972-73; 1979; 1985-90; 1997-99; and 2001-03) in response to domestic economies poor performance. The easing of monetary policy led to sharp increases in money supply growth. Episodes of monetary policy tightening are also evident (1974-76; 1978-81; 1983-85; 1991-96; 1999-00 and 2004) where the growth of money supply fell.

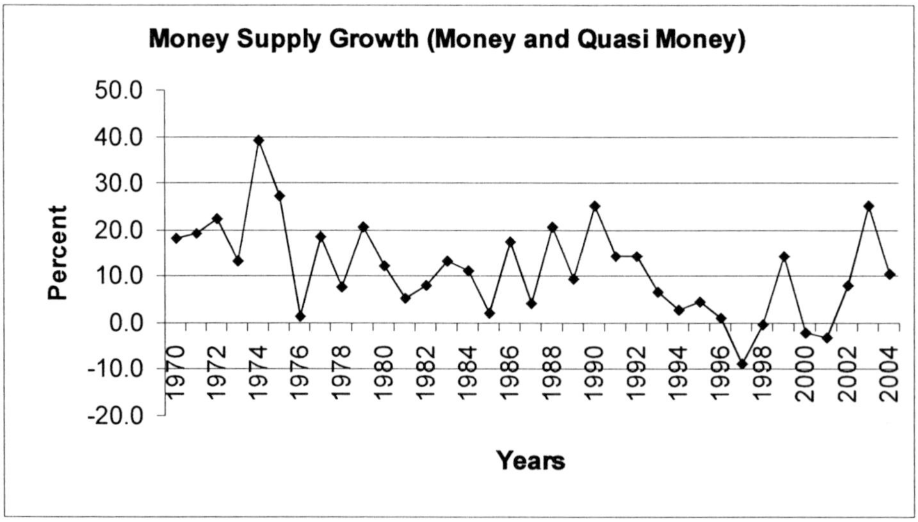

Source of data for Figure 5.4: The World Bank (2004) and Fiji Islands Bureau of Statistics (March 2006).

Figure 5.4.

In late 1980s, rising prices (see Figure 5.1) translated into falling real interest rates (see Figure 5.5 and 5.6) with increased government borrowing (Chapter 4) leading to an explosion in money supply growth (Figure 5.4). From its peak in 1990, money growth slowed as investment levels continued to decline. While inflation continued to decline, nominal interest rate did not keep pace with inflation. It is worth noting that Fiji's interest rate structure has been deliberately maintained at levels that have not followed the workings of a competitive market. Domestic investment in Fiji has been falling in the post-1987 period (Duncan, 2004). Although Fiji's falling investment is attributable to other factors, higher lending interest rates affect domestic investment. However, the Fiji case is quite overt. Despite excess liquidity in the financial system, interest rates on borrowing have remained high while investment has remained low. It seems that Fiji's high lending rates have been deliberately maintained at higher levels with the RBF failing to correct this inefficiency in the financial market. While low levels of investment are directly attributable to Fiji's unresolved political and constitutional issues, lending interest rates are equally important. Had the interest rates being more competitive, this would have certainly beefed up Fiji's gross investment that so far has been heading towards a direction that is uncalled for.

The theoretical argument from a neoclassical perspective is that high interest rates (lending) increase the user cost of capital and so reduces investment. However, in contradiction, the McKinnon-Shaw hypothesis establishes a positive relationship between interest rate and investment (see McKinnon, 1973 and Mishkin, 1995). The interest rate in question is the deposit interest rate. Higher interest rates on deposits will attract more real balances, which allow them to finance more investment. However, low or negative real interest rates discourage savings, which reduce the amount of funds available for investment.

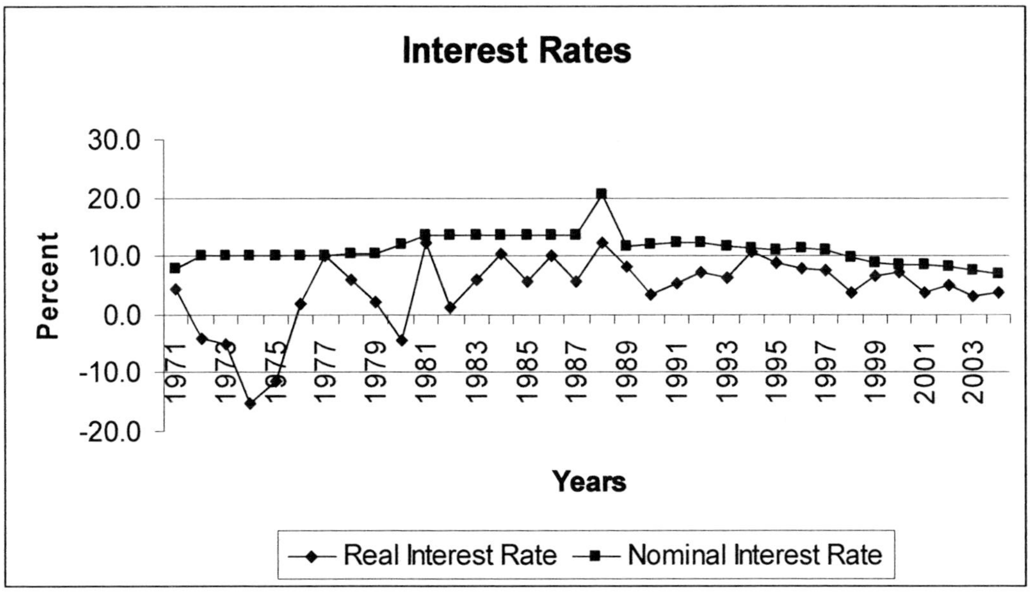

Source of data for Figure 5.5: The World Bank (2004).

Figure 5.5.

A close examination of the data on rates of return in Fiji and its closer trading partner countries reveals wide gaps. At the simplest level of investment in the financial market, the basic indicator: deposit interest rate, is put in perspective for Fiji, Australia and New Zealand (Figure 5.6). The pattern revealed in Figure 5.6 shows that the real deposit interest rates of Australia and New Zealand eventually move together through time. The Fiji interest rate does not share the same pattern as the trading partner countries as revealed by the gap between the two sets. It is obvious that in Fiji, the rates of return are lower than the returns offered in the trading partner countries. Given such low domestic rates of returns compared with those in trading partners, potential investors have been reluctant to invest in Fiji as a result of low returns.

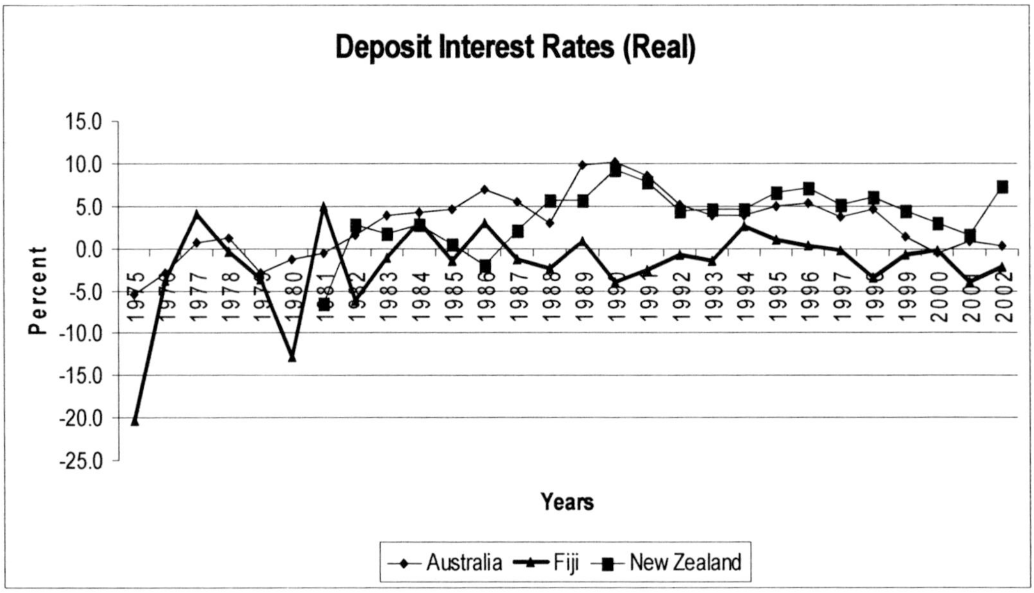

Source of data for Figure 5.6: The World Bank (2004).

Figure 5.6.

In fact, lending interest rates in Fiji are higher than many of its trading partner countries. For example, between 1991-99, lending interest rates in Fiji averaged 11.1% compared to 10.2% in Fiji's largest trading partner, Australia (Gani, 2005). The continuous decline in investment levels in years following the 1987 crises (Chapter 2) has reflected reluctance on part of potential investors to invest in the domestic economy and higher lending interest rates is one factor, although continued political instability has been the prime factor for low domestic investor confidence (Duncan, 2004).

Following the political crises of 1987, monetary reforms were instituted that changed Fiji's framework of monetary policy, that is, a move from regulatory controls towards market based approach (Gani, 1999 and Jayaraman and Ward, 2000). The outcome of this is evident in Figure 5.4 that shows a fall in nominal money supply growth since 1990 to 1997. There was a rebound in 1998 and 1999 so as to accommodate the demand by the private sector for money balances following restored investor confidence in the Fiji's political system after the adoption of the revised constitution acceptable by Fiji's multicultural population. The crisis of

2000 again affected investor confidence that led to a decline in money supply growth while post 2000 saw growth in money supply as a result of gradual normalising political and economic environment. Inflation continued to decline so as the nominal interest rate.

5.7. Liquidity

Available data indicates that there has been excess liquidity in Fiji's banking system.

Excess liquidity in the banking system is measured by the gap between broad money as a percentage of GDP (measures the amount of liquidity available) and the ratio of domestic credit to GDP (which measures the number of bankable projects in the economy). Figure 5.7 depicts evidence of excess liquidity in Fiji's banking system.

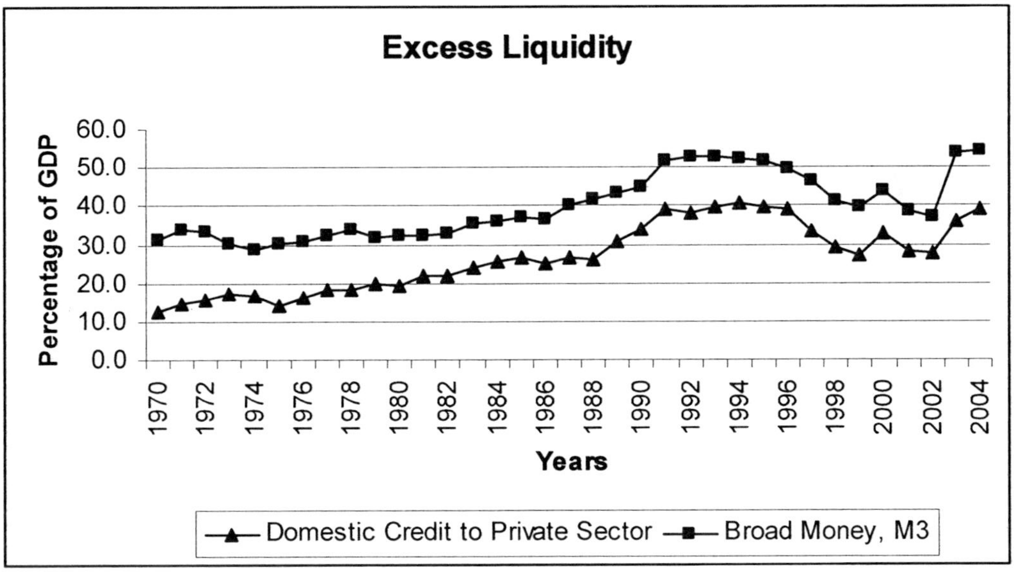

Source of data for Figure 5.7: The World Bank (2004) and Fiji Islands Bureau of Statistics (March 2006).

Figure 5.7.

Several factors are thought to be contributing to the excess liquidity situation in the banking system. These include high lending interest rates, narrow foreign portfolio outlet for Fiji National Provident Fund (FNPF) funds; non-renewal of native land leases and weak legal system in the banking sector (see for example, Asian Development Bank, 2004).

Lending rates are considered to be high and act as a deterrent to potential borrowers. Other than the high lending interest rates, RBFs action to preserve foreign exchange reserves has hindered FNPF from seeking foreign markets for diversification of its portfolio. While domestic investment market is weak, almost of 80 percent of FNPF funds are invested in government instruments with low returns (discussed further in Chapter 6). This provides a deceptive picture of the banking system as it can contribute towards instability because of huge uncertainties about inward and outward movements of large deposits will be put into the banking system. Fiji's land tenure system has compounded this problem of excess liquidity where expiring and non-renewal of land leases have made it difficult for banks to lend using land or leases as collateral. Further, the lack of bankable projects at a reasonable risk, high default (Asian Development Bank, 2004) rate and the difficulty in using the legal system for the collecting of non-performing loans have further added to the high level of liquidity in the banking system.

5.8. CONCLUSION

Fiji's monetary policy conduct has been managed by its Reserve Bank that regulates the commercial banks while ensuring a sound banking system and controlling the quantity of the money that is made available in the economy. The monetary policy framework has largely been determined by Fiji's economic capacity, the development and operational environment of its financial sector and its trade weighted exchange rate system. RBFs main objective has been to maintain price stability by favouring inflation rate of below 3 percent and ensuring foreign reserves equivalent to 3 months of its imports. The RBF abandoned its direct controls on the amount of commercial bank lending and the interest rates at which loans were provided in 1989 and triggered by the crises of 1987 led to the adoption of market based approach of conducting monetary policy, the OMO using the 91-day RBF note rate.

Given Fiji's trade weighted exchange rate, not much intervention in the exchange rate was required other than those led by the crises of 1987 that resulted in the devaluation of the Fiji dollar by 33 percent and a further 20 percent devaluation in 1998. Both these events enhanced Fiji's export competitiveness. This was also aided by the favourable investment climate; manufacturing value added in national output expanded that aided in greater foreign exchange earnings.

In late 1980s, rising prices translated into falling real interest rates with increased government borrowing leading to an explosion in money supply growth. From its peak in 1990, money growth slowed as investment levels continued to decline. It is worth noting that Fiji's interest rate structure has been deliberately maintained at levels that have not followed the workings of a competitive market. Domestic investment in Fiji has been falling in the post-1987 period. Although Fiji's falling investment is attributable to other factors, higher lending interest rates affect domestic investment. However, the Fiji case is quite overt. Despite excess liquidity in the financial system, interest rates on borrowing have remained high while investment has remained low. It seems that Fiji's high lending rates have been deliberately maintained at higher levels with the RBF failing to correct this inefficiency in the financial market. While low levels of investment are directly attributable to Fiji's unresolved political and constitutional issues, lending interest rates are equally important. Had the interest rates being more competitive, this would have certainly increased Fiji's gross investment.

It is obvious that in Fiji, the rates of return are lower than the returns offered in the trading partner countries. Given such low domestic rates of returns compared with those in trading partners, potential investors have been reluctant to invest in Fiji as a result of low returns.

Fiji's monetary policy objective achievements are gauged by its policy targets: price stability and adequate foreign reserves. While, RBF over time has managed to comfortably maintain adequate levels of foreign reserves, it has been less successful in realising its ultimate objective of price stability as maintaining inflation below the 3 percent target mark has been a rare achievement.

REFERENCES

Asian Development Bank. (2004). *Fiji Private Sector Assessment*, Manila. (Available on line at http://www.adb.org/document/reports/psa/fij/fijiislands.pdf). Date of extraction: 10 September 2005.

Ali, F. A. and Jayaraman, T.K. (2001). Monetary and fiscal policy co-ordination in Fiji, Working Paper Number EDWP 2000-01, Reserve Bank of Fiji, Suva.

Duncan, R.C. (2004). The Fiji economy: needing a better investment environment, Paper presented to the 17th Australia Fiji Business Forum, "Fiji and Australia New Partners", held by Australia Fiji Business Council at the Gold Coast, Australia, 17-19 October, 2004.

Fiji Islands Bureau of Statistics. (March 2006). *Key Statistics*. Government Printer: Suva.

Gani, A. (2005). Fiji's emigrant transfers and potential macroeconomic effects, *Pacific Economic Bulletin*, Vol. 20, No. 2, pp. 117-128.

Gani, A. (1999). Drought, the Asian crisis and Fiji's monetary policy response, *Pacific Economic Bulletin*, Vol.14, No.2, pp. 110-122.

Grynberg, R., Munro, D., and White, M., (2002). *Crisis: The Collapse of the National Bank of Fiji*, Crawford House, Adelaide.

Jayaraman, T.K. (2003). *Issues in Monetary Economics of the South Pacific Island Countries*, The University of the South Pacific, Suva.

Jayaraman, T.K. and Ward, B. (2000). Demand for money in Fiji: an econometric analysis, *Pacific Economic Bulletin*, Vol.15, No.1, pp. 81-93.

McKinnon, R.I. (1973). *Money and Capital in Economic Development*. Brookings Institute: Washington.

Mishkin, F. S. (1995). Symposium on the monetary transmission mechanism, *Journal of Economic Perspectives*, Vol. 9, No. 4, pp. 3-10.

Reserve Bank of Fiji. (2004). *Monetary Policy in Fiji*. Suva.

Reserve Bank of Fiji. (1987). *Reserve Bank of Fiji Booklet*. Suva.

Chapter 6

THE FINANCIAL ENVIRONMENT

6.1. INTRODUCTION

The financial sector is an instrumental part of any market economy. It is the hub of the payments systems that facilitates the transactions in an economy. Fiji's financial sector has been largely dominated by the commercial banks, their presence dates back to more than one hundred years. Several non-bank financial institutions got established and these are recent additions to Fiji's financial sector. Fiji has the most developed financial sector among the Pacific Island countries. The government has also played an influential role in terms of regulation and supervision of the financial institutions. Fiji's financial sector has been the major source of facilitating monetary transactions to local and foreign businesses. This chapter provides an overview of Fiji's financial sector. It describes the financial institutions that exist and their strengths in terms of assets and profits. The extent of the diffusion of the financial sectors in the economy is also analysed. The chapter also describes financiers other than commercial banks and non-bank financial institutions.

6.2. FINANCIAL INSTITUTIONS, THEIR ASSETS AND PROFITS

Fiji's financial institutions comprise of an established central monetary institution, the RBF; the commercial banks and non-banks. There are five commercial banks all of which are foreign owned. The non-banks include a superannuation fund, a development bank, a merchant bank, a credit corporation, two housing finance companies, thirty nine credit unions, fourteen insurance companies; one investment corporation and a unit trust (see Reserve Bank of Fiji, 2005).

Commercial banking in Fiji has a historical link with banks from Australia Westpac Banking Corporation (WBC) and Australia and New Zealand Banking Group (ANZ) formerly the Bank of New Zealand, now merged with ANZ Bank. These two banks have been the pioneer's in Fiji's banking industry. Commercial banking in Fiji started in 1880 with Union Bank (merged with Bank of New Zealand in 1955) followed by the Bank of New South Wales (now WBC) in 1901 (see Reserve Bank of Fiji, 1987). Other foreign banks that began operations in Fiji include the Bank of Baroda in 1961 and the Habib Bank in 1991 (Reserve Bank of Fiji, 1987). While these foreign banks had their presence for a long time,

Fiji started with its home grown bank, Savings Bank of Fiji (changed to National Bank of Fiji and now the Colonial National Bank (CNB)) in 1974 (Reserve Bank of Fiji, 1987). In 1995, the National Bank of Fiji became insolvent and its governmental share was bought by CNB in 1998 (see Grynberg, Munro and White, 2002). In 2006, the Commonwealth Bank of Australia bought the remaining governmental share in CNB making Fiji's commercial banking sector fully foreign owned.

Non-bank financial institutions also established their presence in Fiji's financial sector with the FNPF starting its operations in 1966 (see Fiji National Provident Fund, 2005) followed by the Fiji Development Bank (FDB) in 1967. The Housing Authority and Unit Trust of Fiji also joined in and the insurance ACT of 1998 saw ten insurance companies being licensed while the Credit Unions came into the financial market under the Credit Union Act of 1999 (see Asian Development Bank, 2001).

The FNPF is the dominant non-bank financial institution. It is a social security savings scheme jointly supported by the employees, employers and the government. Employers are required to pay an amount equal to 16 percent of their employees' salaries to FNPF, 8 percent of which are deducted from employee salaries (see Fiji National Provident Fund, 2005). All contributions are added to members', that is, employees' balances. As of 2005, FNPF had 306,133 members; 5,620 employers; and a total member's fund of F$2.998 billion (Fiji National Provident Fund, 2005). In 2005, it received approximately F$20 million per month in contributions. Members can withdraw money for education and medical expenses as well as equity for starting a small business. On reaching retirement age (55), the members can take a lump sum, a pension or a combination of both. The entire balance is also payable on the death of the member; when the member is declared medically unfit to work or if a member permanently migrates.

FNPF is allowed to make investments in Commercial Banks, Government Securities, Semi Government Securities and listed securities with a minimum capitalization of F$2 million (Fiji National Provident Fund, 2005). It also invests approximately 10 percent of its portfolio off shore including Australia, Canada, Japan, New Zealand, and United Kingdom. FNPF's investment in the domestic securities is limited at present to 15 percent of its total portfolio. In late 1998, FNPF bought 51 percent of Amalgamated Telecom Holdings Limited from the government (Reserve Bank of Fiji, December 1998). Much of FNPF's portfolio is liquid instruments with over 80 percent of funds in government securities (discussed further in section 6.3). It has substantial property investments in Suva city.

In terms of financial institutions strength, the FNPF is the strongest and the largest asset holder of the financial system followed the commercial banks and then the RBF. The combined assets of non-bank financial institutions (FNPF and FDB) in 2004 was just over F$3,000 million with FNPF's assets alone worth F$1,895.6 million (Figure 6.1). Amongst the commercial banks, ANZ Bank was the largest asset holder in 2004 (F$951 million) followed by WBC (F$758 million) and the CNB (F$361.8 million) respectively (Figure 6.2).

The banks as well as non-banks are largely concentrated in Fiji's main urban centres with a considerable decline in the number of branch and agencies between early 1990s and late 1990s as banks economized on their operations in presence of a booming economy, hence maximizing their returns. This strategy adopted by the banks has led to negative socio-economic outcomes (Sharma and Reddy, 2003). In recent times, at least one commercial bank (ANZ Bank) has taken steps to provide more rural and remote banking services. While commercial banks reduced their number of branches and agencies in remote centres and towns, their financial position has in fact strengthened in the last ten years. For example, commercial banks assets were F$1,668.1 million in 1994 and it rose to F$2,577.2 million in 2004 (Reserve Bank of Fiji, December 2005), a 55 percent increase. The business environment for commercial banks has been generally good with few competitors and so banking operations have been generally profitable.

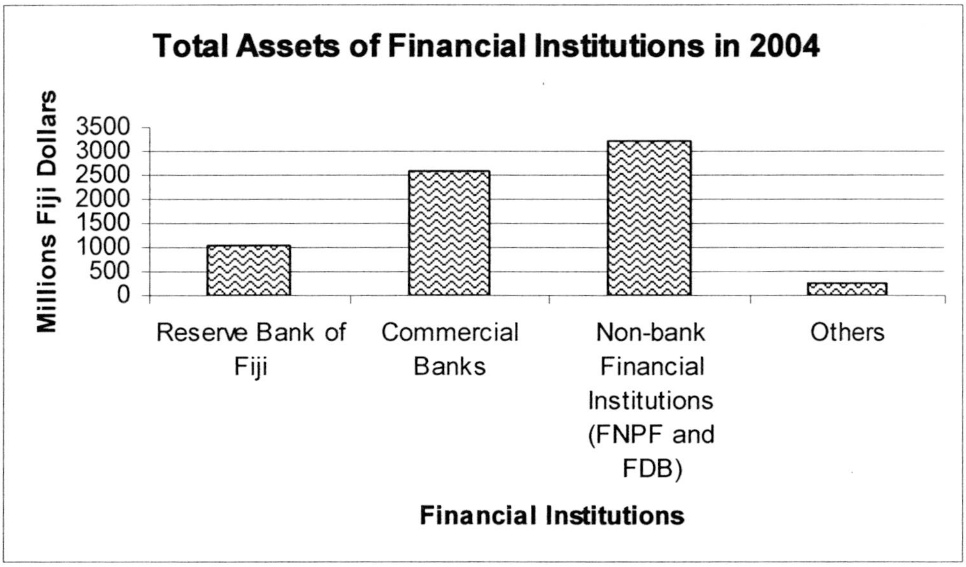

Source of data for Figure 6.1: Reserve Bank of Fiji (December 2005).

Figure 6.1.

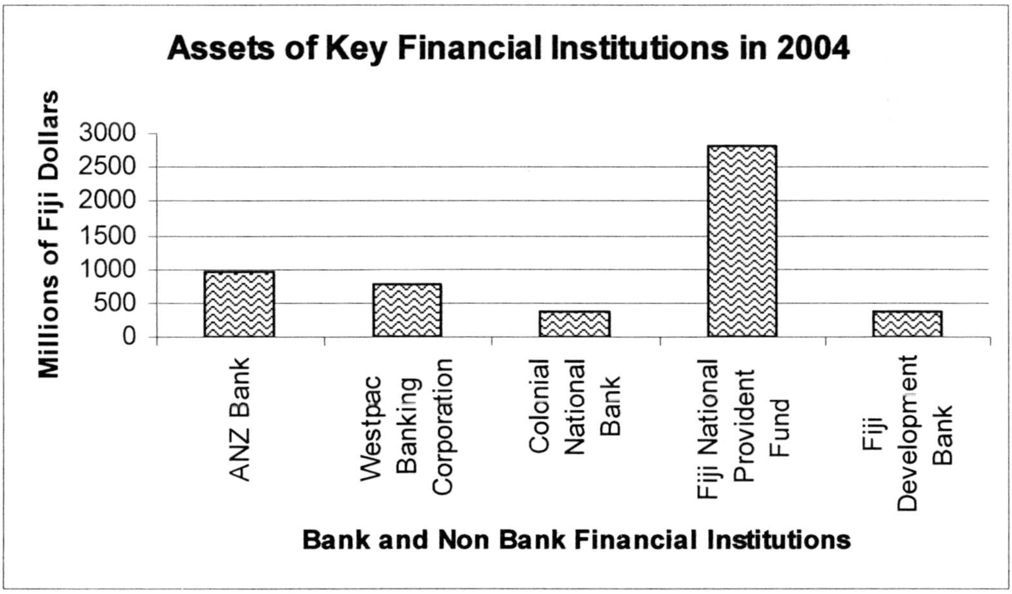

Source of data for Figure 6.2: Reserve Bank of Fiji (December, 2005).

Figure 6.2.

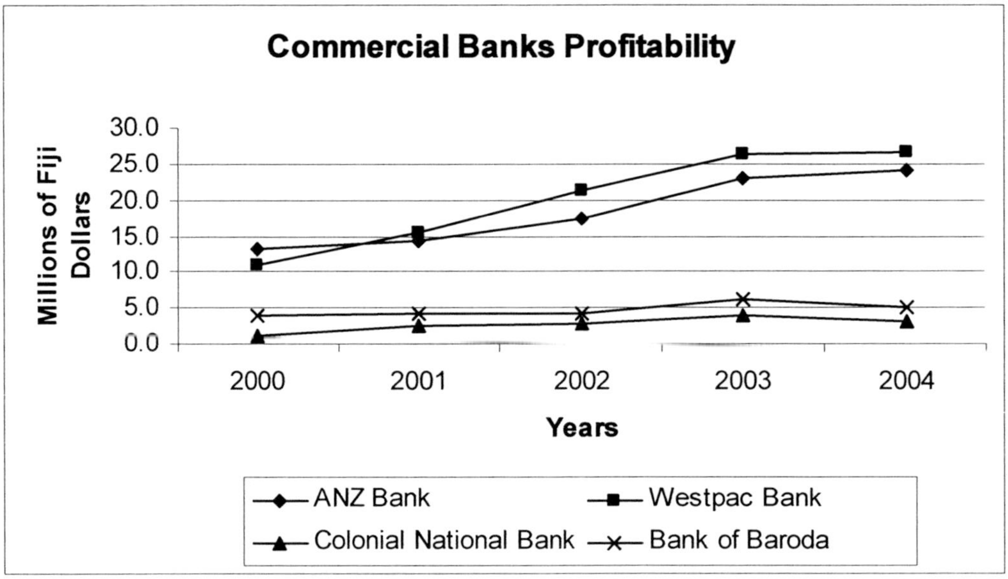

Source of data for Figure 6.3: Reserve Bank of Fiji (December, 2005).

Figure 6.3.

Figure 6.3 depicts the profitability of commercial banks with WBC and ANZ bank's taking the lead roles. While business environment has been good for banks, the credit institutions have equally benefited from the favorable business environment. Their net profit after tax and extra-ordinary items have been positive and on the rise (Figure 6.4). Merchant Finance Limited ranks the top in terms of largest profits amongst the credit institutions followed by Housing Finance Limited and Credit Corporation Limited (Figure 6.4).

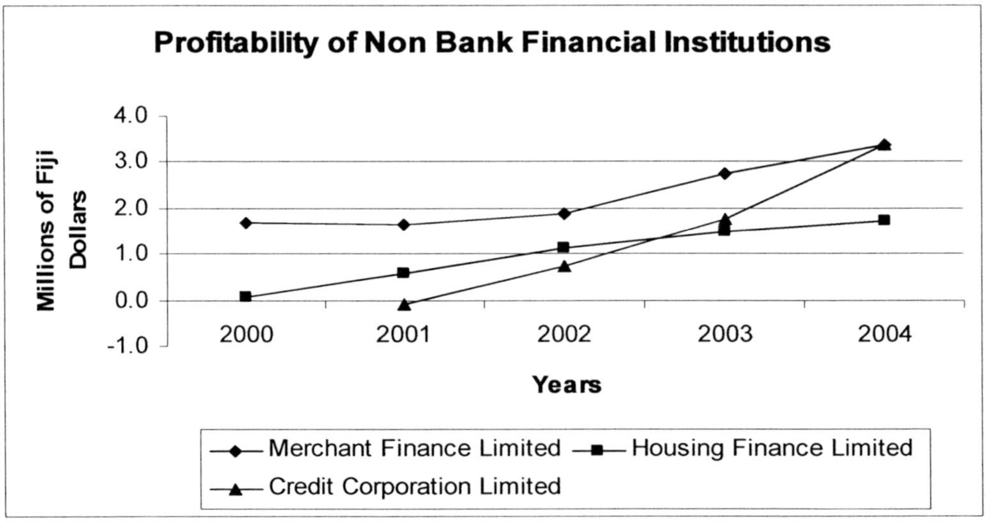

Source of data for Figure 6.4: Reserve Bank of Fiji (December, 2005).

Figure 6.4.

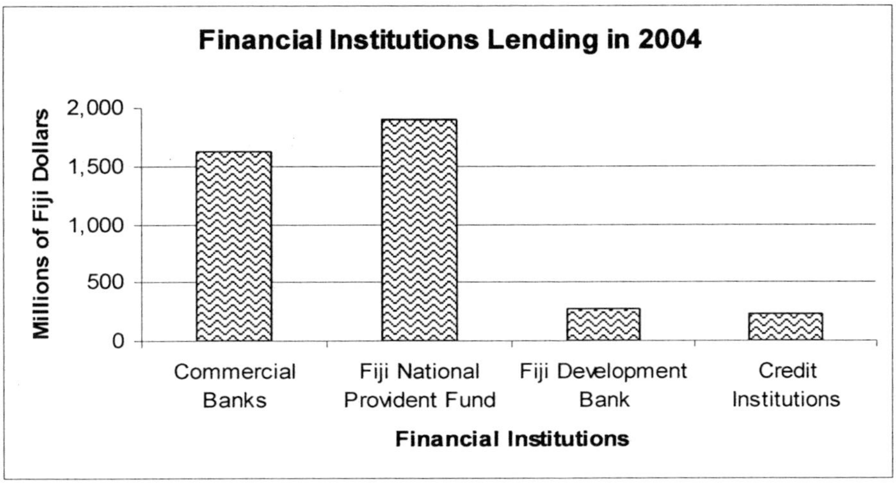

Source of data for Figure 6.5: Reserve Bank of Fiji (December, 2005).

Figure 6.5.

Financial institutions, commercial banks; non-banks; and credit institutions have played a special role in Fiji's economy. They have been the forefront of the domestic and international payments system and facilitated financial transactions in the economy. Their lending has been the major source of financing for local as well as foreign owned businesses. Both banks and non-banks have shown their strong presence in the economy as evidenced by the magnitude of their lending's. Figure 6.5 depicts the extent of the involvement of Fiji's financial institutions in the economy in terms of their total amount of lending. The FNPF, whose funds are treated as investments, is in fact, the prime lender to the government and is regarded as the lender of the last resort for the government. The commercial banks had a continual lending of over F$1,500 million in 2004 followed by FDB and credit institutions.

6.3. Financial Institutions and Economic Diffusion

Financial institutions economic diffusion is analysed in terms of their sectoral lending. In 2004, FNPF has been the largest financier lending close to F$1.9 billion followed by the commercial banks lending that was just over F$1.6 billion (see Figure 6.5 and the Reserve Bank of Fiji, December 2005). A much clearer picture of the economic diffusion of Fiji's financial institutions is seen through their lending's to various production sectors of Fiji's economy. Agriculture, mining, manufacturing, services, government and private individuals have been the key financial recipients and important players in Fiji's economic development. While financial institutions lending has diffused in various production sectors of the economy, the magnitudes of diffusion varies from one sector to another.

Figure 6.6 depicts lending by commercial banks for the period 1994-04 in six key areas. Lending to private individuals has dominated commercial bank lending, rising gradually since 1994 and averaging just over 30 percent of all commercial bank lending (Figure 6.6). Lending to private individuals has been largely for housing and vehicles and for other personal reasons (Reserve Bank of Fiji, December 2005).

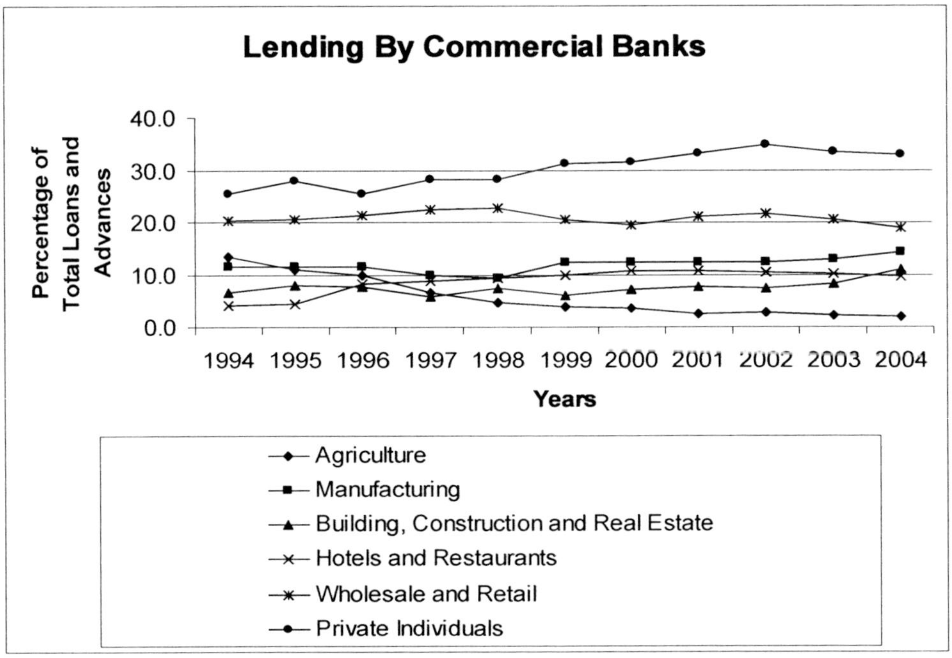

Source of data for Figure 6.6: Reserve Bank of Fiji (December, 2005).

Figure 6.6.

The second largest area of commercial bank lending has been in wholesale and retail that has averaged 20 percent of all commercial lending in the last decade (Figure 6.6). Lending to the manufacturing sector has been in the third place with majority of lending to food, beverage and tobacco industries (Reserve Bank of Fiji, December 2005). While lending to building, construction and real estate development averaged just over 7 percent of all commercial bank lending, it has been on an upward trend in the last three years (Figure 6.6). This is largely a result of the boom in the construction of new houses, commercial premises and real estate development.

A unique feature of commercial bank lending is the downward trend in lending to agriculture, falling from 13 percent of all lending in 1994 to 1.8 percent in 2004 (Figure 6.6). The main contributing factor to this has been the unresolved land lease issue and in particular the non-renewal of leases for agricultural land (see for example, Prasad and Tisdell, 1996). As a result of this, large numbers of sugar cane farmers have been displaced with farm lands out of production (Prasad, 2003). Banks therefore have been reluctant to lend as a result of high levels of risk associated with the ongoing insecurity over land leases to farmers (see Asian Development Bank, 2001).

The non-bank financial institution, FDB, has also played a major role as a provider of finance in Fiji's production sectors. Figure 6.7 depicts lending by FDB with its largest share of lending extended to real estate. While agricultural lending topped in early 90s, lending in this area has declined with lending to wholesale, retail, hotels and restaurants ranked at second place in 2004 (Figure 6.7). Lending to private individuals has also followed a continuous downward trend over the last ten years. However, lending to manufacturing has been on the rise since 2001 and now at levels that were reached in early 1990s (Figure 6.7).

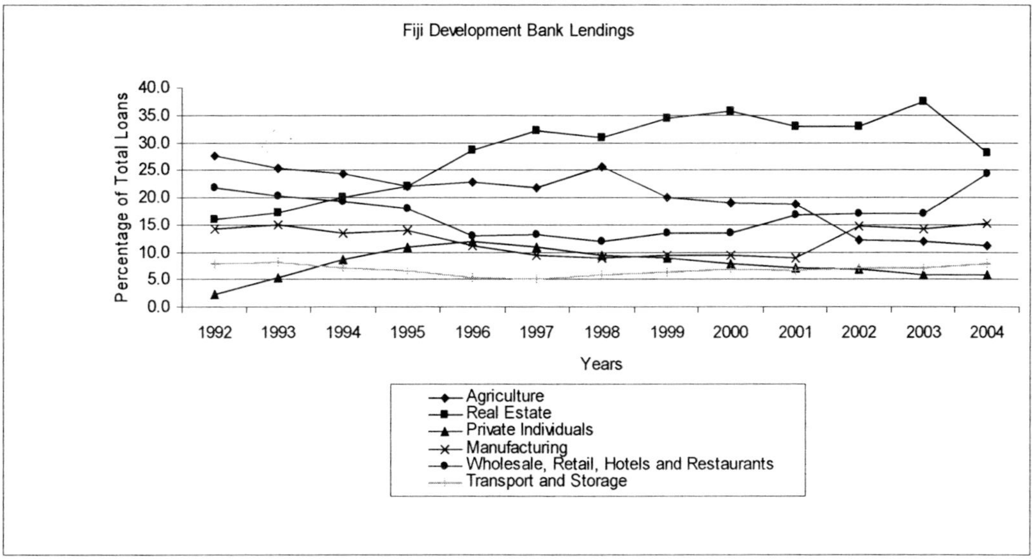

Source of data for Figure 6.7: Reserve Bank of Fiji (December, 2005).

Figure 6.7.

The FNPF's funds have been largely lent to the government. Since 2002, lending to the government increased significantly (Figure 6.8). In 2004, some 80 percent of FNPF funds were lent to the government (see Reserve Bank of Fiji, December 2005). Now the FNPF is the largest buyer and holder of Government securities and acts in effect as a lender of last resort to the government.

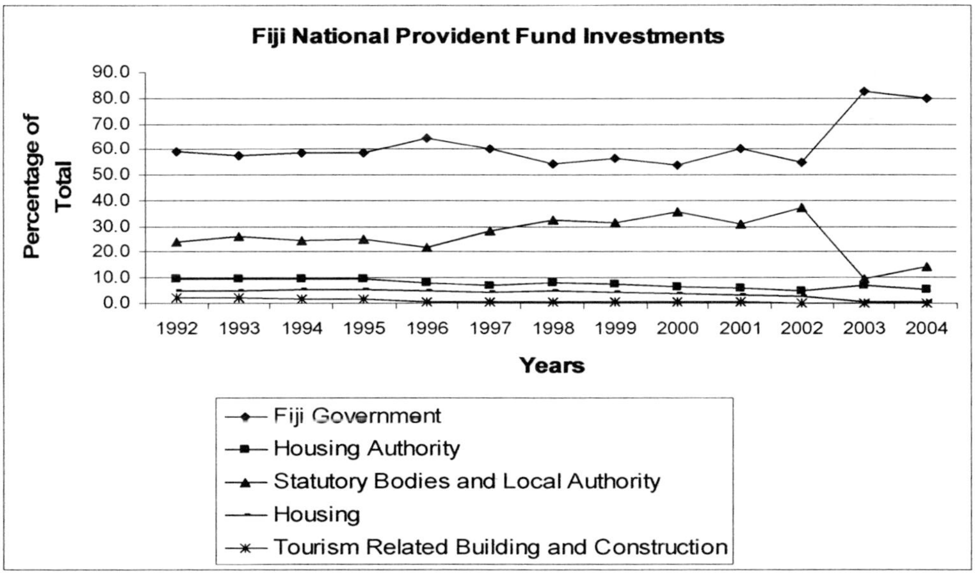

Source of data for Figure 6.8: Reserve Bank of Fiji (December, 2005).

Figure 6.8.

6.4. Commercial Bank Lending and Value Added

Sectoral production data in terms of value added indicate that Fiji has gone through a phase of structural transformation with expansion in manufacturing and services sector value added accompanied by a decline in agricultural value added (see Chapter 8). While Fiji has gone through the dynamic process of changing comparative advantage, financial support to various production sectors as discussed in the previous section has been influential in terms of value added. While the financial sector has also been linked to Fiji's economic growth (see for example, Chand, 2002), it also had some socio-economic effects (Sharma and Reddy, 2003). The relationship between financial support and sectoral value added can be seen through a scatter plot.

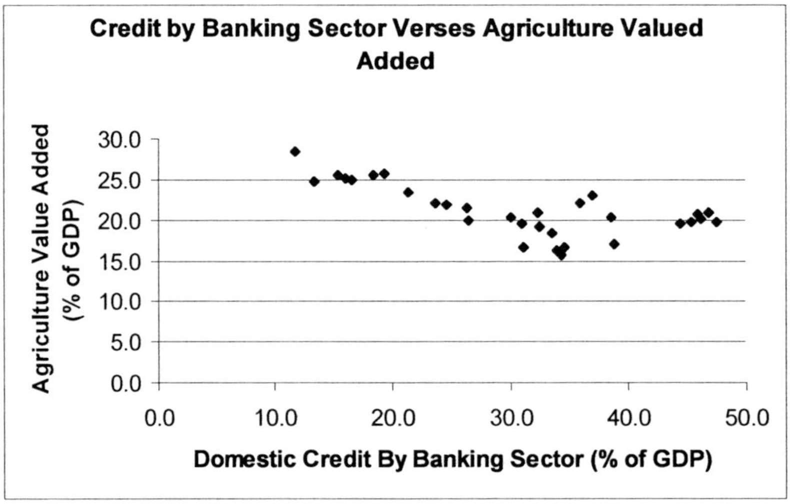

Source of data for Figure 6.9: The World Bank (2004)

Figure 6.9.

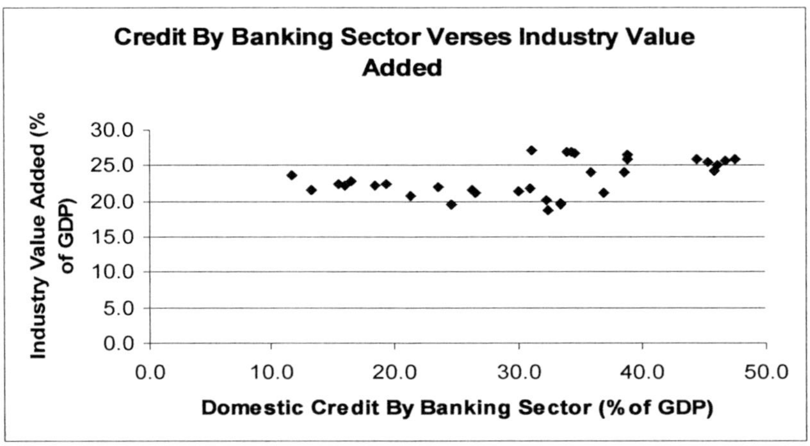

Source of data for Figure 6.10: The World Bank (2004).

Figure 6.10.

Figures 6.9-6.12 present scatter plots that depict the relationship between credit by the banking sector and value added in agriculture, industry, manufacturing and services sectors for the period 1970-02. Figure 6.9 depicts a clear inverse relationship between credit by the banking sector and agricultural value added. As credit by banking sector increased, agricultural value added decreased. The decline in lending to agricultural sector in recent times is therefore not surprising given the falling value added from this sector. Figures 6.10 - 6.12 depict almost a positive relationship between credit by the banking sector and value added in industry, manufacturing and services sectors respectively.

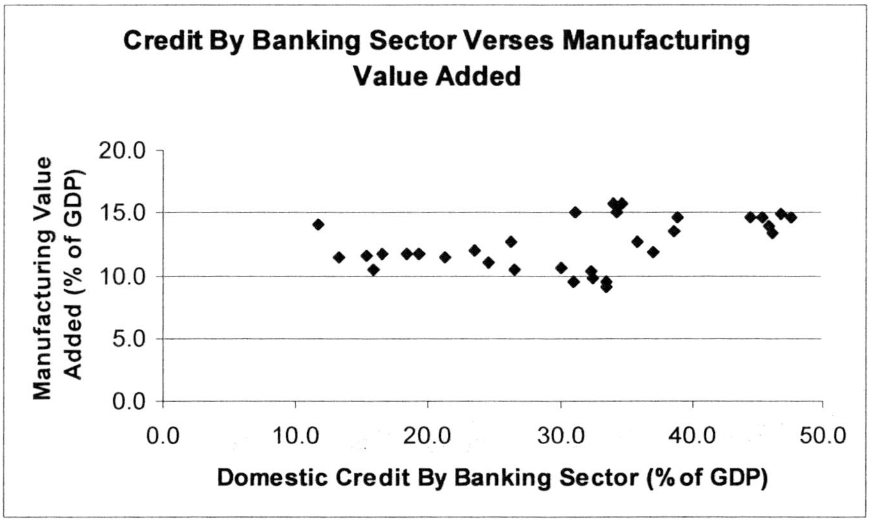

Source of data for Figure 6.11: The World Bank (2004).

Figure 6.11.

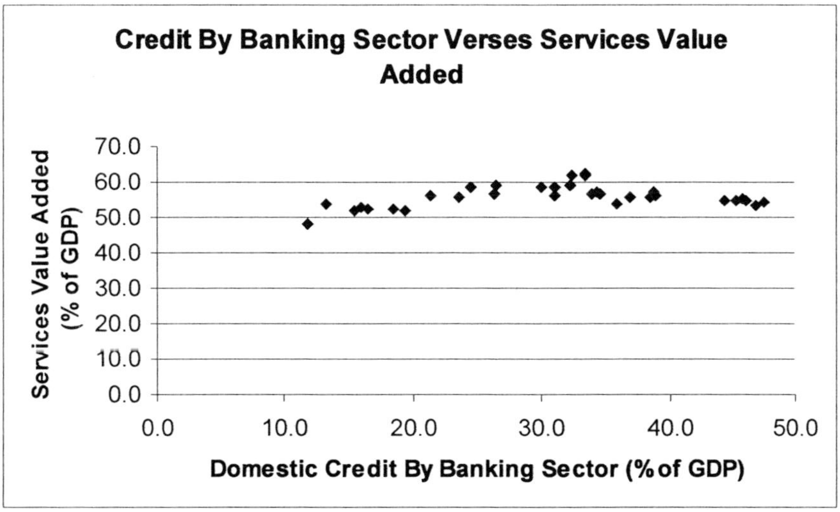

Source of data for Figure 6.12: The World Bank (2004).

Figure 6.12.

6.5. Other Financial Markets

Other than the banks and non-bank financial institutions and credit institutions, Fiji also has an established capital market. The two major players in the capital markets are the Capital Market Development Authority (CMDA) and the South Pacific Stock Exchange (SPSE), formerly the Suva Stock Exchange (SSE). The CMDA was established under the Capital Markets Development Authority Act of 1996 and became fully operational in January 1998 (see CMDA, 2005). The broad purpose of CMDA is to develop efficient and thriving capital market and regulate the activities of various market participants (CMDA, 2005). The CMDA is financially supported by the government. It has focused on trading activities in the stock market, the bond market and the unit trusts market. Other than its involvement in trading activities, its development activity focuses on facilitating the supply of good marketable securities, broadening public participation in the capital markets, and developing the market infrastructure (CMDA, 2005).

SPSE is currently the only licensed securities exchange in Fiji (SPSE, 2005). It was established in 1979 as the Suva Stock Exchange (SSE). The SSE was restructured in late 1990s with two brokerage members: Mercury Securities (owned by FNPF) and the SSE itself. In late 1990s, the Fijian Holding Company (FHL) also formed a stock brokerage company, the FHL Securities while Kontiki Securities became the fourth brokerage company. Because of limited stock volumes, the SSE trades three times a week. At present, the settlements are by exchange of share certificates and checks at SSE premises on the due date of settlement. SSE also receives financial support from the government. SSE over time has developed a viable capital market and with more resources it will be able to list companies at a regional level.

On 30 November 2000, SSE officially changed its name to South Pacific Stock Exchange (SPSE) in line for its vision for a regional exchange (SPSE, 2005). The SPSE is owned by eight financial institutions: FDB, FNPF, Colonial Fiji Life Limited, Credit Corporation Fiji Limited, Kontiki Stockbroking Limited, National MBf Finance Company Limited, FHL Securities Limited and Fiji Stock Brokers Limited (SPSE, 2005). In 2004, it had sixteen listed companies with market capitalization of F$882 million with 881 trades carrying an average value of F$14,415 (SPSE, 2005). It has 19,957 shareholders with all listed companies producing positive total returns (SPSE, 2005).

Fiji also has a bond market but this is still at its infancy stage. Within the confinements of RBFs monetary policy conducted through OMO, the bond market becomes operational. RBF issues government treasury bonds through an auction process while government makes the final decision on the allocation. Trading in secondary market is limited and is largely infeasible as a result of incomplete market (see Asian Development Bank, 2001). This problem is further compounded by the involvement of FNPF which owns 80 percent of government bonds and bills with commercial banks having excess liquidity. Further, the CMDA tends to charge a fee when bonds are traded on the stock exchange and this has been a deterrent to the development of the bond market (Asian Development Bank, 2001).

Fiji has several other providers of capital to the private sector. According to the Asian Development Bank (2001), these include the FDB's equity investment funds; Colonial Fiji Life Limited (an insurance company); Colonial First State Investments (open ended funds with focus on blue chip investments); Fijian Holdings Limited (an investment company enhancing Fijian participation in the economy); Unit Trust of Fiji (open ended equity investment); the FNPF (investment only in blue chip companies); the Kula Fund (regional venture capital fund); and Pacific Islands Investment Facility (provides development finance).

Some micro financing is also present. Fiji's microfinance institutions can be classified as semi-formal and informal. The semi-formal sector includes some 90 registered money lenders; 52 active credit unions with a membership totaling in excess of 10,000; and several non governmental organizations (Asian Development Bank, 2001).

6.6. Conclusion

Fiji's financial sector comprises of an established central monetary institution, the RBF; the commercial banks, and non-banks. They have been at the forefront of domestic and international payments system facilitating monetary transactions to local and foreign businesses. Commercial banking in Fiji that started more than a hundred years ago with foreign banks has now five foreign owned banks. Together with domestically owned non-bank financial institutions and credit institutions, Fiji now has an established financial market with combined assets of over F$3 billion.

Amongst the commercial banks, ANZ Bank was the largest asset holder while FNPF is the dominant non-bank financial institution with assets of close to F$1.9 billion and much of its portfolio is liquid instruments with over 80 percent of funds in government securities.

In recent times, Commercial banks have maximized their returns in presence of a booming economy and few competitors accompanied by a considerable decline in the number of branch and agencies between early 1990s and late 1990s with insufficient diffusion of services to the wider population. Commercial banks have strengthened their financial position with total assets rising by more than 55 percent in the last ten years.

Lending has been the financial institutions major source of financing for local as well as foreign owned businesses while the FNPF has been the prime lender to the government and is regarded as the lender of the last resort for the government.

Financial institutions have diffused their activities widely as seen through their lending's to various production sectors of Fiji's economy with varying magnitudes. Lending to private individuals for housing, vehicles and personal effects has dominated commercial bank lending. The second largest area of commercial bank lending has been in wholesale and retail followed by manufacturing sector in the third place. While lending to building, construction and real estate development averaged just over 7 percent of all commercial bank lending, it has been on an upward trend in the last three years. This is largely a result of the boom in the construction of new houses, commercial premises and real estate development.

A unique feature of commercial bank lending is the downward trend in lending to agriculture standing at 1.8 percent of all lending in 2004 where banks have been reluctant to lend as a result of high levels of risk associated with the ongoing insecurity over land leases to farmers. Financial support has positively aided various sectors revealing positive association between credit by banking sector and value added in industry, manufacturing and services sectors respectively. Fiji has an established capital market with CMDA as major player. Fiji's bond market is still at its infancy stage and micro financing is also present.

REFERENCES

Asian Development Bank. (2001). Financial Sector Development in the Pacific Member Countries: Country Reports, Volume Two Country Report, Manila.

Chand, S. (2002). Financial sector development and economic growth in the Pacific Islands, *Pacific Economic Bulletin,* Vol. 17, No. 2, pp. 117-133.

CMDA. (2005). *CMDA 2004 Annual Report*. Suva.

Fiji National Provident Fund. (2005). *Annual Report*. Available on line at: http://www.fnpf.com.fj/page.asp?frmPageID=13. Date of extraction: 25 January 2006.

Grynberg, R., Munro, D., and White, M., (2002). *Crisis: The Collapse of the National Bank of Fiji*, Crawford House: Adelaide.

Prasad, B.C. (2003). Merging interests in Fiji: essential ingredients for better economic performance, *Pacific Economic Bulletin*, Vol. 18, No.1, pp. 121-130.

Prasad, B.C. and Tisdell, C. (1996). Institutional constraints to economic development: The case of native land rights in Fiji, *Asia Pacific Development Journal,* Vol.3, No.2, pp.49-71.

Reserve Bank of Fiji. (2005). *Annual Report*. Suva.

Reserve Bank of Fiji. (December 1998 and 2005). *Quarterly Economic Bulletin*. Suva.

Reserve Bank of Fiji. (1987). *Reserve Bank of Fiji Booklet*. Suva.

Reserve Bank of Fiji. (December 1998). *Quarterly Economic Bulletin*. Suva.

Sharma, P. and Reddy, M. (2003). Empirical modeling of bank market exclusion, *International Journal of Bank Marketing*, Vol. 21, No. 6/7, pp. 296-303.

SPSE. (2005). *SPSE Annual Report 2005*. Suva.

The World Bank. (2004). *World Development Indicators CD ROM*. Washington, D.C.

Chapter 7

THE LABOUR MARKET

7.1. INTRODUCTION

The labour market plays an important role in terms of a country's process of economic development. Earned income allows workers to maintain an adequate standard of living as well as constitutes to a sense of pride, achievement and belonging (Dalziel and Lattimore, 1996). People who are eligible to work but cannot find a job do not contribute to economy's production of goods and services. On the other hand, country's that are able to keep their workers employed tend to achieve higher levels of growth than those whose workers remain unemployed. This chapter focuses on Fiji's labour market. It begins by analysing Fiji's working age population followed by a discussion of its labour force structure. It discusses labour absorption in key sectors: agriculture, industry and services. Unemployment trends and wage levels are also analysed. It also provides an analysis of brain drain and resulting skill shortage.

7.2. FIJI'S WORKING AGE POPULATION

The working age population usually refers to residents in Fiji who are aged between 15 and 65 years. Fiji's working age population for the period 1970-02 is depicted in Figure 7.1, revealing an increase of 248,000 people over the last 32 years. The working age population grew on an average of 2.4 percent between 1971 to 1986. However, between 1987 and 2002, it grew at an annual average rate of 1.6 percent (Figure 7.1). High levels of emigration in the post-1987 have contributed to the relatively low growth in working age population (see Gani, 2000 and 2005).

Figure 7.2 depicts the labour force participation rate for the 1970-02 period. It is the percentage of population that is in the labour force. The labour force participation rate has gradually increased from 55 percent at independence to 65 percent in 2002. Figures 7.1 and 7.2 provide evidence of Fiji going through demographic changes with its increasing population resulting in increasing number of workers.

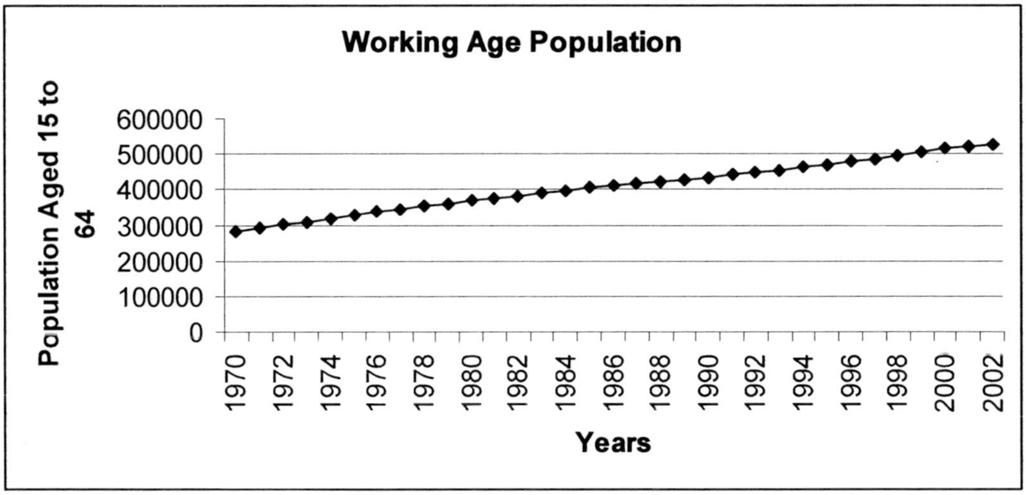

Source of data for Figure 7.1: The World Bank (2004).

Figure 7.1.

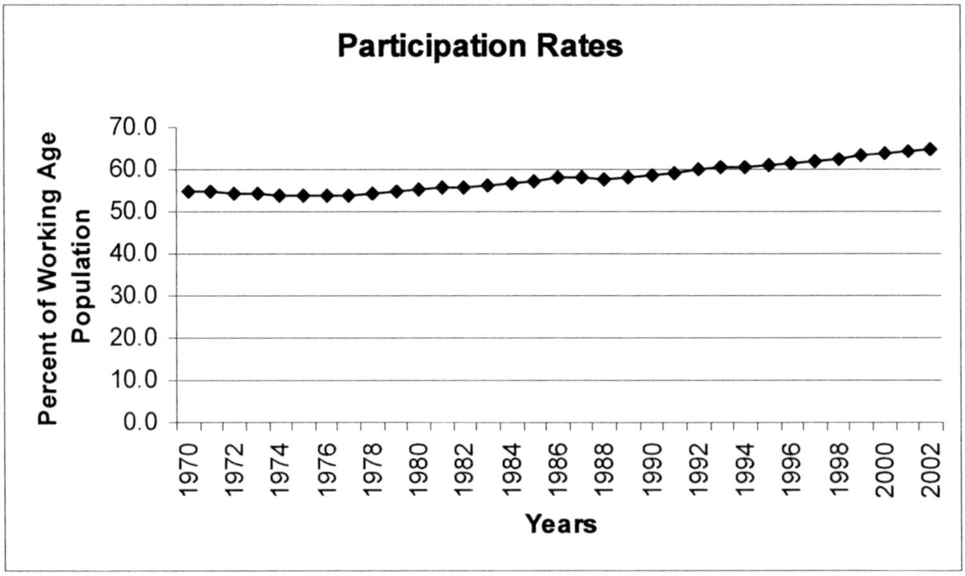

Source of data for Figure 7.2: The World Bank (2004).

Figure 7.2.

7.3. Total Labour Force

The total labour force is the total number of workers, including both employed and unemployed. Fiji's total labour force at independence was slightly over 150,000 (The World Bank, 2004). This has more than doubled in the last three decades to just over 300,000 in 2002 (The World Bank, 2004). Total labour force grew between two to three percent over the entire period (Figure 7.3). Labour force growth rate has followed the population growth rate pattern but remaining almost a percent higher than the population growth as depicted in Figure 7.3. While males dominated the labour force with 88 percent at independence and following a gradual decline to 68 percent in 2002, the female labour force has increased over the same period (Figure 7.3). According to Figure 7.3, at independence, females made up almost 12 percent of the labor force while in 2002, they contributed to just over one third of the labour force. While gradually declining during the 1970-2002 period, the growth rate of female labour force has outpaced the growth rate of male labour force during the entire period (Figure 7.3). Although Fiji is still facing gender imbalance in its labour force, female labour force is likely to continue its current trend in years to come. Fiji's labour force is largely absorbed into its production sectors. This next section discusses this aspect.

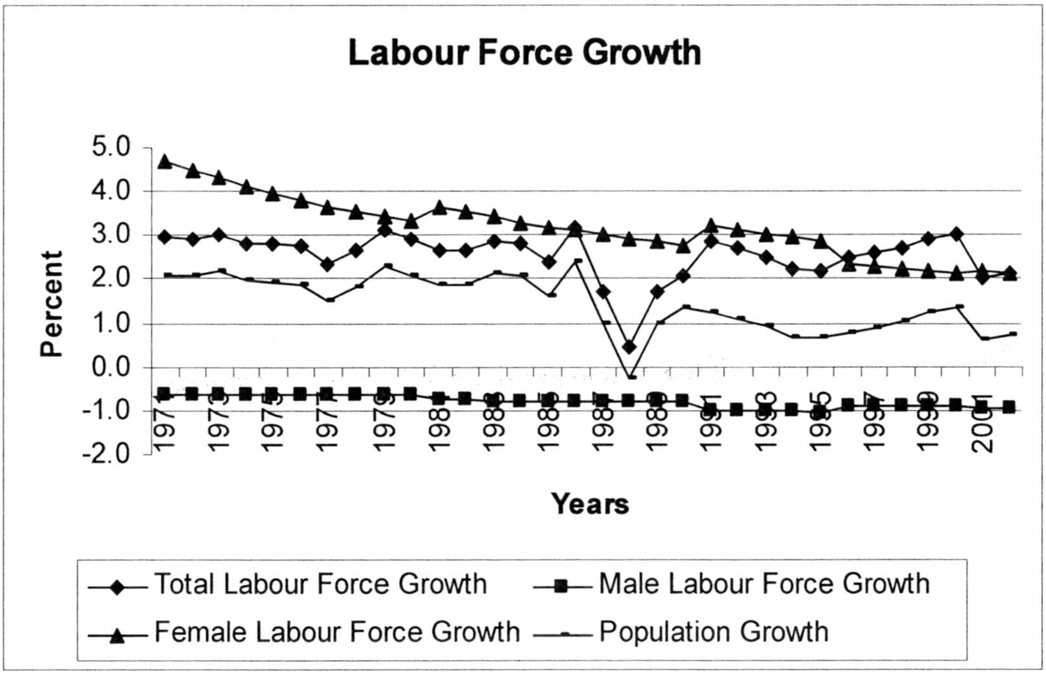

Source of data for Figure 7.3: The World Bank (2004).

Figure 7.3.

7.4. Sectoral Absorption of Labour

Fiji's labour force is absorbed in its agricultural, industrial and services sector. Services sector is the largest employer of the domestic workforce accommodating just over 60 percent of the total workforce. Industry employs almost of 35 percent of the workforce while agriculture between 1.5 to 2 percent of the workforce (Figure 7.4). An interesting observation to note is that Fiji's record of labour absorption through out the last three decades has been poor. According to Figure 7.4, labour force absorption in the agricultural sector has continued to decline from 2.8 percent in 1990 to 1.3 percent in 2003. The industrial sector does not reveal any significant growth in labour absorption other than a decline since 1995 while the services sector showed a slight increase in labour absorption since 1995 (Figure 7.4). Fiji's sluggish economic growth and more so the slow expansion of the private sector has translated into poor labour force absorption rates. Moreover the protected position of labour aristocracy in the public sector has further contributed to slow expansion in paid employment. This has in turn contributed to high levels of unemployment as discussed in the next section.

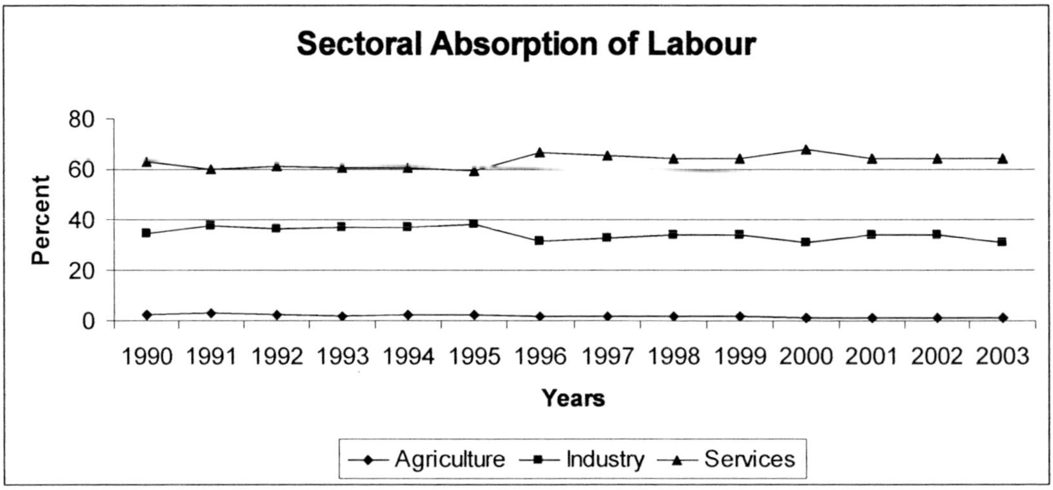

Source of data for Figure 7.4: Fiji Islands Bureau of Statistics (March 2005) and the Reserve Bank of Fiji (March 2006).

Figure 7.4.

7.5. Unemployment

The unemployment rate measures the percentage of labour force that is without paid work. Fiji's unemployment trend is depicted in Figure 7.5. Published data on unemployment rate is available from 1982 to 2000. Fiji's unemployment rate rose gradually since 1982 reaching a high of 9.8 percent in 1988 as a result of political turmoil in this year that translated into a fall in GDP growth (Figure 7.5). Fiji's political crisis of 1987 translated into massive job cuts, redundancies and private sector operating below its pre-1987 capacity. This resulted in job losses for thousands of workers largely in the manufacturing industries. Between 1989 and 1995, the unemployment rate remained below 6 percent (Figure 7.5). This low trend was achieved as a result of economic reforms instituted following the crisis of 1987 (see Prasad, 2003). Of importance has been Fiji's export promotion policies such as the tax free zones and tax free status granted to foreign investors that attracted investment (see Chapter 8), boosted private sector (manufacturing and tourism) and led to job creation (see Elek, Hill and Tabor, 1993). However, unemployment rates deteriorated in the late 1990s (Figure 7.5) largely as a result of falling private investors and rise in number of school leavers (Gani, 1999). It is worth noting that Fiji's unemployment rate is likely to be much higher than as depicted in Figure 7.5. Fiji's labour market does not take into account of all the unemployed labour force as those who live in remote and inaccessible areas are unable to formally get accounted as unemployed by the Fiji Ministry of Labour. Hence, the official published data on unemployment rate is understated and is more likely to be twice that depicted in Figure 7.5.

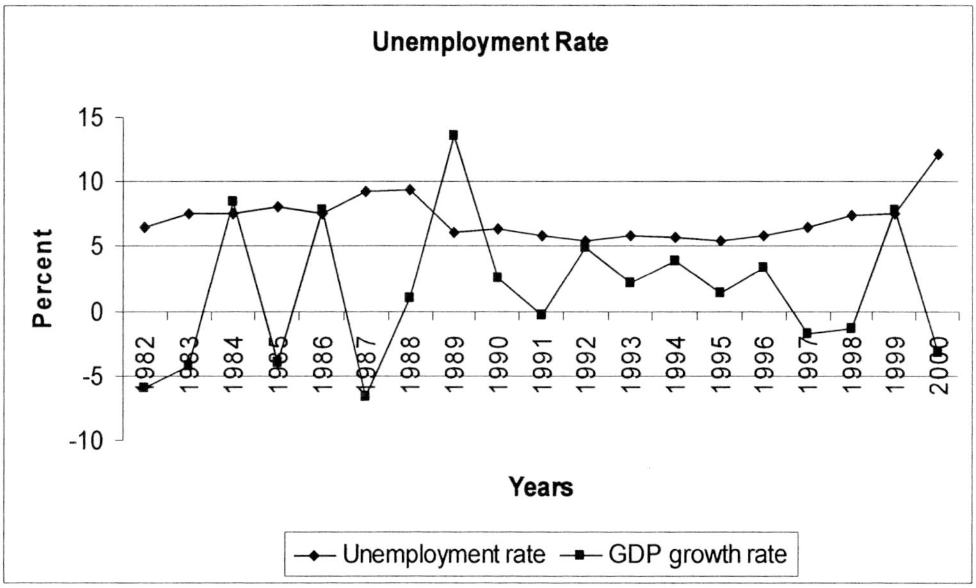

Source of data for Figure 7.5: Asian Development Bank (1990 and 2005).

Figure 7.5.

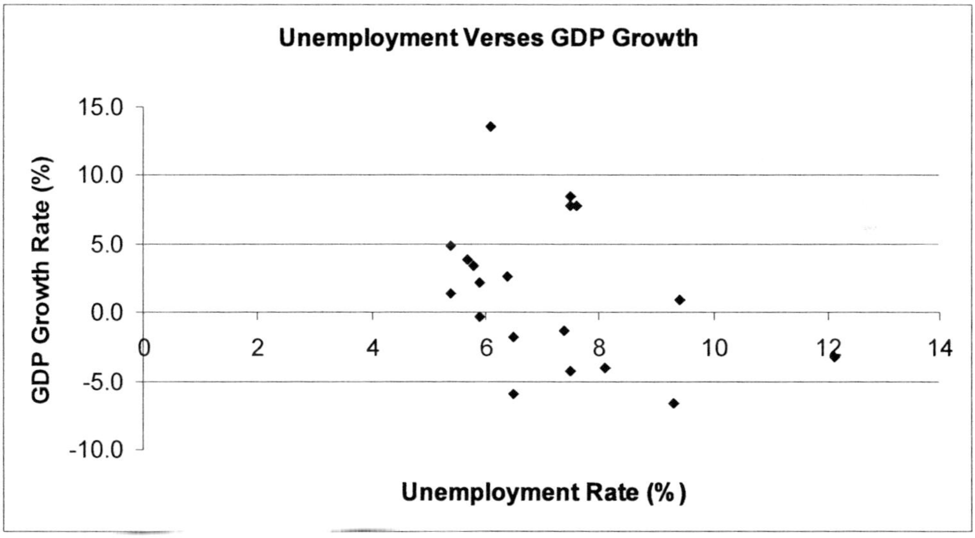

Source of data for Figure 7.6: Asian Development Bank (1990 and 2005).

Figure 7.6.

The rate of unemployment that a country experiences obviously determines its standard of living. When workers are as fully employed as possible, a country can expect high levels of GDP. However, when unemployment rate is high, workers remain idle and do not contribute to economy's production of goods and services. Hence, growth slows. Figure 7.6 shows the relationship between unemployment rate and the economic growth rate as measured by growth in gross domestic product in the form of a scatter plot. The relationship between the two variables is obvious: an inverse pattern, that is, when GDP growth was high, unemployment rate was low while when GDP growth was low, the unemployment rate has been high. The scatter plot in Figure 7.6 confirms that Fiji's sluggish economic growth had a regressive effect on its labour market.

7.6. Wages and Labour Unions

Real wages have been an important component of the Fiji labour market. It is the wage paid to workers measured in terms of real purchasing power, that is, the real wages for a given period is obtained by dividing the nominal (dollar) wage by the consumer price index (CPI) for that period. Figure 7.7 depicts daily mean real wages for all industries while Figure 7.8 depicts real wages by the industry groups. Real wages increased soon after independence peaking in 1977 and then on a declining trend (Figure 7.7). While real wages increased between 1970-77, labour productivity levels have been below relative wages (see for example, Duncan, 1996). This meant rising costs of production. Real wages at the industry level has been no different with declining trends since 1977 among the four core sectors (Figure 7.7). The agricultural sector experienced the lowest real wages while agriculture together with manufacturing was on the same low levels since 1988.

Falling real wages and erratic economic growth has contributed to rising poverty in Fiji including the urban informal sector (see Reddy, Naidu and Mohanty, 2003). A recent report on just wages for Fiji (see Narsey, 2006) provides strong evidence of real incomes of all wage employees not keeping pace with the per capita GDP. Narsey (2006) also provides evidence that some 55 percent of all wage earners were below the poverty line in 1999. While the government legislated minimum wages through Wages Regulation Orders, issued by some ten wages council, on an industry by industry basis, these have been ineffective (Narsey, 2006). As such workers real wages have faced a continual decline over long period of time as revealed in Figures 7.7 and 7.8.

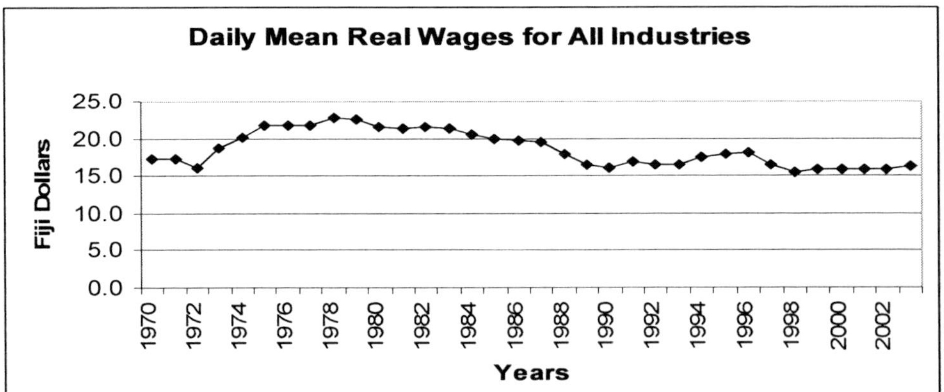

Source of data for Figure 7.7: Fiji Islands Bureau of Statistics (March 2005) and the Reserve Bank of Fiji (March 2006).

Figure 7.7.

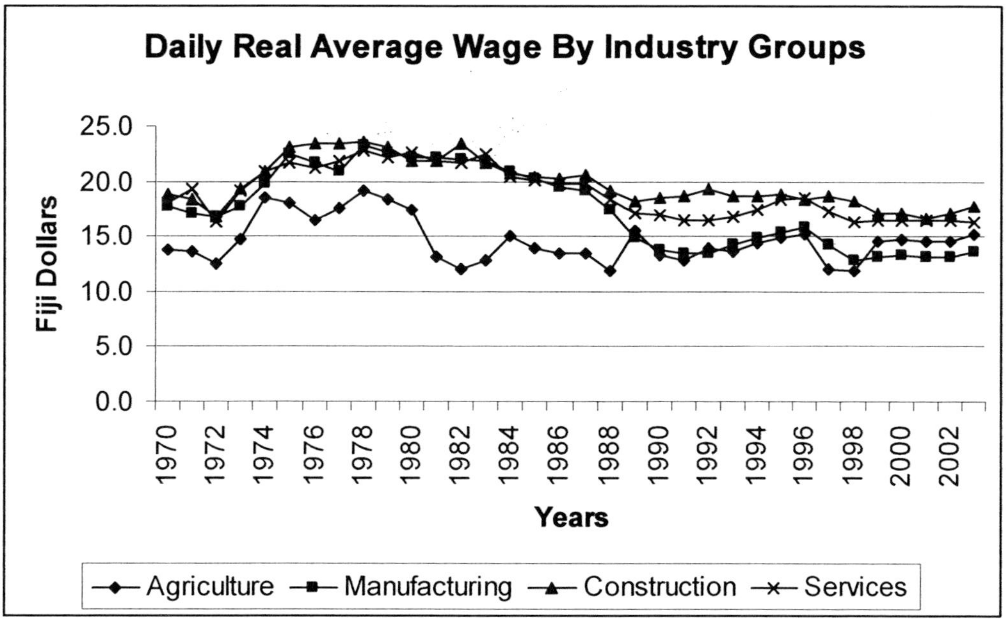

Source of data for Figure 7.8: Fiji Islands Bureau of Statistics (March 2005) and Reserve Bank of Fiji (March 2006)

Figure 7.8.

An important aspect of the Fiji labour market has been the labour unions that have played influential role in Fiji's wage rates setting. Fiji's labour market is represented by two major formal trade unions: the Fiji Trade Union Congress (FTUC) and the Fiji Island Council of Trade Unions (FICTU). The two unions are supported by several industry level sub-unions. Wage policy has been an important component of the trade union movement. The FTUC has been influential beginning with its major role in 1977 agreeing to a regulated wages policy with the government and the Fiji Employer's Federation (see Elek, Hill and Tabor, 1993). This tripartite forum agreed to a centralized wage setting system that linked wages to the consumer price index. This wage setting formula has been revised and now includes a weighted average of movements in the terms of trade, productivity and consumer price index. In response to rising wages experienced in the 1970s, the government at times took harsh stance largely in terms of imposing wage freezes. A major labour market adjustment that took place was a nation wide wage freeze at the end of 1985 (see Browne and Scott, 1989). In 1986, some changes were adopted in wage setting including taking into account of changes of productivity and terms of trade with past inflation, which resulted in restrictive wage increases (Elek, Hill and Tabor, 1993). The political crises of 1987 called for another wages adjustment with the government imposing a 15 percent wage cut in the civil service (Reserve Bank of Fiji, December 1987). The tripartite forum was dissolute in 1987 and wages were frozen for the six months of 1988 (Reserve Bank of Fiji, December 1988). This led to falling real wages and with wages linked to consumer prices, labour costs did fell gradually in the 1980s as depicted in Figures 7.7 and 7.8. However, trade union negotiations led to the successive wage awards between 1989 and 1991 that also included the restoration of earlier wage cuts (Elek, Hill and Tabor, 1993).

Moderate wage outcomes are particularly important for keeping inflation low. However, an agreement between the government and the unions in late 1997 allowed a 6 percent wage increase for public sector workers (Reserve Bank of Fiji, March 1998). In 1998, private sector wage increases were generally around 3 to 4 percent, a good outcome and that was consistent with low inflation (see Gani, 1999). In late 1990s and early 2000, some large private firms and industries have engaged into wage increases of 6 to 10 percent (Reserve Bank of Fiji, December 2000). Such wage increases were likely to be out of line with labour productivity growth. The retention of skilled staff has been an important platform of wage bargaining as emigration of skilled workers from Fiji has been an over-riding issue concerning the private sector (see Gani, 2005).

Fiji policy makers seem to have lost ground in terms of wage negotiations with the labour unions, which seemed to have gained an upper hand during times of crisis. In fact wage adjustments have not realistically reflected the economic realities. Consumer price increases has been the key element for wage bargains by the employees and labour unions yet deteriorating economic conditions and declining economic prosperity seemed to have been left out of equation. The adverse effects of natural disasters that reduced economic activity and export income has not been part of the wage bargaining process either.

Figure 7.9 depicts real wage growth rate against GDP growth. While wage growth rate tended to follow GDP growth up until early 1980s, the late 1980s saw an opposite trend: increases in real GDP with falling real wage growth (Figure 7.9). However, the 1990s saw the normalisation of this relationship with real wage growth rate been aligned to real GDP growth rate (Figure 7.9). Fiji's economic position during years of economic slackness would have been much better had all these factors taken into account in wage increases.

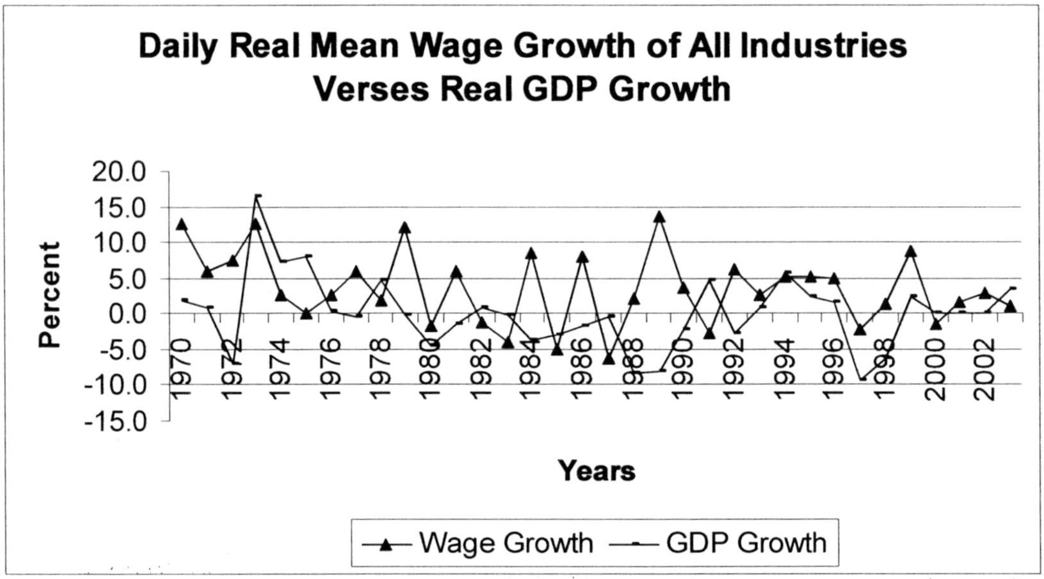

Source of data for Figure 7.9: Fiji Islands Bureau of Statistics (March 2005) and the Reserve Bank of Fiji (March 2006).

Figure 7.9.

While labour unions successfully negotiated wage increases largely on grounds of rising cost of living, Fiji's shortage of skilled workers as a result of emigration seems to have further boosted union representation in terms of labour supply. The government also realized massive skill losses and rewarded existing workers with wage increases so as to retain skilled labour. However, emigration led brain drain continues with Fiji facing massive shortages of educated and workplace trained workers at a time when the private sector has begun to show signs of expansion (Gani, 2005).

7.7. Labour Productivity

Labour productivity measures the average amount of output produced by each worker in paid employment. It can be calculated as the value of real GDP divided by the number of people in full time paid employment. Fiji's labour productivity is depicted in Figure 7.10, revealing sharp declines from 1981 to 1983. However, it grew steadily over the next three years. The crises of 1987 led to a fall in labour productivity that continued a downward trend to 1991 (Figure 7.10). Deterioration in the political environment led to worsening economic performance with several people remain unemployed. Productivity improved slightly in mid-1990s but sliding again in 1998 while the general pattern since 1990 shows a gradual rising trend (Figure 7.10). Since 1990, labour productivity rose significantly reaching levels experienced in mid-1980s. The political crisis of 2000 led to another decline in productivity as a result of massive job losses in the garment industry and other sectors of the economy. Productivity picked up in early 2001 (Figure 7.10) and has risen over the 2001-04 period.

7.8. Brain Drain and Skill Shortage

The emigration of educated and skilled and trained people from developing economies where they received their training and work experience to high income or developed countries is referred to as brain drain. Fiji is long associated with international migration that has implications in terms of loss of skilled work force. Historically, it has been a migrant recipient country (the arrival of Melanesians many hundreds of years ago; the arrival of European explorers and settlers between 1800 and 1850 and then the importation of Pacific island labourers in 1860s). The large scale importation of labourers from India by Britain, the then colonial ruler, to fill the gap in the supply of labour on the sugar plantations was the hallmark of Fijian immigration history. This indentured emigration ceased in 1916. Since World War II, greater international exposure and closer economic relations with high-income countries, together with the Fiji Indian migrant family and friend's network in other countries, saw a notable change in Fiji's immigration patterns. This change involved Fiji becoming a migrant sending country with Fijians, largely Fiji Indians seeking permanent residency in high-income countries mainly in Australia, Canada, United States of America, and New Zealand (see Gani, 2000 and Narayan and Smyth, 2005).

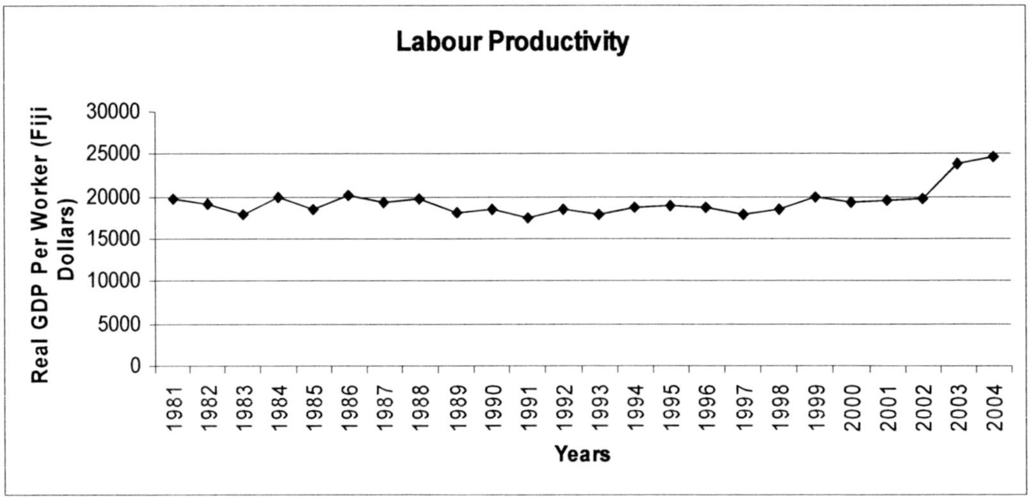

Source of data for Figure 7.10: Asian Development Bank (2005) and the Reserve Bank of Fiji (March 2006).

Figure 7.10.

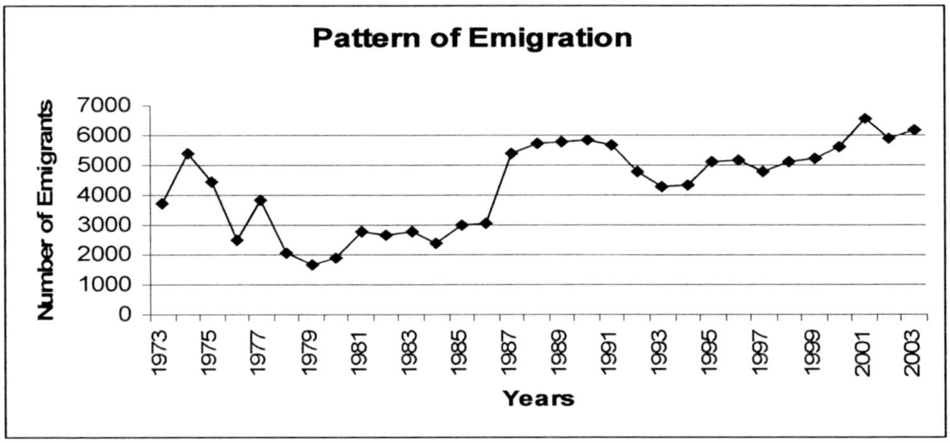

Source of data for Figure 7.11: Fiji Islands Bureau of Statistics (March 2006).

Figure 7.11.

In recent years the emigration of people from Fiji has assumed significant proportions to its neighbouring high-income countries: Australia and New Zealand as well as other distant high-income countries (Canada and the United States of America) as a result of the first political crises that eventuated in 1987. The expectations of the people of Fiji for the country returning to normality following the implementation of a revised constitution in mid-1998 were short-lived when the democratically elected government of the FLP was seized at gunpoint in May 2000 giving further impetus to emigration (Gani, 2000).

It is useful to first look at the patterns of Fiji's emigration so as to set a way toward the analysis of brain drain. Figure 7.11 depicts the trends in Fiji's emigration, rising dramatically from 1987. Despite a slowdown in Fiji's emigration numbers in late 1990s, emigration has been provoked again in year 2000, as it happened in 1987 (Figure 7.11). Within one year, following the events of May 2000 only, some 6,000 Fiji Indians, and 600 indigenous Fijians emigrated with large numbers of skilled workers (Gani, 2000).

Gani (2000) notes that one feature of emigration in the post-1987 period is that, on an annual average, many emigrants were occupational migrants. The emigration of Fijians with special attributes of high education levels, skills and work experience is a pure case of brain drain and is considered to high for a very small developing country. With the exception of some skills at the minor occupational category, information on skills of Fijian emigrants at a disaggregate level is scarce. Data on occupational characteristics of Fiji emigrants is available by major occupational categories (Figure 7.12) and some minor occupational categories (Table 7.1). These data give a broad indication of occupational characteristics of emigrating Fijians.

Since 1987, emigrants were largely from the professional and technical workers category (Figure 7.12). This included scientists, engineers, architects, doctors, dentists, accountants and teachers (Table 7.1). Among these occupations, the largest number was teachers, followed by architects, engineers and related technicians, then accountants and finally doctors and dentists. The second major occupational category included clerical workers followed by administrative and managerial workers (Figure 7.12). The production and equipment workers' occupational category included machine fitters and assemblers, electricians, plumbers, welders, carpenters and cabinet makers. Emigrants from these occupations had high qualification levels and work experience, occupations vital for developmental which Fiji could ill afford to lose. At the same time, high-income countries have certainly attracted the highly skilled and competent workers as these occupational categories command better remuneration in destination than origin country. All the occupational areas in Figure 7.12 and Table 7.1 are of critical importance to Fiji and the loss of these skills has been severe, creating an acute bottleneck to rapid and sustainable growth.

Table 7.1. Emigration by minor occupational group - professional, technical and related workers

Year	Architects, engineers and related technicians	Accountants	Teachers	Medical, dental, veterinary and related workers	Total
1987	127	103	125	83	438
1988	135	97	166	86	484
1989	114	96	188	72	470
1990	...	...	...	...	...
1991	127	81	173	66	447
1992	113	61	167	65	406
1993	80	62	99	60	301
1994	49	40	90	30	209

... indicates data unavailable.

Source: Fiji Islands Bureau of Statistics (March 1995).

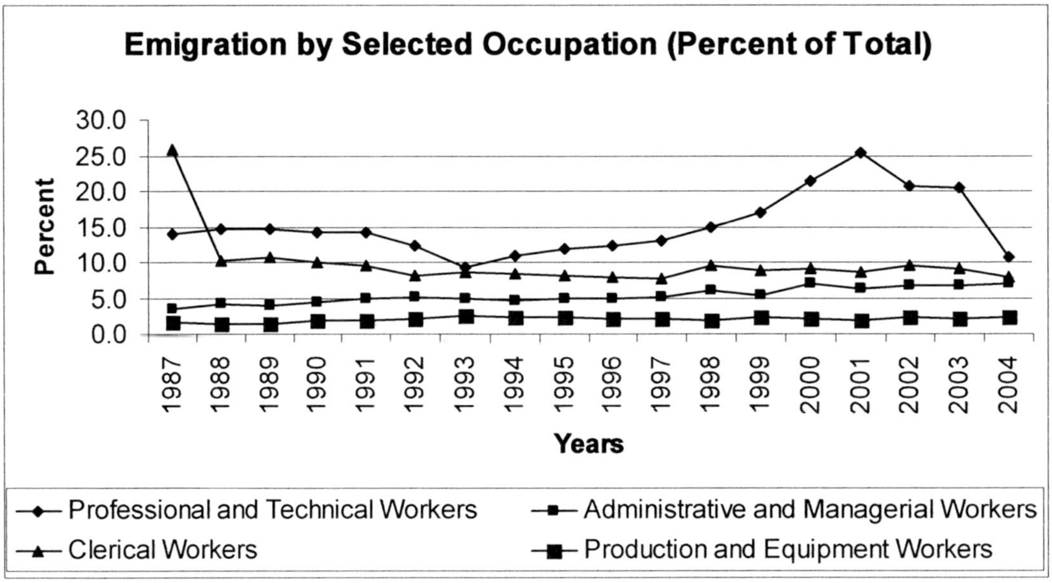

Source of data for Figure 7.12: Fiji Islands Bureau of Statistics (March 1990, 2000 and 2005).

Figure 7.12.

The importance of the role of human capital in growth has been well expounded in the development literature (see Galor and Tsiddon, 1997; Beine et al. 2001; and Barro, 1991). A fall in investment in human capital is likely to adversely affect long-term growth. Government funding in terms of human resource development through education has remained almost steady in the post-1987 period as discussed in chapter four. However, Fiji's stock of human capital has suffered as a result of emigration of highly educated and skilled people as revealed in Figure 7.12. According to the Construction Industry Council, the construction industry of Fiji has been at static manning levels for over a decade as a result of migration of skilled workers that has left the industry with an under-trained and inexperienced workforce and is constraining growth that the current booming economic climate presents (see for example, Fraser, 2004).

7.9. Conclusion

Fiji's labour market developments since its independence reveal patterns consistent for countries passing through structural and demographic shifts. With a working age population of 248,000 people, emigration of skilled workers in the post-1987 had a regressive effect in its working age population.

Labour force growth rate has been almost a percent higher than the population growth. While the female labour force has increased over the same period and now representing just over one third of the labour force, this gender imbalance is likely to continue.

Fiji's record of labour absorption through out the last three decades has been poor with declining absorption in the agricultural sector while the industrial sector does not reveal any significant growth either. Opportunities are likely to be in the services sector, currently accommodating some 60 percent of the total workforce and likely to increase as potentials for this sector to expand prevails.

Fiji's political crisis of 1987 translated into massive job cuts, redundancies and private sector operating below its pre-1987 capacity resulting in job losses for thousands of workers largely in the manufacturing industries. Unemployment rates are rising as a result of sluggish job creation in private sector and rise in number of school leavers. It is worth noting that Fiji's unemployment rate is likely to be more than double the current numbers officially published as the labour market does not take into account of all the unemployed labour force as those who live in remote and inaccessible areas are unable to formally get accounted as unemployed. Over long-term, there is strong evidence that Fiji's sluggish economic growth had a regressive effect on its labour market.

While real wages increased for the first few years following independence and that real wages have been on a declining trend since 1978. Labour productivity has not revealed any marked improvement either other than a slight improvement in the post-2000 period. The labour unions have played influential role in Fiji's wage rate setting with trade union negotiations led to the successive wage awards.

While wage growth rate tended to follow GDP growth up until early 1980s, the late 1980s saw an opposite trend: increases in real GDP with falling real wage growth. The long-term trend has been falling real wages and rising poverty amongst Fiji's wage and salary earners. However, the late 1990s saw some normalisation of this relationship with real wage growth rate been slightly aligned to real GDP growth rate largely on grounds of rising cost of living and emigration of skilled workers. This seems to have boosted union representation in terms of labour supply.

Emigration led brain drain continues with Fiji facing massive shortages of educated and workplace trained workers at a time when the private sector has begun to show signs of expansion. Emigration of skilled people from Fiji has continued as a result of continued political instability and massive wage differentials between Fiji and high-income countries. Since 1987, emigrants were largely from the professional and technical workers category (scientists, engineers, architects, doctors, dentists, accountants and teachers); clerical workers; administrative and managerial workers; and production and equipment workers' (machine fitters and assemblers, electricians, plumbers, welders, carpenters and cabinet makers). Emigrants from these occupations had high qualification levels and work experience, occupations vital for developmental which Fiji could ill afford to lose. The loss of these skills has been severe, creating an acute bottleneck to rapid and sustainable growth. Fiji's labour market outcomes are generally poor with high unemployment rate, falling real wages, static levels of labour productivity and shortage of qualified and skilled workers. Fiji lives with an untrained and inexperienced workforce particularly in the construction and manufacturing sectors, sectors showing strong signs of growth that the current economic climate presents.

REFERENCES

Asian Development Bank. (1990 and 2005). *Key Indicators*. Manila.

Barro, R.J. (1991). Economic growth in a cross-section of countries, *Quarterly Journal of Economics*, Vol. 106, No. 10, pp. 407-443.

Beine, M., Docquier, F., and Rapoport, H. (2001). Brain drain and economic growth: theory and evidence, *Journal of Development Economics*, Vol. 64, pp. 275-289.

Browne, C. and Scott, D.A. (1989). *Economic Development in Seven Pacific Island Countries.* International Monetary Fund: Washington, D.C.

Dalziel, P. and R. Lattimore. (1996). *The New Zealand Macroeconomy: A Briefing on Reforms,* Oxford University Press: Auckland.

Duncan, R. (1996). Unit labour costs in manufacturing in Fiji and Papua New Guinea, *Pacific Economic Bulletin*, Vol. 11, No. 2, pp. 39-47.

Elek, A., Hill, H., and Tabor, S. R. (1993). Liberalisation and diversification in a small economy: Fiji since the 1987 coups, *World Development*, Vol. 21, No. 5, pp. 749-769.

Fraser, C. (2004). Building the foundation for growth, Construction Industry Conference Paper, Suva.

Fiji Islands Bureau of Statistics. (Various issues). *Key Statistics*. Government Printer. Suva.

Galor, O., Tsiddon, D. (1997). The distribution of human capital and economic growth. *Journal of Economic Growth*, Vol. 2, No. 1, pp. 93-124.

Gani, A. (2005). Fiji's emigrant transfers and potential macroeconomic effects, *Pacific Economic Bulletin*, Vol. 20, No.2. pp. 117-128.

Gani, A. (2000). Some dimensions of Fiji's recent emigration, *Pacific Economic Bulletin*, Vol. 15, No. 1. pp. 94-103.

Gani, A. (1999). Drought, the Asian crisis and Fiji's monetary policy response, *Pacific Economic Bulletin*, Vol. 14, No. 2, pp. 35-48.

Narayan, P. and Smyth, R. (2005). Modeling immigration flows: an application of the bounds test to Fiji-Australia migration, *Pacific Economic Bulletin*, Vol. 20, No.2, pp. 104-116.

Narsey, W. (2006). *Just Wages for Fiji: Lifting Workers Out of Poverty*. Vanuavou Publishing: Suva.

Prasad, B.C. (2003). Merging interests in Fiji: essential ingredients for better economic performance, *Pacific Economic Bulletin*, Vol. 18, No.1, pp. 121-130.

Reddy, M. and Mohanty, M. (2003). The urban informal sector in Fiji: results from a survey, *Fijian Studies*, Vol. 1, No. 1, pp. 127-154.

Reserve Bank of Fiji. (December 1987, 1988 and March 2006). *Quarterly Economic Bulletin*. Suva.

The World Bank. (2004). *World Development Indicators CD ROM*. Washington, D.C.

Chapter 8

The Industrial Sector

8.1. Introduction

The development of the industrial sector is an important part of any economy's growth strategy. Fiji has been a late comer in terms of its industrial expansion with a boost to its industrial sector eventuating in the post-1987 period. From a strategy emphasizing protectionism and production for the home market, the Fijian government moved to export oriented model of industrialisation which privileges foreign direct investment and production for foreign markets. Fiji's economic structure changed dramatically since then. The industrialisation of the Fiji economy has been accompanied by an increase in per capita incomes. This chapter presents an overview of Fiji's industrial sector addressing some of its key aspects such as the structure of production, the extent of industries economic diffusion and industry policies.

8.2. Structure of Industrial Production

Fiji's economic performance has been dictated by changing structure of sectoral production in the last four decades. Sectoral production data indicates that Fiji has gone through structural transformation. Theoretically, it has been posited that in a growing economy, the decline of the agricultural sector has generally been accompanied by the strong expansion of the manufacturing and or services sector (see for example, Kuznets, 1966 and Chenery and Syrquin, 1975). Based on Hecksher-Ohlin (Heckscher, 1919 and Ohlin, 1933) trade theory (for a review of this, see Krugman and Obstfeld, 2000) we would expect that changing economic structure and, therefore, changing factor endowments would result in shifts in the structure of trade. Taking a historical perspective and in line with the theoretical arguments as noted above, available data reveals that structural transformation has been fundamental in Fiji. Fiji has experienced the dynamic processes of changing comparative advantage as depicted in Figure 8.1.

According to the trends depicted in Figure 8.1, the agricultural sector has declined gradually over time with its value added in GDP falling steadily from 39 percent in 1965 to 16 percent in 2002. In contrast the share of industry rose from a low of 18.3 percent of GDP in 1985 to 27 percent of GDP in 2002 while the manufacturing sector also expanded since mid-1980s: its contribution to GDP rose from 9.2 percent in 1983 to 15.7 percent in 2002 (Figure 8.1). The trends depicted in Figure 8.1 also confirm that since 1965, services have been the largest sector and currently accounts for just over 57 percent of GDP. The progress noted in terms of the contribution of the industry, manufacturing and services to GDP particularly since late 1980s is largely attributable to major reforms undertaken by the interim government in 1987 following the political crises as mentioned in the earlier chapters. These reforms led to a more outward looking economy.

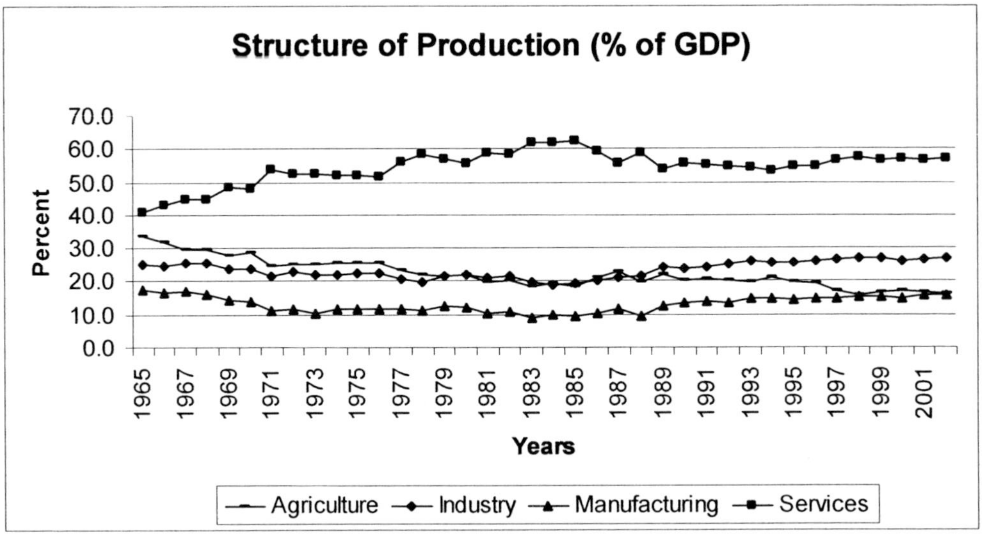

Source of data for Figure 8.1: The World Bank (2004).

Figure 8.1.

8.3. Industry Economic Diffusion

While services sector remains the dominant contributor to Fiji's GDP, the industry and manufacturing sectors contribution has been on the rising trend in the post-1987 period. In 2002, industry share in GDP was 27 percent while manufacturing share in GDP was 16 percent. Fiji's industrial valued added comes from several production sectors with varying magnitudes. Agriculture, industry, manufacturing and services sectors have been the core contributors to value added. Other important ones are community, social and personal services and transport and communication. Community, social and personal services have the largest monetary representation in terms of value added followed by wholesale, retail trade, restaurants and hotels and agriculture, forestry and fishing in third place (Table 8.1).

Providing employment to the domestic labour force has been a key feature of Fiji's production sectors. Community, social and personal services sector is the largest employer of the domestic workforce with manufacturing falling in the second place followed by wholesale, retail trade, restaurants and hotels in the third place (Table 8.2).

Table 8.1. Economic Diffusion: Value Added (F$000, 1995 Constant Prices)

Activity	1995	2004
Agriculture, forestry and fishing	475,901	458,046
Mining and quarrying	37,650	43,384
Manufacturing	330,612	506,482
Electricity and water	76,438	112,905
Construction	132,179	141,595
Wholesale, retail trade, restaurants and hotels	361,484	538,387
Transport and communication	293,624	396,918
Finance, insurance, real estate and business services	383,412	338,757
Community, social and personal services	433,579	515,089

Source: Fiji Islands Bureau of Statistics (March 2005 and 2006).

Table 8.2. Economic Diffusion: Number of Paid Workers

Activity	1990	2003
Agriculture, forestry and fishing	2,312	1,800
Mining and quarrying	1,660	1,800
Manufacturing	21,051	31,600
Electricity and water	2,059	2,900
Construction	5,727	4,600
Wholesale, retail trade, restaurants and hotels	14,849	21,900
Transport and communication	9,520	9,900
Finance, insurance, real estate and business services	5,633	7,300
Community, social and personal services	29,296	38,200

Source: Fiji Islands Bureau of Statistics (March 2005 and 2006) and the Reserve Bank of Fiji (March 2006).

Table 8.3. Manufacturing Industries Value Added (F $ millions)

Industry	1995	2003
Sugar	454.4	306.9
Canned Fish	34.2	2.4
Beverages and Tobacco	0.5	3.1
Mineral Water	0.0	45.7
Timber	53.1	33.2
Coconut Oil	3.9	4.0
Chemicals	5.4	13.4
Textiles	9.9	9.9
Garments	185.0	252.7
Footwear	15.5	21.2
Gold	58.6	76.5

Source: Fiji Islands Bureau of Statistics (March 2005 and 2006).

Manufacturing industries are more or less comprised of resource based product (Table 8.3). Cane sugar is still the largest contributor of manufactured value added followed by garments and then gold in third place. The composition of manufacturing value added has changed since independence. While sugar remains as the dominant manufactured item, garments, footwear and mineral water are some of the newer additions.

Commercial bank lending to various industry groups is another evidence of their growing role supporting the industrial expansion. As a percentage of total lending by commercial banks, the wholesale, retail, hotels and restaurants sector has been the largest recipient of bank loans. The growth in wholesale, retail trade, restaurants and hotels have also meant more borrowings from commercial banks (Table 8.4). Lending to the construction and real estate sectors increased since 1994 as a result of recent growth in this industry and boom in real estate development.

Table 8.4. Economic Diffusion: Lending by Commercial Banks in 2002

Activity	Percentage of Total Lending	
	1994	2005
Agriculture, forestry and fishing	12.7	1.3
Mining and quarrying	0.6	0.1
Manufacturing	11.6	10.8
Wholesale, retail, hotels and restaurants	24.4	27.5
Transport and communication	2.5	3.1
Building and construction	3.4	4.7
Real estate, non-bank financial institutions, public enterprises and business services	5.7	15.7

Source: Reserve Bank of Fiji (March 2006).

8.4. Industry Policy

To promote the expansion of the industrial sector, countries need to implement effective industrial policies. Industrial policies need well defined objectives, justification and scope. According to the World Bank (1998), the working definition of industrial policy is "government's efforts to alter industrial structure to promote productivity growth." Industrial policies in practice have multiple objectives including employment creation, increasing output; enhancing technological capacity; and allowing more equal distribution of income (see for example, Warr, 1993). Fiji's industrial policy has been largely formulated within the framework of these broad objectives with a number of instruments that focused on external market interventions. External market interventions involve protecting domestic industries from imports as well as using export promotion measures (export subsidies, export promotion zones and subsidized credit).

At independence, Fiji did not have a strong industrial policy in place. Its industrial sector was small and represented about 25 percent of GDP. From then onwards, industrial output has been sluggish and almost following a downward trend for most of 1970s and first half of 1980s as depicted in Figure 8.1. A number of factors are thought to have contributed to this sluggish development of Fiji's industrial base during this time as discussed in chapter two. First, economic policy making focused largely on import substitution and a pronounced bias against export led industries where the government relied on tariffs as a major source of its revenue (Browne and Scott, 1989). Second, domestic market has been small and producers found no incentive to produce for a small consumer market. Third, Fiji's high wage rates made production highly cost ineffective, again creating disincentive amongst the producers (see Duncan, 1996).

The scope for the expansion of Fiji's industrial base largely came in 1981 when SPARTECA was created that allowed duty free access to Fiji's goods to Australian and New Zealand markets (see Chandra, 1989). The government also realised the importance of developing the industrial base and the foreign exchange that would come from this sector. As such it provided fiscal incentives, including income tax breaks and duty drawbacks on imported materials so as to encourage increased levels of industrial investment (Chandra, 1989). However, rapid expansion of the industrial base could not be realised because of other structural deficiencies such as rigidities in the labour market, high transportation costs, poor physical infrastructure and lack of commercial and marketing skills amongst domestic producers.

Since the beginning of Fiji's political crisis in 1987, there has been a major shift in industrialization in Fiji – industrialization becoming a key aspect of Fiji's development strategy in particular by making manufacturing sector more outward oriented. As such a major industrial policy change was the introduction of the tax-free system (commonly known as export processing zones so as to boost manufacturing exports). The tax free system usually comprise of two aspects: tax free zones and tax free factories (Warr, 1993), where the condition for enterprises to qualify for tax free benefits was to export 95 percent of their production. The key feature of this policy change was the overly generous tax concessions granted to foreign investors that in effect led to the erosion of Fiji's tax base (Gani, 2005). Investors that qualified under the tax-free system were not required to pay tax on corporate profits for up to a period of thirteen years (Chandra, 1989). But more importantly there have been no restrictions on repatriation of capital and profits (see Fiji Trade and Investment Board, 2005). Although, the tax free system encouraged the expansion of Fiji's manufacturing (which in fact was expanding prior to the introduction of the tax free system largely as a result of Fiji's preferential market access to New Zealand and Australia), the lack of restrictions on capital repatriation for those enterprise qualifying under the tax free system has not only eroded Fiji's tax base but has clearly contributed towards a wholesale free flow of vital financial capital out of Fiji (Gani, 2005).

Capital outflows can also adversely affect the government's tax effort and budget performance in the sense that in the presence of capital outflows the actual government tax revenue is likely to fall short of the initial projections. In contrast if all capital outflows were subjected to taxation, the taxable income base would increase government revenues. In Fiji, it seems that there exists a bi-directional causality between tax revenues and economic downfall. Falling tax revenues has contributed to economic slowdown (Gani, 2005). As discussed earlier, it is to be noted that for years the government has extended extravagant tax concessions for investors, for example, the overly generous tax holidays to the garment factories and the gold mining industry. In the export processing zones firms have made little contribution to tax revenue and have been equally true in countries that have granted company tax holidays and those which have not (Warr, 1993). As a result of such generous tax holidays, Fiji has lost millions of dollars of legitimate tax revenue (Gani, 2005).

Following the industrial policy reforms of 1987 as discussed above, the government realised the benefits such policies brought about largely the expansion of the manufacturing base and creation of jobs. The boost in manufacturing industries made the case clear to the government in terms of further reforming its industrial policies so as to boost its domestic investment and production (see for example, Narayan and Prasad, 2003). In 1993, Fiji directed its overall economic policy as one of deregulation so as to encourage investment in all areas of economy and from all sources (see Fiji Trade and Investment Board (FTIB), 2005). The governments core focus became market driven investment as opposed to government directed. The government engaged into reforming several sectors of the economy. It tasked FTIB to promote, facilitate and stimulate equally local and foreign investors in all areas of the economy. The FTIB engaged itself in facilitating investment by acting as a liaison between potential investors and the government. More specifically, FTIB fulfilled this by promoting Fiji's incentive schemes; conducted investment seminars and promotion missions; targeted overseas and local investors in advertising and promotional campaigns; identified and prepared industrial project profiles in key development sectors; provided guidance and advice on investment policies and provided information on overseas market trends and opportunities (FTIB, 2005).

According to the FTIB (2005), in 2001, the government carried out a major review of its investment incentives targeting various sectors of the economy. The industry specific incentives are offered to industries with high potential for expansion and development. The specific industry incentives targeted two major sectors: the tourism and mining industries.

The incentives extended to the tourism industry included: the exemption of hotel developer profits; tourism vessel investment allowance of 55 percent of the cost; projects approved for hotel building or expansion may receive an investment allowance of 55 percent of the approved cost to offset against chargeable income and the Hotel Aid Act's Short Life Investment Package (SLIP) (FTIB, 2005). According to the FTIB (2005), the SLIP allowed several concessions: carrying forward losses up to 8 years; duty free import of all capital equipment, machinery and plant for initial development; no corporate tax on profits for 20 years for capital investments exceeding F$40 million; and concessionary fiscal duty on building materials (3 percent); furnishing and fittings (10 percent); specialised boats and vessels and sports equipment (10 percent); and heavy plant and machinery for resort project development (5 percent).

To the mining industry, major incentives extended included a loss carry forward of 8 years; export tax of 3 percent on gold; duty free importation of capital plant and equipment (FTIB, 2005).

In addition to the above two industry incentives, the government has extended its guarantees to investors in several areas: freedom to invest; the repatriation of profits at any point in time once exchange control guidelines are met; ensures protection of intellectual property; compensation to property when expropriation occurs (FTIB, 2005).

Fiji has also implemented taxation reform with simplification and rationalisation of its tax system. High tariffs, personal and corporate income taxes have been progressively reduced. According to the FTIB (2005), the elements of Fiji's competitive taxation regime include: corporate tax rate of 31 percent and is scheduled for further reduction to 30 percent; double taxation agreements with major trading partners; the alignment of resident and non-resident personal tax rates; corporate dividends are taxed only once; and a generous eight year period is offered for business loss carried forward.

Government has also encouraged competitive domestic financial market with local investors are freely able to seek finance for their investments from domestic financial institutions. Foreign investors are allowed to borrow F$3 for every F$1 invested up to a total of $10 million from local lending institutions (FTIB, 2005).

8.5. Conclusion

Fiji's industrial development over long term shows that structural transformation has been fundamental with a decline in agricultural value added but a rise in industry and services value added. Services have been the largest sector and currently accounts for close to two thirds of Fiji's GDP. Other than the monetary value added, Fiji's industrial development has played an equally important role in terms of providing paid work for the domestic labour. Fiji's industrial sector is well linked with other sectors of the economy, particularly the financial sector that has played a growing role in terms of financial support. The wholesale, retail trade, hotels and restaurants sector has been the largest recipient of bank loans while the boom in the construction and real estate sectors saw a rise in commercial bank lending in recent times.

Fiji's industrial development has been assisted by its industrial policies. Of importance has been the SPARTECA that came into to effect some 25 years ago and it allowed duty free access to Fiji's goods in the Australian and New Zealand markets. However, structural deficiencies such as high transportation costs, rigidities in the labour market, poor physical infrastructure, poor regulatory policies and shortage of skills have constrained rapid long-term industrial expansion. The overly generous introduction of the tax free zones and tax free factories was a major industrial policy change triggered by the political crises of 1987. While it worked to the benefit of investors and the country, it did erode Fiji's tax base. The government has continued to support industrial expansion and creating and ongoing investor friendly environment through reforming several sectors of the economy; providing industry specific incentives; guarantees on freedom to invest and repatriation of profits; simplification of the tax system; reduction in tariffs and corporate income taxes; and borrowings in the domestic lending institutions of up F$10 million.

Industrialisation in Fiji is now closely bound with its manufacturing and services sectors. The experiences suggest that while Fiji's industrial expansion is largely attributable to domestic industrial policy in post-1987 period. Fiji's long-term industrialisation has been greatly affected by policies of protectionism pursued at independence. Fiji's late industrialisation illustrates high levels of intervention by the state. The economic boom following the 1987 political crises saw an increase in per capita incomes which resulted in an increase of the purchasing power by majority of the population which also created opportunities for expansion of domestic small businesses. The Fijian economy will continue to see a significant presence in its services and manufacturing production for export in years to come.

REFERENCES

Browne, C. and Scott, D.A. (1989). *Economic Development in Seven Pacific Island Countries.* International Monetary Fund: Washington, D.C.

Chandra, R. (1989). The political crisis and the manufacturing sector in Fiji, *Pacific Viewpoint*, Vol. 30, pp. 163-178.

Chenery, H. B. and M. Syrquin. (1975). *Patterns of Development, 1950-1970.* Oxford University Press for the World Bank: London.

Duncan, R. (1996). Unit labour costs in manufacturing in Fiji and Papua New Guinea, *Pacific Economic Bulletin*, Vol. 11, No. 2, pp. 39-47.

Fiji Islands Bureau of Statistics. (March 2005 and 2006). *Key Statistics*. Government Printer: Suva.

Fiji Trade and Investment Board. (2005). *Investment Incentives*, Suva. (Available on line at http://www.ftin.org.fj/show/contents/invest_incentives/new_incentive.html).

Date of extraction: 15 February 2006.

Gani, A. (2005). Fiji's emigrant transfers and potential macroeconomic effects, *Pacific Economic Bulletin*, Vol. 20, No. 2, pp. 117-128.

Heckscher, Eli. (1919). The effects of foreign trade on the distribution of income, originally published in 1919. In *Readings in the Theory of International Trade*, Eds, Howard. S. Ellis and Lloyed, .M. Metzler (1949). Blakiston: Philadelphia.

Krugman, P.R. and Obstfeld, M. (2000). *International Economics Theory and Policy*. Addison-Wesley Publishing Company: New York.

Kuznets, S. (1966). *Modern Economic Growth: Rate, Structure and Spread.* The Yale University Press: New Haven, CT.

Narayan, P. K. and Prasad, B. C. (2003). Fiji's sugar, tourism and garment industries: a survey of performance, problems and potentials, *Fijian Studies: A Journal of Contemporary Fiji*, Vol. 1, No.1, pp. 2-23.

Ohlin, B. (1933). *International and Interregional Trade*. Cambridge, MA: Harvard University Press.

Reserve Bank of Fiji. (March 2006). *Quarterly Economic Bulletin*. Suva.

The World Bank. (2004). *World Development Indicators CD ROM*. Washington, DC.

The World Bank. (1998). *World Development Report*. Oxford University Press. Oxford.

Warr, P. (1993). The potential for export processing zones, *Pacific Economic Bulletin*, Vol. 8, pp. 19-26.

Chapter 9

GOOD GOVERNANCE AND THE MACROECONOMY

9.1. INTRODUCTION

Following independence in 1970, Fiji took over the reins of its colonial power, United Kingdom. The post independence constitution gave the government the right capacity to self rule for all its multicultural population. While the government over time diffused its role into all sectors of the economy, its economic and social progress has been disappointing: economic growth has been sluggish, governmental policies have been questioned and general elections of 1987 led to Fiji's first political crisis with the over throw of the democratically elected government. In 2000, the events of 1987 were repeated with the country continuing to ride on the track of political vulnerability. On 6 December 2006, the Fiji Military Forces removed the government from office due to escalating corruption and poor governance. Such political developments make a pressing need to look at the quality of governance, institutions and the macroeconomy in Fiji. It is now well known that good governance is positively correlated with macroeconomic fundamentals: economic growth, job creation and better quality of life. Poor governance not only hinders the macroeconomy but also contributes of social deprivation. This chapter looks at Fiji's governance structures and achievements and its link with the macroeconomy largely in the post-1987 era.

9.2. TRACING THE SYMPTOMS OF POOR GOVERNANCE IN FIJI

There have been strong signs that government in Fiji has performed inefficiently and ineffectively since independence. This ineffectiveness has surrounded areas of law and order, provision of basic services and inefficiencies attached to a highly regulated economy (see for example, Prasad, 2003 and Duncan, 2003). Over time, several symptoms of Fiji's poor governance have surfaced. The most obvious ones have been long periods of political instability, high levels of public sector corruption, collapse of financial institutions, institutional failures and weak executive governments.

Achieving and maintaining good governance and strong institutions is an issue concerning many countries. The issue has become a focal point for Fiji given its poor economic and social progress. Duncan and Chand (2002) argued that the economic and social progress of several countries in the South Pacific region has been disappointing over many years. Equally disappointing have been achievements in good governance. Saldanha (2004) argued that governance problems in the Pacific find their roots deeply embedded in political and social issues such as the structures of government, the quality of leadership, and the capacity of civil society to hold government accountable.

Fiji is no exception in respect to concerns about governance. Following its independence in 1970 from United Kingdom, the post independence constitution gave the government the capacity to self rule. While the government over time diffused its role into all sectors of the Fiji economy, its economic and social progress has been disappointing (Prasad, 2003 and Kumar and Prasad, 2004): economic growth has been sluggish, governmental policies have been questioned and general elections of 1987 led to Fiji's first political crisis with the over throw of the democratically elected government. The events of 1987 led to continued political instability resulting in falling investments, sluggish economic growth, slow progress in economic reforms and deteriorating institutional infrastructure. In 2000, the events of 1987 were repeated with the country continuing to ride on the track of political vulnerability. As of January 2006 and again in November 2006, a near coup became possible with a continued standoff between the government and the military.

The overthrowing of the democratically elected government in 1987 led to continued political instability and this has been the foremost factor undermining the establishment of an effective government. Fiji's continued political instability that has now taken more than 18 years has undermined other dimensions of good governance: deterioration in law and order; corrupt civil servants; excessive bureaucracy; regulated business environment and control of public voice and freedom. Fiji has struggled to maintain a strong and effective government that has served the welfare of its multicultural population. Fiji's continued political instability has disrupted the emergence of consistent and stable economic and commercial polices, it has encouraged political interference in its civil service and private sector that has affected efficiency and cost effectiveness, and led to the emergence of corruption and rent seekers (see Duncan, 2005).

While Fiji cannot be said to be corrupt free following its independence, the post 1987 period has been marked with extensive corruption and has persistently characterized Fiji's record of poor governance. Political instability continues to compound Fiji's corruption that has become so intrusive that has involved politicians, key position holders in the government and elites of the business community. Although Fiji inherited the right institutions from its colonial power (police and judiciary) to curb corruption, such institutional presence has been ineffective due to lack of financial and physical (equipment) resources compounded by the presence of corrupt elites at political and civil service executive levels.

Another obvious symptom of Fiji's poor governance has been the institutional watch dog. Government institutions such as the Auditor Generals Office, the Office of the Ombudsman, Prosecutions and the Courts and the Reserve Bank of Fiji have in many cases failed to act swiftly and effectively. With the exception of the Reserve Bank of Fiji, all other institutions have been inherently constrained in terms of financial and technical support. Their roles have been to a large extent undermined. There have been cases where the recommendations and findings of these institutions in key areas that determine good governance have been cast aside. The collapse of the National Bank of Fiji (see Grynberg, Munro and White, 2002) has reflected major institutional failure of the financial sector watch dog, the Reserve Bank of Fiji.

9.3. The Dimensions of Good Governance

Governance is primarily concerned with the process by which governments are selected and replaced; the government's ability to effectively formulate and implement sound policies; and the respect of citizens and the state for the institutions that govern economic and social interactions among them (see for example, Kaufmann, Kraay and Mastruzzi, 2003; Polidano, 2000; and Neumayer, 2002). The appropriateness and effectiveness of a country's institutions and its governance outcomes can be argued to be reflected in various ways including political participation, voter awareness, and transparency in government accounts, media attention, and corruption.

Given that governance outcomes are wide and varied, an attempt has been undertaken by the staff of the World Bank (Kaufmann, Kraay and Mastruzzi, 2003 and 2004) to choose governance dimensions that largely reflect the definitions of governance as mentioned above. These authors have identified and developed measures of core dimensions that contribute to good governance. These include the rule of law, government effectiveness, regulatory quality, control of corruption, political stability and voice and accountability. These dimensions can exert significant influence on a country's macroeconomic behaviour.

Upholding the *rule of law* can attract investors (see Barro, 2001) while long periods of *political instability* can reduce the risk of doing business. *Government effectiveness* can facilitate investment (see Chong and Calderon, 2000 and Romer, 1998) while governments that exert discretionary power over economic affairs can deter would be investors (for example, Fischer *et al.*, 2001). Similarly, countries rife with *corruption* in their public sector can negatively affect economic activity and deter investment. *Regulatory intrusion* into market enterprise activities can lead to corruption and larger unofficial economies, thus working against the interest of foreign investors (Safavian et *al*, 2001; Djankov, et al, 2002; and Gausch and Hahn, 1997). *Voice and accountability* can also influence growth for the need to encourage public input is important for democratic development (see for example, Bardhan, 2002 and Pande, 2003).

9.4. Achievements in Fiji's Governance

The most widely quoted governance indicators, based on perceptions, are those developed for 199 countries (for the years 1996, 1998, 2000, 2002, 2003, 2004 and 2005) by researchers at the World Bank (see Kaufmann, Kraay and Mastruzzi, 2004 and the World Bank, 2006). Figures 9.1 and 9.2, utilizing Kaufmann, Kraay and Mastruzzi (2003) data, depict trends in six core dimensions of governance for Fiji. In Figures 9.1 and 9.2, higher point estimates means improvements in each of the six dimensions of governance.

The trends presented in Figures 9.1 and 9.2 are obvious. There has been deterioration in political stability (since 1996); corruption (since 2000); government effectiveness (since 2002); and regulatory quality (since 2002). However, the rule of law has improved since 2000. A limitation of Kaufmann, Kraay and Mastruzzi (2003) data as depicted in Figures 9.1 and 9.2 is that they are based in perceptions. These author's acknowledge the limitations of their indicators due to the unreliability of the polls or survey results, and notes that "the margins of error associated with the governance indicators remain large relative to the units in which governance is measured." The arbitrary nature of qualitative information derived from surveys and expert opinions is in itself a limitation of governance measures.

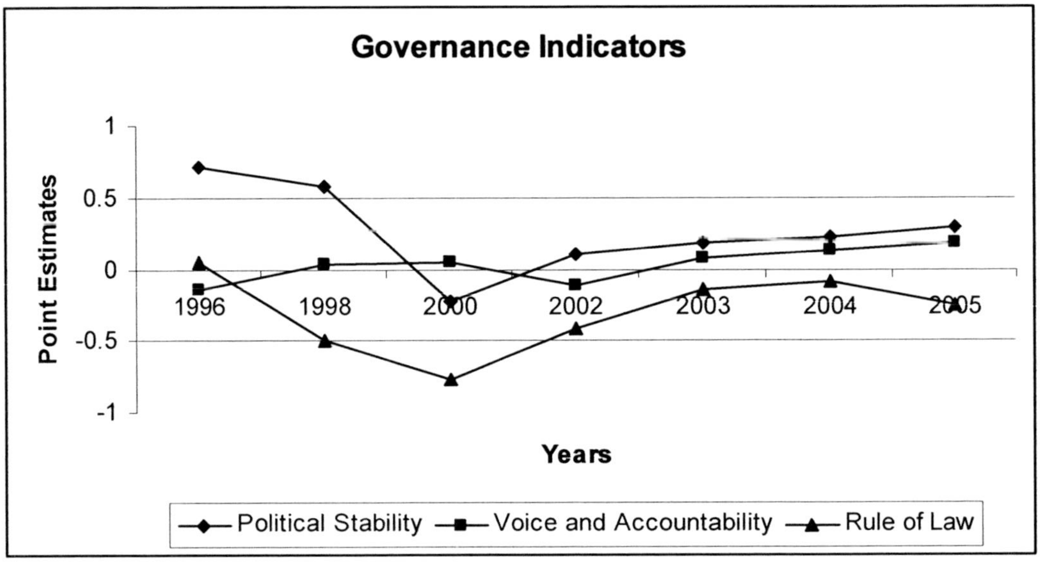

Figure 9.1.

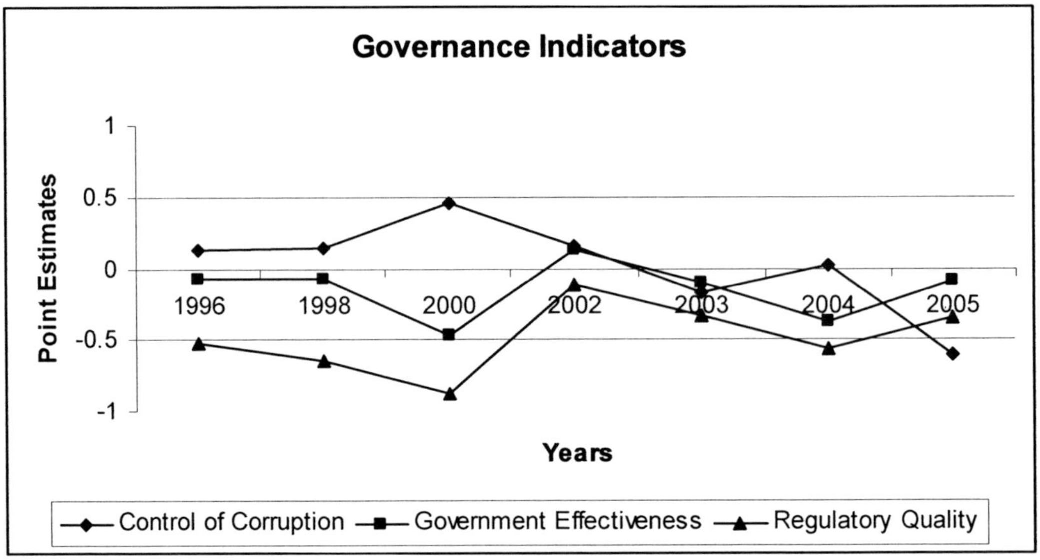

Figure 9.2.

An alternative to the use of such "soft" qualitative information is to use "hard" information, i.e., quantitative data drawn from official publications. An attempt has been made to construct an index of governance performance for Fiji using published time-series data for the period 1985 to 2005 comprising of twenty-five variables (see Gani and Duncan, 2006) with key results presented in Table 9.1. The composite index of governance, which is measured over the range from zero to 1.0, is based on three core dimensions: *the rule of law*, *government effectiveness* and *regulatory quality*, all widely believed to reflect governance performance. The interpretation of the core dimensions and the overall governance index is that a value closer to zero indicates a lower level of achievement.

Table 9.1. Fiji's Governance Index

Year	Rule of Law Index	Government Effectiveness Index	Regulatory Quality Index	Governance Index
1985	0.841	0.320	0.402	0.521
1986	0.859	0.424	0.443	0.575
1987	0.660	0.433	0.451	0.515
1988	0.263	0.440	0.432	0.378
1989	0.401	0.498	0.356	0.418
1990	0.210	0.532	0.418	0.387
1991	0.208	0.522	0.429	0.386
1992	0.279	0.421	0.499	0.400
1993	0.534	0.456	0.624	0.538
1994	0.492	0.466	0.576	0.512
1995	0.420	0.519	0.528	0.489
1996	0.439	0.503	0.475	0.472
1997	0.430	0.531	0.454	0.472
1998	0.468	0.684	0.563	0.572
1999	0.495	0.694	0.544	0.578
2000	0.662	0.453	0.632	0.582
2001	0.317	0.420	0.549	0.429
2002	0.510	0.297	0.555	0.454
2003	0.543	0.332	0.711	0.529
2004	0.515	0.373	0.633	0.507
2005	0.527	0.390	0.719	0.545

Source: Gani and Duncan (2006a and b).

The overall governance index is depicted in Figure 9.3. It shows that the coups of 1987 and 2000 had a significant detrimental impact on governance so that despite periods of substantial improvement, the overall governance indicator was much the same at the end of the period as at the beginning. In 1986, prior to the first political crisis (1987), the governance index was 0.470 and then took a sharp dive to its lowest level for the whole period, reaching 0.324 in 1988. As can be seen from Table 9.1, the sharp decline in the rule of law was almost the sole contributor to this decline in the overall governance indicator. The modest decline in regulatory quality also was a contributor.

After 1988, Fiji's governance performance improved but at a slow pace, so that it took until 1994 to return to the 1987 level. During the 1988-94 periods, the rule of law dimension continued to deteriorate, reaching a low of 0.208 in 1991 and then gradually improved. Over this same period, other dimensions of governance followed a pattern of their own. The government effectiveness dimension continued to improve from 1985 to 1990, deteriorated between 1991 and 1993 and then peaked in 1999. The regulatory quality dimension continued to improve from 1988 (0.432) until 2005 (0.719).

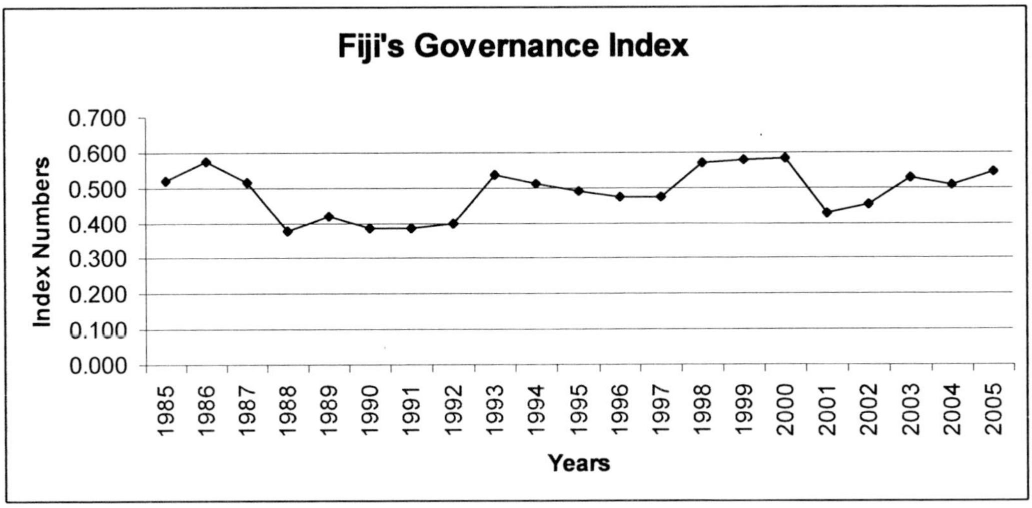

Figure 9.3.

9.5. GOVERNANCE AND THE MACROECONOMY

Governance can directly affect the behaviour of the macroeconomy. Good governance can lead to a stable macroeconomic environment where market participants can interact freely without disruption to their economic activities (see for example, North, 1990; Rutherford, 2001; and Black, 2000). The rule of law component of governance addresses the interactions between citizens and the institutions that assist in governing these interactions. As an ingredient to rule of law, political freedom is an important aspect of human welfare and reflects the extent to which the rule of law is observed. Good governance and the freedom to choose not only have a direct effect on people's happiness but can enhance a country's long-term investment capacity (Sen, 1999). The rule of law can also be influenced by political instability: where the governing régime is vulnerable, it may prevent the emergence of strong governing institutions such as the judiciary. National progress extends beyond investment in capital and a stable macroeconomic environment to the protection of property. Here maintaining law and order, minimizing governmental interference in the people's activities can facilitate a stable economic atmosphere. The quality and independence of the media can also influence the rule of law. The civic involvement in government through newspapers, television, radio, telephone, and the internet can have an important bearing on government responsibility (financial and macroeconomic policies) and economic progress. This can strengthen the accountability of governments which would enable them to tread more cautiously on public funds and have sound fiscal policies in place.

The government effectiveness component of governance captures the ability of governments to develop and implement sound policies, efficiently deliver public goods and services, and enforce rules uniformly. Other than its fiscal responsibilities (taxing and spending) governmental roles extend to the establishment of property rights, provision of security to public and private infrastructure a well functioning judiciary national defence and regulation of market activity, all important for economic activity. Bureaucratic efficiency in these areas can promote speedy progress in nation building and improvement in the welfare of society. Subsidies, regulations, and direct participation in economic activity by the government are some of the violations of free markets (Krueger, 1990).

The presence of corruption in the public sector can negatively affect government effectiveness (see for example, May, Pyle and Sommers, 2002). The abuse of public power for private benefit can arise as a result of intense governmental regulation of many economic activities: price ceilings or floors, quantitative restrictions on imports, regulations about types of workers to hire, etc. Further, the complexity of taxation and other laws may allow scope for evasion or for the exercise of rent seeking by public officials. Heavy regulatory intrusion results in considerable time spent with officials, coupled with attempts to evade taxation and other repressive regulations, firms and/or individuals often bribe public officials. There is ample evidence that corruption is linked to the loss of foreign investment, the sustained existence of inefficient state-owned enterprises, wage differentials between public employees and poverty and income inequality.

Regulatory quality refers to the extent to which government policies promote or inhibit market activity. Regulatory intrusion into enterprise activities may be manifested in a variety of forms: obstacles to entry in the form of registration permits and licenses; repressive, unpredictable and arbitrary taxation; required compliance with wide-ranging, superfluous statutes and regulations; significant statutory power given to regulatory officials charged with monitoring and enforcing compliance among firms (Safavian *et al.*, 2001 and Gausch and Hahn, 1997). Regulations that are costly to firms or people can induce bribes or other lobbying activities to bring about changes or, at least, waivers of the regulations in question. Regulatory intrusion is notable for its various negative effects including less democratic government, corruption, and development of informal activity; deterrence of domestic and foreign investors; and overall undesirable economic consequences (Djankov, *et al.*, 2002).

Improvements in societal welfare can also reflect the quality of governance. An effective public sector, with good management and without problems of corruption, means government can provide higher quality welfare at the same cost.

9.6. Governance and its Relationship with Fiji's Macroeconomic Aggregates

Good governance and its dimensions (rule of law, quality of government bureaucracy and the extent of corruption) can influence macroeconomic performance and overall growth as discussed in the previous section. Figures 9.4 to 9.7 drawing on data from Gani and Duncan (2006) and the World Bank (2004) depict the relationship between Fiji's governance and macroeconomic aggregates: GDP growth, inflation, unemployment and trade. All these macroeconomic aggregates reveal evidence of correlations with the governance index as discussed below.

The scatter plot in Figure 9.4 provides evidence that as governance improves, GDP growth also improves. Thus, good governance is important for promoting economic growth.

Figure 9.5 depicts the relationship between governance and inflation. The scatter plot shows a clear inverse relationship: as governance improves inflation falls and vice versa.

Again, it provides confirmation that good governance is associated with lower levels of inflation.

The relationship between governance and investment is depicted in Figure 9.6. Again the relationship is clear: as governance improves, investment rises and vice versa. Thus, good governance is associated with more investment.

Finally, Figure 9.7 depicts the relationship between governance and trade. The scatter plot depicts a clear pattern: as governance improves, the level of trade increases, hence a positive association. Thus, it can be concluded that good governance encourages international trade.

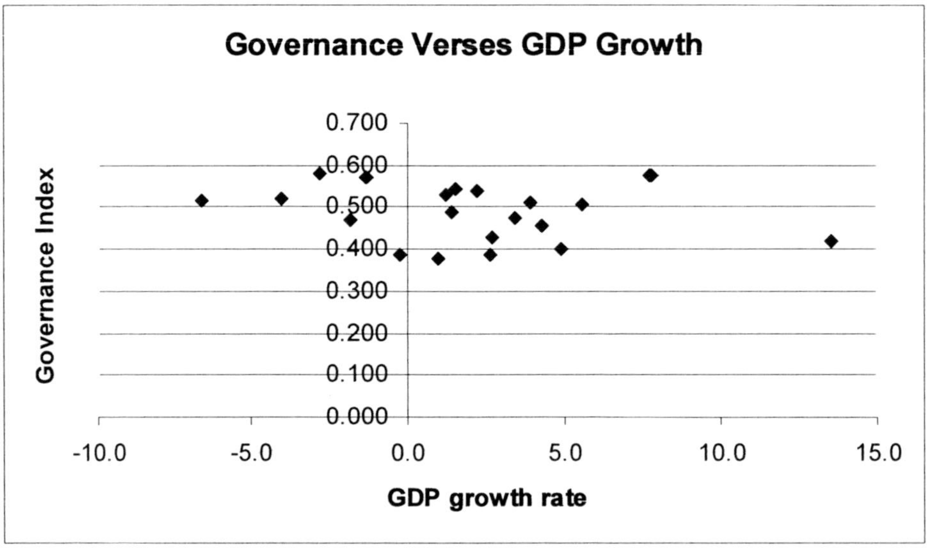

Figure 9.4.

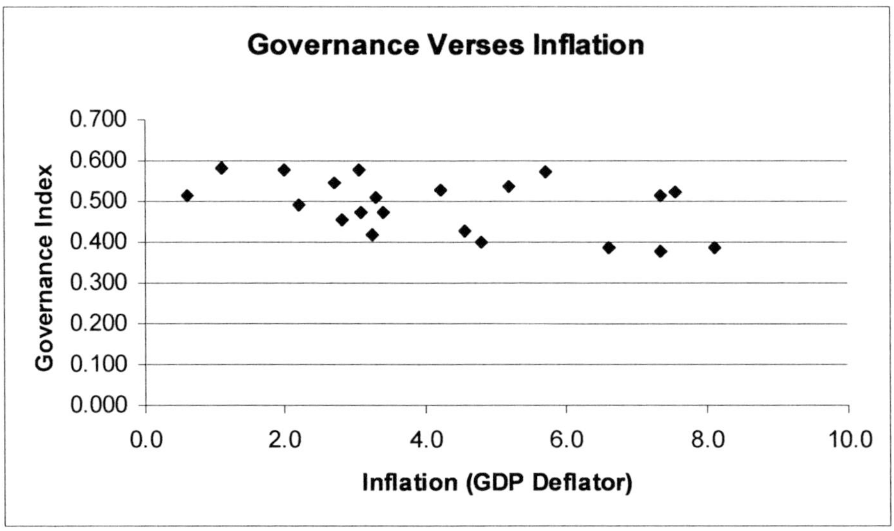

Figure 9.5.

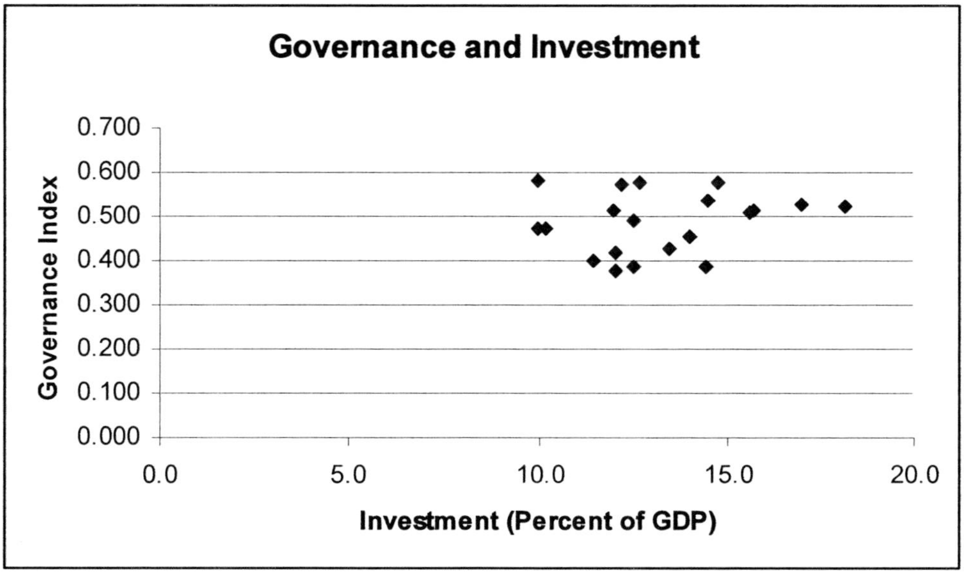

Figure 9.6.

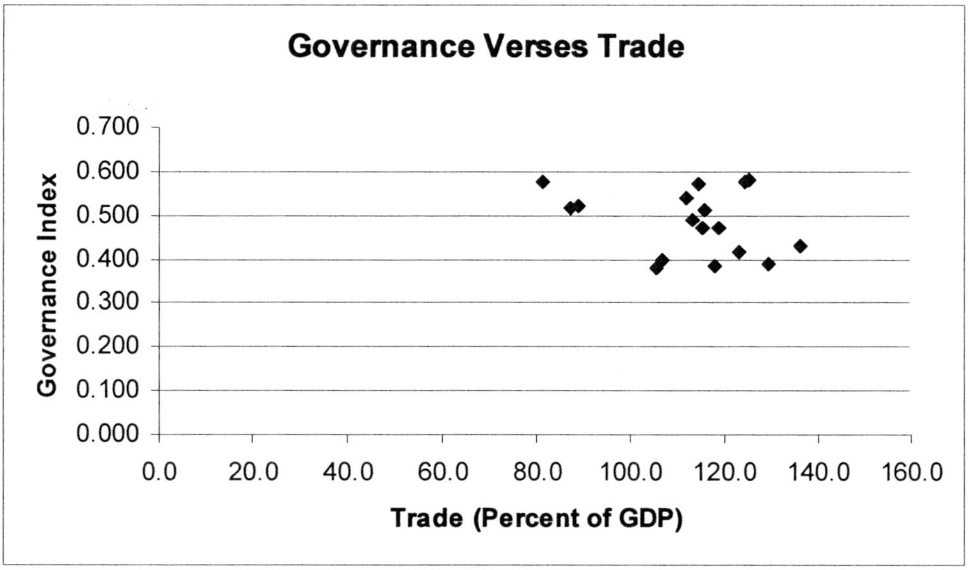

Figure 9.7.

9.7. Conclusion

This chapter has supplemented other chapters in emphasizing the importance of governance for macroeconomic performance. The rule of law, government effectiveness, regulatory quality, control of corruption, political stability and voice and accountability have been identified by the World Bank as the core dimensions of good governance. Based on these dimensions, there have been strong signs of poor governance in Fiji that has surfaced more strongly in the post-1987 period. The most obvious ones have been long periods of political instability, high levels of corruption, institutional failures and weak executive governments. Fiji's continued political instability that has now taken more than 18 years has undermined several dimensions of good governance. Fiji has struggled to maintain a strong and effective government and its political instability has encouraged political interference in its civil service and private sector that has affected efficiency and cost effectiveness, and led to the emergence of corruption and rent seekers. Extensive corruption has persistently characterized Fiji's record of poor governance in post 1987 period. Fiji's institutional watch dog such as the Auditor Generals Office, the Office of the Ombudsman, Prosecutions and the Courts and the Reserve Bank have in many cases failed to act swiftly and effectively. An index of governance performance for Fiji has been developed using mostly published time-series data for the period 1985 to 2005 showing that the coups of 1987 and 2000 had a significant impact on governance so that despite periods of substantial improvement, the overall governance indicator was much the same at the end of the period as at the beginning. Good governance and its dimensions have influenced Fiji's macroeconomic performance and overall growth. Good governance is found to be important for promoting economic growth; is associated with lower levels of inflation, improvements in investment and aids international trade. The evidence presented here suggests that good governance directly facilitates and improves macroeconomic environment.

REFERENCES

Banerjee, A.V. (1997). A theory of misgovernance, *Quarterly Journal of Economics*, Vol. CXII(4) 4, pp. 1289-332.

Bardhan, P. (2002). Decentralization of governance and development, *Journal of Economic Perspectives*, Vol. 16, No. 4, pp: 185-205.

Barro, R. J. (2001). Human capital: growth, history and policy. *The American Economic Review,* Vol. 19, No. 2, pp: 12-7.

Black, R. M. (2000). When can public policy makers rely on private markets? The effective provision of social services, *The Economic Journal*, Vol. 110, No. 462, pp: C34-C49.

Chong, A. and Calderon, C. (2000). Institutional quality and income distribution, *Economic Development and Cultural Change*, Vol. 48, No. 4, pp: 761-86.

Djankov, S. et. al. (2002). The regulation of entry, *Quarterly Journal of Economics*, Vol. 117, No. 1, pp: 1-37.

Duncan, R.C. (2005). Fiddling with the books: where does the buck stop?, Paper presented to the Prime Minister's Corporate Governance Summit held at The Warrick Fiji, on 11-12 March, 2005.

Duncan, R.C. (2003). Governance and growth, paper presented to the Symposium on Governance held at the University of the South Pacific, Suva, September.

Gani, A. and Duncan, R.C. (2006a). Fiji's governance index. Paper presented at the Fiji Update and Pacific 2020, The Australian National University and the University of the South Pacific, Holiday Inn: Suva.

Gani, A. and Duncan, R.C. (2006b). Measuring good governance using time-series data: Fiji, *Journal of Asia Pacific Economy*. (Forthcoming).

Grynberg, R., Munro, D., and White, M. (2002). *Crisis: The Collapse of the National Bank of Fiji*. Crawford House: Adelaide.

Guasch, L. and Hahn, R. W. (1997). *The costs and benefits of regulation*, Policy Research Working Paper No. 1773, World Bank, Washington D.C.

Fischer, S., Alonso-Gamo, P., and Von Allmen, U. E. (2001). Economic developments in the West Bank and Gaza since OSLO, *The Economic Journal*, Vol. 111, No. 472, pp: F254-F275.

Kaufmann, D., Kraay, A., and Mastruzzi, M. (2004). Governance matters III: Governance indicators for 1996, 1998, 2000, and 2002. *The World Bank Economic Review* Vol. 18, No. 2, pp: 253 – 287.

Kaufmann, D., Kraay, A., and Mstruzzi, M. (2003). *Governance matters III: governance indicators for 1996-2002*, Policy Research Working Paper No. 3106, The World Bank.

Krueger, A. O. (1990). Government failures in development, *Journal of Economic Perspectives*, Vol. 4, No. 3, pp: 16-7.

Kumar, S. and Prasad, B. (2004). Politics of race and poverty in Fiji: a case of Indo-Fijian community, *International Journal of Social Economics*, Vol. 31, No. 5/6, pp. 469- 486.

May, J.W., Pyle, W. and Sommers, P.M. (2002). Does governance explain unofficial activity? *Applied Economics Letters*, Vol. 9, No. 8, pp: 537-39.

Neumayer, E. (2002). Is good governance rewarded? A cross-national analysis of debt Forgiveness, *World Development*, Vol. 30, No. 6, pp: 913-30.

North, D.C. (1990). *Institutions, Institutional Change and Economic Performance*, Cambridge University Press: Cambridge.

Pande, R. (2003). Can mandated political representation increase policy influence for disadvantaged minorities? Theory and evidence from India. *The American Economic Review,* Vol. 93, No. 4, pp: 1132-51.

Prasad, B.C. (2003). Institutional economics and economic development – the theory of property rights, economic development, good governance and the environment, *International Journal of Social Economics*, Vol. 30, No. 6, pp. 741-762.

Polidano, C. (2000). Measuring public sector capacity, *World Development*, Vol. 28, No. 5, pp. 805-822.

Romer, P. M. (1998). Economic Growth in David R. Henderson, (ed.). *The Fortune Encyclopedia of Economics*. Warner Books: New York.

Rutherford, M. (2001). Institutional economics: then and now, *Journal of Economic Perspectives*, Vol. 15, No. 3, pp: 173-94.

Safavian, M.S., Graham, D. H. and Gonzalez-Vega, C. (2001). Corruption and micro enterprises in Russia, *World Development*, Vol. 29, No. 7, pp: 1215-24.

Sen, A. (1999). The possibility of social choice, *American Economic Review*, Vol. 89, No. 3, pp: 358-9.

The World Bank. (2006). Governance Indicators. Available on line at http://country_report_table. Date of extraction: 9 October 2006.

Wei, S-J. (1997). *Why is corruption so much more taxing than tax? Arbitrariness kills*, National Bureau of Economic Research Working Paper No. W6255. Cambridge: NBER, November.

Chapter 10

CONCLUSION

The macroeconomic performance noted for Fiji during 1970-04 period indicates that economic growth has been less than satisfactory; unemployment has been twice high of that been officially recorded; real wages have been declining; current account and government budget continuing to remain in deficits and getting worse; inflation remaining above the desired level; and investment remaining below the desired levels. Over the long-term, Fiji's economic growth has been below the average for the lower-middle- income and East Asia and the Pacific group of countries.

While good growth results were achieved in the early years following Fiji's independence, this trend could not be maintained for long. Although external economic shocks and natural disasters had some serious negative effects on the economy during some years of the 1970-04 periods, Fiji could have performed much better. Much of the blame on less than satisfactory level of achievements can be directed towards Fiji's economic policies which seem to have been rather short-sighted and didn't direct the country in terms of setting the right pre-conditions to economic growth and broadening its economic export base. Much has to do with policies that did not enhance the degree of Fiji's market orientation with lack of focus on private ownership, domestic market liberalisation, institutional improvement and domestic investment. Long periods of political instability, falling investment, brain drain, corruption, financial scams, mismanagement of public funds and unresolved land tenure issues had major regressive effects on Fiji's economic growth in the post-1987 period.

Fiji's long-term social progress and achievements measured by per capita GNP, reveals that Fiji has been better than the average achievement for the lower-middle-income countries as well as the average for the countries in the East Asia and the Pacific region. Fiji, with close to a million people is a very small highly open lower-middle-income country. While a steady improvement in human development is revealed by HDI over the long-term, the HDI remained below the average for countries in the East Asia and the Pacific region in the post-2003 period. Despite aggregate measures like the per capita GNP and HDI revealing long-term improvements in human well being, micro data indicate worsening levels of human well being as falling real wages has translated into worsening poverty.

It looks as if Fiji throughout the post independence period has dwelled on a thin economic line. Economic policy makers were heavily relied on sugar as the prime income earner. The sugar industry has been taken as a guaranteed stance towards Fiji's economic sustenance without much thought of expanding the private sector, strengthening the dimensions of good governance and moving the economy more broadly through diversifying the economic base. Today, the main source of Fiji's GDP has been its services sector comprising of wholesale and retail trade, restaurants and hotels, manufacturing and transport and communications. While services have added value significantly, agricultural valued added has declined with sugarcane production, which for long has dominated the Fiji economy is no longer the dominant income earner. The tourism sector has propelled over the last fifteen years, receiving some half a million visitors in 2004, is now the largest foreign exchange earner.

Fiji seems to have fallen short of its broad economic thinking and also its ignorance on setting the right conditions to economic growth. Much effort seems to have been placed on the political process and formation of the government, both from ruling and opposition political parties. For most of the time since independence, Fiji lacked constructive debates and policies in terms of directing the country on a path of long-term economic growth. As such, it has remained highly inward oriented and lost grounds in capitalising on frugal opportunities such as the expansion of the private sector, reducing the role of state in market activities and strengthening of institutions and resolving land tenure problems.

Fiji's unsatisfactory economic performance is not a huge mystery. Despite the constraints to growth, Fiji has the potentials to achieve higher levels of economic prosperity. Fiji's growth performance can be improved through improvements on several macroeconomic fronts that pose major challenges for the government and its policy makers in the short to medium term.

On the *trade* front, international trade has been important to Fiji and will continue to remain one of the prime movers of the economy. Over long-term, Fiji has lived with long periods of trade deficits, importing more than exporting. Trade reforms in the post-1987 period led to major improvements as export of goods and services as a share of GDP increased significantly. Tourism is now the leading income earner with earnings amounting to almost 60 percent of total exports. Fiji's industrial expansion including the establishment of light manufacturing industry, has led to newer export products such as woodchips, textiles, chemicals, vegetables and mineral water. The potentials for additional newer export commodities and services such as high quality agricultural produce, pharmaceutical drugs, information technology centers and film making look promising in the short to medium term. The performance of Fiji's predominant industry, sugar, has deteriorated and is no longer the top income earner. Of all the commodities exported in the last five years, mineral water recorded the largest growth in terms of export earnings. Fiji, while maintaining stronger comparative advantage in its largely primary products, does face strong competition from other primary producers around the world. Fiji's major imports are machines and transport equipment. This together with imports of mineral fuels, crude materials and chemicals are vital inputs to the production process.

For long, Fiji's main export and import markets have been high-income countries: Australia, New Zealand, Japan and the United States. Today, Australia continues to remain the major import market while USA is the main export market. The first major challenge for Fiji's trade is to strengthen trade links with its traditional high-income partners as well as with its newer markets particularly in Asia (Singapore, China, Hong Kong, Thailand, India and Indonesia) that are cheaper than the traditional high-income country markets. Second, Fiji certainly needs to diversify its export base so as to dampen the possibility of exogenous shocks. Fiji has a high level of structural openness as reflected in the share of its trade in

GDP/GNP often close to and in some years over 100 percent. Third, the developments in the global trading environment will continue to affect Fiji's long-term trading pattern. The phased introduction of global trade reform within the principles of World Trade Organisation hold both opportunities (overcome any diseconomies of scale through the expansion of markets) and threats (falling income and contraction in employment creation) to its growth prospects. Therefore, Fiji certainly needs to diversify its export base perhaps into high technology and high value added products to reap the benefits of global freer trade regimes. Fiji also needs to engage into more bilateral trading relationships and in continued search for more export markets and cheaper import markets.

On the *fiscal* front, continued budget deficits, mounting national debt and government involvement in private production has characterized Fiji's fiscal position since independence. Fiji's fiscal deficit has averaged 3 percent of GDP and in recent time's budget deficits has been close to 7 percent of GDP. This is certainly beyond sustainable levels for any developing country. While the government maintained a contractionary fiscal stance following the crises of 1987, an expansionary fiscal environment followed since 1990 that led to mounting debt with national debt now remaining 52 percent of GDP, landing Fiji into the moderately indebted category of countries. Fiji, while representing the features of a mixed economy does reveal that the government involvement in private production remained extensive over long-term. This has reduced the prospects of a fast growing competitive market and at the same time it has crowded out private sector expansion. In view of inefficiencies experienced as a producer of goods and services, the government has embarked with major reforms in order to improve efficiency and quality of services, its regulatory environment has been overly burdensome to domestic and foreign investors alike. Fiji's major fiscal policy challenge is to curb its mounting national debt, reduce exploding budget deficit and quickly establishing the environment which facilitates the independent functioning and prosperity of the private enterprises while reducing its role in private production.

On the *monetary* front, the RBF is well able to act as the regulator of the commercial banks while ensuring a sound banking system and controlling the quantity of the money that is made available in the economy. While, RBF over time has managed to comfortably maintain adequate levels of foreign reserves (equivalent to three months of imports), it has been less successful in realising its ultimate objective of price stability as maintaining inflation below the 3 percent target mark has been a rare achievement. Its adoption of market based approach of conducting monetary policy, the OMO using the 91-day RBF note rate and the trade weighted exchange rate neither has nor called for aggressive intervention in the monetary area. While its crises led devaluation of the Fiji dollar by 33 percent in 1987 and a further 20 percent devaluation in 1998 were of major concern to investors, both these events enhanced Fiji's export competitiveness. Given the looming political instability as a result of stand off between the Fiji Military and the Government as of November 2006 translating into worsening foreign reserve position and economic growth, the prospects of further devaluation of the Fiji dollar in the short-run is a possibility. In face of falling investment levels together with the excess liquidity in the financial sector, Fiji's major monetary policy challenge is to maintain competitive interest rates that so far have been deliberately maintained at levels that have not followed the workings of a competitive market. At the same time, the RBF faces a major task of maintaining price stability in the short to medium term given rising oil and commodity prices in the 2006 – 06 periods.

On the *financial* front, Fiji has a well established financial sector comprising of the RBF; the commercial banks, and non-banks and these have efficiently facilitated monetary transactions. Fiji now has an established financial market with combined assets of over F$3 billion. Amongst the commercial banks, ANZ Bank is the largest asset holder while FNPF is the dominant non-bank financial institution with assets of close to F$1.9 billion and much of its portfolio is liquid instruments with over 80 percent of funds in government securities.

Fiji faces a number of challenges on the financial front. First, while commercial banks have maximized their returns in presence of few competitors, there is clear evidence of insufficient diffusion of services to the wider population as commercial banks while strengthening their financial position have considerably reduced the number of branches and agencies over time. Given their frugal financial position, financial institutions need to make a wider economy wide presence.

Second, the FNPF has been the prime lender to the government and is now regarded as the lender of the last resort for the government. With over 80 percent of lending to the government, FNPF should move away from this uncompetitive form of lending and diversify its investment portfolio towards more competitive markets where returns are likely to be higher than its current funds in government securities.

Third, while financial institutions have diffused their activities widely, much of their lending has been to private individuals for housing, vehicles and personal effects have dominated commercial bank lending. Financial markets need to play an active greater role in encouraging investment for production rather than consumption.

On the *labour market* front, Fiji's labour market developments since its independence reveal that labour force comprises of 30 percent of the working age population. Fiji has a huge gender imbalance with females representing just over one third of the total workforce. Other than this, Fiji's labour market over long-term has been characterised as one with high levels of unemployment, falling real wages, static labour productivity levels and skill shortages. Fiji faces major challenges in its labour market. First, rising structural unemployment, rising number of school leavers, declining labour absorption in sectors other than the services is a major threat to further worsening in unemployment levels. Fiji needs to create opportunities in the private sector to absorb its growing pool of workforce.

Second, the long-term trend in wage growth rate has been disappointing with increases in real GDP failing to translate into increases in real wage growth. Falling real wages has been one factor contributing to rising poverty amongst Fiji's wage and salary earners. Real wage rate needs to be aligned with real GDP growth rate. This misalignment is also a contributory factor towards rising emigration of skilled workers.

Third, closely associated with falling real wages is the emigration led brain drain creating massive shortages of educated and workplace trained workers at a time when the private sector has begun to show signs of expansion. Emigration of skilled people from Fiji has continued as a result of continued political instability and massive wage differentials between Fiji and high-income countries. Fiji's skilled workers are vital assets for developmental needs which Fiji could ill afford to lose. The loss of these skills has been severe, creating acute bottlenecks particularly in the construction and manufacturing sectors, sectors showing strong signs of growth that the current economic climate presents. Fiji needs to create a competitive labour market environment so as to retain its skilled workforce at a time when growth prospects are brighter.

Finally, Fiji faces a major challenge in terms of uplifting its labor productivity that has not revealed any marked improvement.

On the *industrial* front, industrialization in Fiji is now closely bound with its manufacturing and services sectors. The experiences suggest that while Fiji's industrial expansion is largely attributable to domestic industrial policy in post-1987 period, Fiji's long-term industrialization has been greatly affected by policies of protectionism pursued at independence. Fiji's late industrialisation illustrates high levels of intervention by the state. The Fijian economy continues to see a significant presence in its services and manufacturing production for export in years to come and this is where its major industrial challenge lies.

Services have been the largest sector and currently accounts for close to two thirds of Fiji's GDP, and provides paid work for thousands of the domestic labour. Fiji needs to closely associate its industrial sector links with other sectors of the economy, particularly the financial and agricultural sectors.

Fiji needs to focus on reform of its industrial policies. Structural deficiencies such as high transportation costs, rigidities in the labour market, poor physical infrastructure, high telecommunication costs, poor regulatory policies and shortage of skills and access to markets have constrained rapid long-term industrial expansion. In additions, its overly generous introduction of the tax free zones and tax free factories has eroded Fiji's tax base. While, the government continues to support industrial expansion and creating and ongoing investor friendly environment through reforming several sectors of the economy and providing industry specific incentives; it needs to aggressively move forward in terms of reducing tariffs, investment in infrastructure and communication, reforms of its regulatory policies and training its workforce with skills that the current industrial expansion demands.

On the *institutional* front, Fiji's governance index for the 1987-2005 period revealed that the coups of 1987 and 2000 had a significant impact on governance so that despite periods of substantial improvement, the overall governance indicator was much the same at the end of the period as at the beginning. The rule of law, government effectiveness, regulatory quality, control of corruption, political stability and voice and accountability deteriorated in the post-1987 period. Good governance and its dimensions have influenced Fiji's macroeconomic performance and overall growth. Good governance is found to be important for promoting economic growth; is associated with lower levels of inflation, improvements in investment and aids international trade. The evidence presented here suggests that good governance directly facilitates and improves macroeconomic environment and Fiji needs to improve on its core dimensions of governance (rule of law, regulatory quality, control of corruption, political stability and government effectiveness) over long-term.

INDEX

A

B

C

D

J

K

L

Q

R

S

T

U

V

W

Z